RAYMOND PACE ALEXANDER

Raymond Pace
Alexander

A NEW NEGRO LAWYER FIGHTS
FOR CIVIL RIGHTS IN PHILADELPHIA

David A. Canton

University Press of Mississippi / Jackson

www.upress.state.ms.us

Margaret Walker Alexander Series
in African American Studies

The University Press of Mississippi is a member of the
Association of American University Presses.

All photographs are courtesy of Collections of the
University of Pennsylvania Archives.

First printing 2010

∞

Library of Congress Cataloging-in-Publication Data

Canton, David A.
Raymond Pace Alexander : a new Negro lawyer fights for civil rights in
Philadelphia / David A. Canton.
p. cm. — (Margaret Walker Alexander Series in African American
Studies)
Includes bibliographical references and index.
ISBN 978-1-60473-425-6 (cloth : alk. paper) 1. Alexander, Raymond Pace,
1898–1974. 2. African American lawyers—Pennsylvania—Philadelphia—
Biography. 3. African Americans—Pennsylvania—Philadelphia—
Biography. 4. Civil rights—Pennsylvania—History—20th century. I. Title.
KF373.A385C36 2010
340.092—dc22
[B]   2009043743

British Library Cataloging-in-Publication Data available

CONTENTS

vii   Introduction

Part One
Alexander's Race Radicalism and the New Negro Lawyer,
1898–1937

3   CHAPTER ONE
The Origin of a New Negro Lawyer, 1898–1924

27   CHAPTER TWO
Using the Left to Fight for What Is Right
Civil Rights Law and Radicalism, 1925–1935

Part Two
From Race Radical to Racial Reformer, 1936–1953

61   CHAPTER THREE
Making a National Movement Local
The Civil Rights Struggle in Philadelphia, 1936–1948

93   CHAPTER FOUR
The Cold War, Northern Scottsboro, and the Politics of
Civil Rights, 1949–1953

Part Three
A New Negro Judge During the Civil Rights/Black Power Era, 1954–1974

125   CHAPTER FIVE
Participating in the Civil Rights Movement from the Bench, 1954–1964

158   CHAPTER SIX
A New Negro Judge in Black Power America, 1965–1974

189   Conclusion

195   Notes

215   Bibliography

227   Index

INTRODUCTION

The most powerful recollection of what made Raymond Pace Alexander a leading civil rights attorney in Philadelphia came from his wife, Sadie Tanner Mossell Alexander, who also became a successful lawyer. In 1965, the *Philadelphia Evening Bulletin* published a twenty-page report titled "The Negro in Philadelphia," chronicling the history of African Americans in that city. Sadie recounted in the report an incident that had occurred while she was an undergraduate student at the University of Pennsylvania. In December 1918, Sadie asked her classmate Raymond Pace Alexander to escort her and two friends visiting from Cornell University to the movie theater. Raymond and the other man purchased four tickets to the Schubert Theater in downtown Philadelphia. When the four students arrived at the theater, the young men presented their tickets to the theater's manager, but he prohibited them from entering, saying that there had been a mistake and some other people had purchased their tickets for the same seats. Furious, "Alex began excitedly talking in Spanish," and the other three "chimed in with French phrases." After witnessing their foreign language proficiency, the theater manager said, "Why, they are not Niggers!" and allowed them to enter the theater. Once inside, they looked over to the seats they had purchased and noticed that they were empty. After the incident, Raymond Pace Alexander and Sadie Tanner Mossell vowed "if we ever become lawyers, we are going to break this thing— segregation and discrimination. And, yes—we are going to open up those restaurants, too. You just wait! Just wait!"[1] This incident exemplifies just one of the many racial barriers that African Americans in northern cities encountered during the first two decades of the twentieth century.

The theater incident occurred six months after W. E. B. DuBois wrote his controversial editorial, "Close Ranks," for *The Crisis*, the magazine of the National Association for the Advancement of Colored People (NAACP). DuBois contended that African Americans must "forget our special grievances and close our ranks shoulder to shoulder with our white fellow citizens and the allied nations that are fighting for democracy" in the Great War. After the war "to make the world safe for democracy," however, African Americans continued to meet with racial terrorism and hostility, ranging from lynching and race riots in the South to segregation and political marginalization in the North. Black citizens' heightened expectations were met with white backlash.[2]

When Americans reflect on the civil rights struggle, they immediately think of the southern movement, of Rosa Parks and Martin Luther King Jr., Montgomery and Birmingham, the March on Washington, the 1964 Civil Rights Act and the 1965 Voting Rights Act. From 1865 to 1965, the South was politically, socially, economically, and culturally committed to white supremacy and de jure segregation. Southern Democrats used racism to destroy the economically radical, biracial Populist movement, advocated violence and lynchings to intimidate southern blacks, and disfranchised both blacks and poor whites. African Americans responded by constructing their own community institutions, creating mutual aid societies, and relocating to more promising places.[3]

De jure segregation started in the South; however, historian C. Vann Woodward argues, "One of the strangest things about the career of Jim Crow was that the system was born in the North and reached an advanced age before moving South in force." By 1830, most northern states had abolished slavery and replaced it with segregation, a system that denied African Americans equal access to public resources, funds for education, relief, and municipal employment. Whites segregated blacks in public spaces such as parks, theaters, beaches, and other public accommodations. African Americans in the North struggled for civil rights continuously, first in the abolitionist movement and then in black regiments during the Civil War. After Emancipation, black citizens in the North joined their emancipated brothers and sisters in the South to defend personal liberties from Reconstruction until the 1896 U.S. Supreme Court decision in *Plessy v. Ferguson* declared "separate but equal" constitutional.[4]

Despite the long history of civil rights activism in the urban north, it was the southern movement that historians studied and a paradigm emerged that views the civil rights struggle as a southern movement. The first generation of civil rights scholarship used a "top down" approach and concentrated on male figures, such as Martin Luther King Jr., the role of the federal government, and the activities of national civil rights organizations, such as the NAACP and the Congress on Racial Equality (CORE). Charles Eagles argues that historians who had participated in the civil rights movement were unable to be critical of the movement's leaders, tactics, and goals.[5] During the last twenty years, civil rights historiography working from the "bottom up" emphasized the importance of grassroots activism, especially women leaders, and explored the tactical and ideological tensions among civil rights leaders and organizations. The new approach demonstrated African American agency and organizational sophistication of southern black communities.[6]

Recent studies have begun to chronicle the civil rights struggle in the North, and these scholars contend that a northern civil rights struggle existed simultaneously with the southern civil rights movement. By the mid-forties, the growing black population in northern cities began to protest their exclusion from beaches and amusement parks, union jobs, and federally funded housing projects. Black voters provided black leaders political power that they transformed into municipal and union jobs and greater access to local and state resources. Unlike the southern movement, the northern civil rights struggle does not have a national figure such as Martin Luther King Jr. As a result, there is not a national narrative that focuses on the civil rights activity of King. The northern civil rights struggle was a local affair that consisted of a plethora of individuals and organizations.[7]

In order to set the civil rights activism of black northern city-dwellers in historical perspective, however, we must begin much earlier in the twentieth century with the Great Migration. World War I transformed the situation of African Americans and laid the groundwork for the northern civil rights struggle. Before the war, 90 percent of the U.S. black population lived in the South. In most northern cities, the black community was too small to pose a threat to white political and economic power. Race relations were relatively trouble-free as long as African Americans remained in their place. The onset of the Great War in Europe led to a precipitous decline in the number of European immigrants, and northern employers facing labor shortages recruited black workers. The first Great Migration from the rural South to the urban North began during World War I, and, according to Woodward, the "trend toward racism in the North was amply illustrated in the years immediately following the First World War." Instead of embracing these new

American migrants, northern whites met the influx of African Americans with hostility and intensified segregation.[8]

World War I changed race relations in the North forever. Over a million African American men enlisted in the military, and African American college students such as Alexander joined their local Reserve Officers' Training Corps (ROTC) programs in college. After the war, black veterans "retuned to the nation fighting" for civil rights. Some uniformed black veterans refused to obey Jim Crow laws and defended themselves against insults, triggering race riots in southern cities. During the "Red Summer" of 1919, a wave of lynchings and twenty-five race riots occurred across America. The poet Claude McKay wrote "If We Must Die," encouraging African Americans to "face the murderous, cowardly pack, pressed to the wall, dying, but fighting back!"[9] The violence that erupted after World War I forced some African Americans to advocate self-defense. This new generation of African Americans, or New Negroes, was not going to die quietly at the mercy of white mobs. David Levering Lewis argues that "the new mood of militancy was genuine and widespread" but that "pragmatic New Negroes 'elected to survive while striving.'" According to August Meier, the term "New Negro," made famous by Alain Locke in 1925, may have first been used in an 1895 editorial in the *Cleveland Gazette*, a black newspaper. The editorial stated that "a class of colored people the New Negro," had emerged and that they had "education, refinement and money." The "New Negro" included educated African American doctors, dentists, teachers, artists, businessmen, and lawyers.[10]

According to sociologist Monroe Work, by 1928, there were eighty thousand black professionals in the United States. As philosopher Alain Locke describes their politics, the New Negro did not reject Booker T. Washington's accommodation and economic self-help but refused to tolerate segregation and second-class citizenship. Locke notes that the New Negro was "radical on race matters," but "a social protestant rather than a genuine radical."[11] Some New Negroes, particularly West Indian-born journalists Hubert Harrison and Cyrill Briggs, embraced socialism and criticized black leaders who sought racial equality in a racist capitalist state, but, in 1920, a black person demanding full citizenship in a racist society was a radical concept, and New Negro attorneys were in the forefront of this radical movement. Trained at prestigious law schools, they opened their own firms that protected African American civil rights, improved the status of black lawyers, and assisted the NAACP lawyers. In her pathbreaking essay, "Black Lawyers and the Twentieth-Century Struggle for Constitutional Change," Darlene Clark

Hine laments, "historians have neglected to analyze the roles played by the individual local black attorneys who labored behind the scenes." Raymond Pace Alexander of Philadelphia exemplifies the black attorneys in northern cities whose contributions to the northern civil rights struggle have been overlooked.[12]

The leading roles played by a few African American lawyers in dismantling segregation and obtaining civil rights are well known. Charles Hamilton Houston, head counsel for the NAACP Legal Committee; William Hastie, the first African American federal appointed judge; and Thurgood Marshall, who would become the first African American Supreme Court Justice, achieved legal victories of national significance. These three lawyers fought segregation throughout the nation, but they are known for their civil rights activity in the South. Alexander's civil rights struggle in Philadelphia complemented the work accomplished by his nationally known colleagues and demonstrates the post–World War I origins of the civil rights struggle in the North. While Supreme Court rulings applied to the entire nation, Alexander's civil rights struggle in Philadelphia sought to improve black employment, housing, and educational opportunities for African Americans in Philadelphia. Alexander's civil rights struggle laid the foundation for Philadelphia's Black Power movement.[13]

From 1920 to 1930, the number of black attorneys in Philadelphia had increased from 13 to 30. During the same decade, the number of black attorneys in New York rose from 50 to 103. According to Carter G. Woodson, in Cleveland, New York, and Boston, black lawyers actively participated in the white local bar. In southern cities, such as Baltimore, Maryland, and Wilmington, Delaware, white attorneys prohibited black attorneys from joining the white bar association. In Philadelphia, Alexander joined the Philadelphia Bar, but beyond the courtroom, black and white attorneys in Philadelphia rarely interacted outside of the courtroom. Segregation pervaded public space in "the City of Brotherly love." In 1950, Alexander wrote:

> Excepting only the restaurants in the John Wanamaker store and the Broad Street Station, a Negro in 1923 could not be served in the restaurant or café of any first class hotels in Philadelphia, nor could he obtain food in any of the Central City restaurants . . . I know it will surprise you to know that was the rule even in such great restaurants as the Horn & Hardart chain, Lintons, Childs and the like the only place he could obtain food in central Philadelphia was in the Automats, which

were color blind . . . restaurants away from the central section and those
in the suburban area were even worse. Their method of refusal sometime took the form of violence.[14]

Some white businesses posted signs: "No Negroes allowed." The 1920s are
famous for the Harlem Renaissance, but this decade also witnessed the birth
of the northern civil rights struggle.

During the 1920s, African Americans in northern cities hired black attorneys and used the courts to fight for civil rights. It took Alexander, the black
community, and white allies forty years to eliminate de jure segregation in
Philadelphia's schools, public parks, restaurants, hotels, theaters, and beaches.
Northern civil rights activists also sought to increase the number of black
employees in municipal service, well before the federal government endorsed
equal opportunity in employment. They also pressed for equal distribution of
public services, such as relief. The northern civil rights struggle expands the
definition of equality. Most Americans assumed that once southern blacks
obtained the right to vote, equality would arrive. Blacks voted in the North but
understood that their vote did not entitle them to all of the rights and privileges
of whites. These entitlements included safe playgrounds, high-quality schools,
and going to the beach or park without being attacked by racist whites. Alexander's achievements in Philadelphia came not only in the courtroom but also
through the voting booth and on the city council. The combination of voting
with litigation and protest proved potent for black Philadelphians and serves
as a model to study the northern civil rights struggle.

Alexander's civil rights struggle in Philadelphia can be divided into three
stages. From the 1920s through the mid-1930s, Alexander fought to force
northern states to enforce their state Equal Rights Laws. In 1883, the United
States Supreme Court declared the 1875 Civil Rights Act unconstitutional,
and, as a response, between 1885 and 1905, sixteen northern states passed
Equal Rights Laws making segregation a crime. But the state governments
failed to enforce the law unless African Americans protested. Nevertheless,
Pennsylvania's 1887 Equal Rights Law, while it lacked "teeth," provided Alexander with a basis to file suits against discrimination. Alexander's civil rights
cases, the boycotts, and the black vote assisted the passing of the 1935 Pennsylvania Equal Rights Law. According to Alexander, unlike the 1887 law, this
law had "some nasty sharp-edged teeth."[15]

The second phase of Alexander's northern civil rights struggle in Philadelphia began during World War II and extended through the 1950s. Black labor

leader A. Philip Randolph threatened a mass demonstration in the nation's capital to protest discrimination in hiring at war plants, forcing President Franklin Delano Roosevelt to issue Executive Order #8802, which prohibited discrimination in federal employment and by plants holding federal contracts and established the Fair Employment Practices Committee (FEPC). During the 1940s, a number of northern states passed their own FEPC laws. Since the 1930s, African Americans had organized "Don't Buy Where You Can't Work" campaigns to force white businesses to hire African Americans. Civil rights activists and black leaders viewed equal employment opportunities as a civil right. Alexander advocated African Americans to support their own businesses, and he fought to increase black employment in the city and federal government.[16]

The final phase of the northern civil rights struggle started in 1960, the same year as the direct action protests in the South. African Americans in northern cities remained trapped in low-paying jobs, poor neighborhoods, and inadequate schools. Taking a cue from the southern movement, northern local leaders used demonstrations to protest these inequities, but they were unable to capture national attention. In August 1964, an African American woman in North Philadelphia went into a white-owned store and got into an argument with the proprietor. The owner called the police, who arrested the woman, but a rumor circulated that the police had murdered her. Rioting broke out during the next two nights, and the mayor issued a curfew. The next week, the *Philadelphia Inquirer* reported that the riot was caused by "alleged police brutality and lack of jobs." The 1964 Philadelphia race riot foreshadowed the unrest that soon engulfed many other cities. Most civil rights scholarship views the Watts riot of 1965 as the event that marked the beginnings of Black Power, but the causes of the Philadelphia race riot of 1964 should have warned government officials of the problems in northern cities.[17]

Alexander's ideological transformation is a major theme of this book. During the 1920s and 1930s, Alexander was a race radical who used litigation and supported mass protests to obtain civil rights for African Americans. Starting in the twenties, the NAACP launched a successful litigation campaign to desegregate graduate and professional schools in the South. Pullman porters unionized and engaged in community-based political activism to improve their wages and working conditions and engaged in community-based political activism. Litigation was Alexander's main tactic. In Philadelphia, Alexander used the courts and, unlike Walter White of the NAACP, embraced mass politics and allowed leftist organizations to participate in local movements. The NAACP's legal campaigns were successful, but the Great Depression forced black leaders to consider using mass-based protest to demand change. Kenneth Mack argues that civil rights scholarship has created a false dichotomy between legal strategies and mass-based protests. As a result, all black lawyers are categorized as opposed to protest, and the claim that "lawyers deradicalize social movements has proceeded with little sustained analysis of lawyers' everyday work." In fact, during the apogee of Alexander's radicalism he was "sympathetic to the radical's arguments" and synthesized "legalism with mass politics." Consequently, Alexander built coalitions in Philadelphia with the left and the black masses. After World War II and during the Cold War, however, Alexander's radicalism shifted to reform, and he avoided working with the left, which was increasingly stigmatized and persecuted. Alexander believed in racial uplift, but, unlike many of his contemporaries, he did not blame poor blacks for their condition. Kevin Gaines notes that "black lawyers were solidly in the more group-oriented uplift tradition of socially responsible education."[18]

Another major theme of this work is explicating Alexander's ideological differences with the leadership of national civil rights organizations. When the Student Nonviolent Coordinating Committee formed in 1960, older black ministers did not agree with direct action tactics. Thurgood Marshall, who had witnessed the devastating impact of southern race riots, took a "negative view of King's rhetoric and mass protests," and after the successful Montgomery Bus Boycott, he "grew irritated at the front-page attention being showered on King." The black ministers' views of SNCC and Marshall's view of King were shaped by the experiences of their generation and egos. When Alexander returned to Philadelphia to practice law in 1923, he was critical of black leaders such as John C. Asbury who failed to demand more from Philadelphia's white political machine. Asbury belonged to the "older Negro Bar," those who passed the Pennsylvania Bar before 1920. The thirteen New Negro lawyers, who, like Alexander, passed the bar between 1920 and 1933, "had been trained at the larger and more prominent schools and universities of the North" and belonged to the Philadelphia Bar Association." As Alexander aged, he expressed serious reservations about Black Power, and on numerous occasions he expressed that he had never received the recognition that he deserved."

Alexander's New Negro generation took full advantage of the new political and economic opportunities for the black elite. In 1948, President Harry S. Truman and the Democratic Party made a strong commitment to civil rights.

In 1946, Truman appointed a fifteen-member Committee on Civil Rights, including Alexander's wife, Sadie Tanner Mossell Alexander. The committee's 1947 report, "To Secure These Rights," recommended far-reaching changes in federal policy that would dismantle racial segregation. When Truman appointed Sadie, the Alexanders were Republicans, but after her appointment, both had joined the Democratic Party and Raymond immediately started campaigning for Truman. In 1948, a vacancy opened on the federal bench. Alexander and William Hastie were the two front-runners, but Truman nominated Hastie, who was a lifelong Democrat. Alexander was nationally respected in black America, but only locally known in white America. In Philadelphia, however, he was extremely influential. Alexander played a major part in the city's political reform movement, a coalition of black and white middle-class liberals that challenged the city's governing Republican machine. In 1951, the reform movement ended Republican rule. According to Matthew Countryman, three years earlier, the civil rights struggle in Philadelphia had secured "one of the country's first municipal fair employment practices law."[20]

The Cold War provided career opportunities for black elites in foreign service. Prior to the Cold War, the only diplomatic position African Americans obtained was in Haiti, whose population was predominantly of African descent. The Cold War forced the United States to improve its image in the rest of the world, so the diplomatic corps was opened to a few African Americans. During the 1940s and 1950s, Alexander wrote numerous letters to government officials trying to obtain an appointment in the foreign service. In 1965, the U.S. State Department hired Alexander as a Special Assistant and sent him to the Far East to discuss race relations. Alexander criticized American racism in the United States, but when he worked for the U.S. State Department, he told his audience that Communist nations' discussion of American racism was propaganda. Alexander's Far East speeches emphasized racial cooperation rather than racial tension, the image that predominated in foreign media. In 1968, the U.S. State Department rehired Alexander to serve as an American Specialist to the Middle East. These lectures highlighted the impact of the civil rights movement, and they discussed the perils of institutionalized poverty and racism. Alexander's two stints with the State Department represented the ideological shift that resulted from the radical views articulated by King after 1965. On his first foreign speaking tour, Alexander emphasized civil rights, but by the late sixties, he also discussed the impact of institutionalized racism and poverty.

This study examines Alexander's civil rights activism in Philadelphia and his struggle for status in the legal profession. [Alexander provided the groundwork for the civil rights generation and the next wave of black lawyers in Philadelphia.] African American activists of the sixties used the same protest tactics—boycotting, and voting, picketing—that had been used earlier in the twentieth century. Historical understanding can bridge the ideological gap between generations. Alexander and the younger leaders both sought equal access to education, employment, health care, and housing. Litigation sought to eliminate de jure segregation by utilizing the power of the state. Mass protest accompanied legal initiatives and generated public support for change. Boycotts used the power of the black dollar for African Americans to obtain jobs in white-owned businesses. Voting mobilized the strength of numbers to attain access to municipal employment and public services. Many Black Power and civil rights activists of the 1960s failed to see the world from Alexander's perspective. The young activists were not aware of the amount of segregation that existed in Philadelphia during the 1920s and could not appreciate the effectiveness of the combination of litigation and politics with protest. Alexander expanded opportunities for black lawyers and the black community in Philadelphia.

In order to comprehend Alexander's impact on the civil rights struggle Philadelphia, one must understand how the white establishment denied resources to the black community. During the 1920s, Philadelphia was an extremely racist city. Assaults by white citizens on black citizens were frequent occurrences, especially in public places of recreation. Black neighborhoods lacked public parks, decent schools, and police protection. Alexander understood that the city government had systematically denied public resources to African Americans, despite their being voters and taxpayers. Working downtown and in City Hall, he learned how white power worked. From 1923 to 1960, Alexander fought to desegregate the city and to ensure that it provided its black residents with their fair share of public resources.

The majority of post–World War II northern civil rights struggles are community studies. This biography complements the expanding body of literature on the civil rights struggle in the North by providing insight from a New Negro lawyer's perspective. It also roots the northern civil rights struggle in the 1920s. Growing up in Philadelphia and spending his entire life in the North, Alexander encountered a different type of racism than did black southerners. Alexander realized that African Americans lacked political power and that the only way to improve the city was to become part of

Philadelphia's power structure and work with white liberals. This book consists of three parts that chronicles Alexander's shift from a New Negro race radical to a racial liberal.

Part I: Alexander's Race Radicalism and the New Negro Lawyer, 1898–1937

In chapter 1, "The Origin of a New Negro Lawyer, 1898–1924," I examine the social forces that shaped Alexander and the New Negro Lawyer generation, including Alexander's social, educational, and intellectual influences as he matured from a working-class African American youth to a well-trained black professional. As he encountered segregation and discrimination, his understanding of black history and culture strengthened him. Born to a working-class Philadelphia family but enjoying significant attention from both black and white educators, he became active in African American social and political organizations and, at the same time, in white professional organizations.

In chapter 2, "Using the Left to Fight for What Is Right: Civil Rights Law and Radicalism, 1925–1935," I chronicle the development of Alexander's race radicalism. From 1923 to 1935, the fight to end segregation in public accommodations was a radical concept in Philadelphia. In 1923, Alexander started to practice law in Philadelphia and initiated lawsuits to desegregate white businesses. In this chapter, I examine Alexander's synthesis of litigation and mass-based protest. During the 1930s Alexander and other members of the black bar were open to working with leftist organizations. This is evident with the 1932 Berwyn, Pennsylvania, school desegregation. The Berwyn school district built a new elementary school for white students. Black parents protested by participating in a two-year boycott. The parents hired Alexander and planned a protest march with support from left-wing organizations such as the International Labor Defense (ILD). One year after this case, Pennsylvania passed the 1935 Equal Rights Law.

Part II: From Race Radical to Racial Reformer, 1936–1953

In chapter 3, "Making a National Movement Local: The Civil Rights Struggle in Philadelphia, 1936–1948," I explore Alexander's civil rights activity within the context of the long civil rights movement and his shift from race radical to reformer. In 1936, Alexander had joined the National Negro Congress (NNC) a black radical organization, and the NNC held its second annual conference in Philadelphia. On numerous occasions when Alexander reflected on his civil rights activity in Philadelphia he recalled that during the 1920s he was not welcomed in city hall. Alexander used this story to demonstrate to younger activists the amount of discrimination that existed in Philadelphia and the radicalism of what he was trying to accomplish. By the 1930s, the New Deal and a cadre of black leadership made civil rights a national issue and Alexander's desire for racial equality became reformist rather than radical. Among educated black and white liberals, black equality was becoming a more acceptable position, and the "Double V" campaign for victory over fascism abroad and over racism at home forced the nation to address civil rights, and ending segregation in northern cities was no longer a radical notion.

In chapter 4, "The Cold War, Northern Scottsboro, and the Politics of Civil Rights, 1949–1953," I examine Alexander's efforts to translate his civil rights activism into larger political ambitions. As the New Deal and the Democratic Party created opportunities for black professionals, Alexander continued with his campaign to become the first black judge in Philadelphia. Winning important civil rights cases such as the Trenton Six, however, did not secure him white support or a nomination from Harry S. Truman to become the first black federal judge. In the Trenton Six Case, known as the "Scottsboro North," six young black men were accused of murdering a white store owner in Trenton, New Jersey, in 1949. The NAACP hired Alexander to represent two of the six men. Unlike in the thirties, when Alexander obtained support from the left, he did not want the Civil Rights Congress, a leftist organization, to defend the men. In 1951, the Democrats won the mayoral election and Alexander became the first African American elected to the city council. Serving until 1958, he secured the extension of city services and provision of public resources to African Americans.

Part III: A New Negro Judge During the Civil Rights/Black Power Era, 1954–1974

In chapter 5, "Participating in the Civil Rights Movement from the Bench, 1954–1964," I investigate Alexander's judicial activism in Philadelphia as well as his views on the Black Freedom Movement in the South and in

Philadelphia. Alexander created the Community Legal Services (CLC), an organization intended to provide free legal assistance for the poor. From 1954 to 1958, Alexander fought to desegregate Girard College, a privately funded but publicly administered school for poor white orphans in Philadelphia. From the late forties, Alexander was active alongside white middle-class liberals in the Democratic Reform Movement in Philadelphia. As a local judge, Alexander could no longer participate actively in Philadelphia's civil rights movement, but he observed and commented on the civil rights movement in the South and in Philadelphia. Cecil B. Moore, a black lawyer and president of the Philadelphia branch of the NAACP castigated Alexander and referred to him as an "Uncle Tom." Alexander viewed Moore as a radical and believed his mass demonstrations were not needed in Philadelphia.

In chapter 6, "A New Negro Judge in Black Power America 1965–1974," I investigate Alexander's views about Black Power, the role of black attorneys during the Black Power Era, and his shift toward addressing institutionalized inequality. Alexander was anti-Black Power, but, on one occasion, he compared Black Power to the Harlem Renaissance. Both movements had recognized the important of black history and culture, and young people led both movements. After dedicating his life to dismantling segregation, Alexander was unable to understand why black college students desired a "segregated space." Ironically, however, Alexander was nurtured in a "segregated space." He belonged to two black fraternities, Alpha Phi Alpha and Sigma Pi Phi, and numerous black professional organizations, such as the National Bar Association and the National Conference of Black Lawyers.

Raymond Pace Alexander: A New Negro Lawyer Fights for Civil Rights in Philadelphia chronicles Alexander's life and civil rights struggle in Philadelphia. I argue that the origin of the urban crisis, the northern civil rights struggle, and the movement for Black Power began during the 1920s. It took years of legal, political, and mass-based activism to desegregate northern cities. Alexander's civil rights struggle reflected the political ideology of the day. During the thirties, Alexander supported mass-based politics; after World War II and during the Cold War, he advocated litigation and voting. His civil rights struggle in Philadelphia encompassed civil rights cases, criminal cases, the desegregation of schools and public accommodations desegregation, coalition building, and electoral activism. Toward the end of Alexander's life, he became more critical of liberal whites and cognizant of the impact of institutionalized black poverty. Like most African Americans, the longer he lived, xxINTRODUCTION

the more cognizant he became of what novelist Ralph Ellison refers to as "the changing same of racism." In 1971, Senior Judge Raymond Pace Alexander spoke at the NAACP's Testimonial Dinner. Alexander discussed how he used "non-violent, yet vigorous action rather than . . . explosive methods" to obtain civil rights. He believed that his "approach to these problems was right and I still have faith in God and my country." Alexander promised his audience that he could answer all of their questions in a "full biography of his life," but he died before the biography was completed. This biography will answer the audience's questions and transmit his legacy to all Americans.[21]

Part One

ALEXANDER'S RACE RADICALISM AND
THE NEW NEGRO LAWYER, 1898–1937

Chapter One

Raymond Pace Alexander was born on October 13, 1898, to Hillard Boone Alexander and Virginia Pace Alexander of Philadelphia. His father had been born a slave on November 22, 1856, to James and Ellen Alexander in Mecklenberg, Virginia, a town southwest of Richmond near the North Carolina border. In 1880, Hillard and his brother Samuel migrated to Philadelphia. There are no records of their movements, and Alexander provides no details about his father, but most black southern migrants to Philadelphia experienced mixed results. Compared to New York and Boston, it was more difficult for black men to obtain skilled jobs in Philadelphia. According to Roger Lane, "in terms of skilled jobs the situation was worse on Philadelphia's side of the Mason-Dixon line." When Hillard and Samuel arrived in Philadelphia, the 1880 census reported that "80 to 90 percent of black adults could read and write." Even if black men were literate, whites employed them as unskilled laborers. It would not be surprising if the two future entrepreneurs had lived in Washington, D.C., or Baltimore for a while before coming to Philadelphia. Historian Robert Gregg maintains that financially successful black migrants often had some prior experience with urban life. Virginia Pace, Raymond's mother, was born a slave in 1854 to Thomas and Jenne Pace in Essex County, Virginia, seventy-five miles south of Washington, D.C. Virginia and her brother John Schollie Pace migrated to Philadelphia in 1880. Two years later, Virginia and Hillard Alexander married.[1]

Alexander's parents were part of the first wave of a black migration out of the Deep and Upper South that occurred between the end of Reconstruction and the turn of the twentieth century. After Reconstruction, the federal and southern state governments attempted to ensure that black labor remained in the South. African Americans worked primarily as sharecroppers and tenant farmers for white landowners. In response to the challenge of Populism, whites used legal as well as illegal means to disfranchise African American men. By the late 1870s, some southern African Americans were moving from rural communities to the West and the urban South. Growing numbers of African Americans from Virginia, Maryland, and North Carolina migrated north to Baltimore, Philadelphia, and New York City. Black men and women left in search of economic opportunities and to escape the wanton violence associated with Jim Crow.[2]

When Alexander's parents arrived in Philadelphia during the 1880s, the city was in transition. As the population grew, economic opportunities became available for African Americans. By the 1890s, the city was building trolley tracks and improving its infrastructure. Alexander's parents were part of what Roger Lane refers to as the "unskilled majority." The wages that the Alexanders earned in Philadelphia were an improvement over the wages in the rural South. In addition, racial tensions between blacks and the Irish had decreased, which allowed African Americans to establish their own communities. However, by the turn of the century, blacks had to compete with Italian immigrant workers. Whites confined black residents of Philadelphia and other northern cities to decaying housing in densely populated neighborhoods.[3]

The growth of the black community in Philadelphia affected city politics. Two years before Hillard and Samuel arrived in Philadelphia, two African Americans were serving on the school board in the Fifth and Seventh Wards, both black neighborhoods. Philadelphia was divided into thirty wards, and each had a common councilor. By 1891, the black community elected "three common councilors and five sectional school directors." Class played a role in local elections, as the black elite organized political organizations such as the "Committee of One Hundred" to protect their interests. While the black elite obtained the highest paid positions, by 1891 there were "60 policemen, one fireman, eight public school janitors" from Philadelphia's African American population. Hillard was a Republican, but he was a southern migrant and part of the black working poor, and obtaining a civil service job depended upon having local connections. Racism and poverty made it difficult to develop and sustain an independent black vote. By the late 1880s, there was not one African American common councilor. Black political power depended upon the expanding black population as well as patronage.[4]

According to DuBois, between 1870 and 1890, the city's black population increased from 22,147 to 39,371; by 1900, it had risen to 62,613. When Hillard Alexander arrived, the majority of the black community lived in the Seventh Ward, and the majority of African Americans were working class. The year Alexander was born, his family lived at 534 South 24th Street, in what DuBois classified as the ""fair to comfortable" section of the ward. Their home was located at the edge of the neighborhood on a predominantly white block. DuBois's occupational study listed one horse trainer aged 31–40, who may well have been Alexander's father or uncle.[5] In Philadelphia and most other northern cities, a significant proportion of black married women had to work to supplement their husband's income. However, according to Alexander's birth certificate, at the time of his birth, Virginia Pace Alexander did not have any paid employment. Virginia could have taken in washing or sewing to make money. Perhaps Hillard made enough money to enable her not to seek outside employment; perhaps, like many men, he did not want his wife to work for whites and deal with racism and sexism. DuBois described southern migrants who had lived in Philadelphia for a decade or two as ambitious, literate, and active in the church; most encouraged their children to attend school past the sixth grade. The black working class lived in the "midst of discouragements" as they encountered the city's pervasive white racism. According to DuBois, 56 percent of the black families in Philadelphia were working class and adhered to the respectable values that Alexander internalized, especially hard work, thrift, education, church, and family.[6]

During the late nineteenth century, whites denied African Americans opportunities to learn skilled trades and get industrial jobs, confining them to menial labor and service work. In Philadelphia, whites excluded black men and women from employment in the many small manufacturing workshops located near their neighborhoods. The majority toiled as longshoremen, caterers, day laborers, and domestic workers. Many African Americans viewed an occupation that served wealthy whites as a high-status position. Hillard Alexander occupied such a situation. Many black service workers relied on formal good manners to preserve their dignity in such close-contact situations; often, indeed, they out-polited white folks. But they also dissembled, wearing masks that employers found inscrutable. Raymond Pace Alexander's birth certificate listed his father's occupation as a "Riding Master." Hillard and his brother Samuel Alexander rented stables at the Alpine Riding Academy and gave riding lessons to some of Philadelphia's wealthiest white families for approximately twenty years. By 1915, however, black entrepreneurs who served whites faced increasing difficulties. Roger Lane found that "just as white men were increasingly unwilling to patronize black barbers," the Seventh Ward "was getting big and black enough to scare off white women."[7] As more African Americans moved into Philadelphia and the black residential area grew in size, the white elite stopped patronizing black businesses. Barbers, caterers, and other businesses that relied on whites failed. Raymond Alexander recalled that his father and uncle "did not have the foresight to abandon" their horse training business, and his father's horse riding lessons ended because of the emergence of the "automobile era in 1910–1915."[8] Elite white Philadelphians replaced African American employees and service providers with working-class whites and immigrants. The Alexanders lacked the capital to purchase their own stables, so they had no property to sell.

On June 17, 1903, shortly after his younger brother Schollie was born, Alexander's mother died of pneumonia. In 1896, the death rate for Negroes from pneumonia was 293.62 per 100,000, almost twice as high as that among whites. DuBois attributes the prevalence of pneumonia and consumption to poor housing conditions in the Seventh Ward. Alexander's father's long work days made it difficult for him to take care of his five children. Alexander's father decided that Raymond and his four siblings, Irene, Hillard Jr., Virginia, and Schollie, should live with their maternal aunt, Georgia Chandler Pace, in North Philadelphia. Born in 1866 in Richmond, Virginia, Georgia Chandler graduated from high school and taught in King and Queen County, Virginia. In 1887, she migrated to Philadelphia and married Alexander's maternal uncle John Schollie Pace, who was from Essex County, Virginia. Initially the Paces lived in South Philadelphia, but in 1902 they moved to North Philadelphia, an expanding black community. They joined Zion Baptist Church, the third largest black church in Philadelphia, where Alexander remained a member for the rest of his life. Zion Baptist played an important role in Alexander's life. Before Alexander and his siblings moved in, the Paces adopted a daughter named Alice. Georgia Pace's husband John was a waiter. With a family of eight, the Paces represented the African American working poor.[9]

At the age of eight, immediately following his mother's death, Raymond started working to assist his family. As soon as he was old enough to earn money, he told his father "to count him out of his calculations" because he would take care of his own expenses. Hillard Alexander gave money to help Georgia and John take care of the children. Initially Raymond worked on the docks unloading fish. Later on, he sold newspapers. He started at 6:00 A.M., finished delivering the papers at 7:30, went home for breakfast, and then went to school. He earned twelve dollars a week. Alexander also owned a bootblack stand where he worked six days a week. On Sundays, he paid a friend to tend the stand while he attended church and participated in the Boy's Choir of Zion Baptist Church. Despite his long workdays, Alexander made time for school. In 1905, he entered John Hancock Elementary School. The majority of black children attended integrated schools in Philadelphia, but black teachers were prohibited from working in them. By 1910, Philadelphia had nine separated black schools, all of which promoted industrial education.[10]

When Alexander attended school, most white educators blamed African Americans for their below-average academic achievements. Instead of recognizing the significance of class, white teachers viewed race as the problem, so black children had to prove to white teachers that they were smart. In 1910, Philadelphia school district superintendent Dr. Martin G. Brumbaugh hired Howard W. Odum, a white sociologist, to conduct a study of black children in the elementary schools. Odum studied black "retardation," which he defined not as mental incapacity but as the slower advancement of black students through the elementary grades. In 1910, white sixth graders were, on average, 12.4 years of age while black sixth graders were, on average, 13.9. Black students were much more likely to leave school early as well. By the eighth grade, there were 6,869 white children and alarmingly few black children—just 186—in the city school system. Only 4 percent of whites and 2.3 percent of black students reached the eighth grade, and most of them did not attend high school. Odum attributed black students' retardation to "poor sleeping habits, lack of concentration, poor attendance, lateness, black working mothers, poor body hygiene and partly because of innate traits." What Odum failed to mention was the impact of racialized poverty, which meant that a higher proportion of black mothers and children had to work.[11]

Given his family's poverty, Raymond Pace Alexander could not take his education for granted. In a 1956 letter to Reverend Leon Sullivan, Alexander recalled that his aunt and uncle told him and his siblings that they had to leave the household after they completed high school; they "did not want him to go to college." Although his aunt had been a teacher, she "discouraged him from getting an education."[12] Perhaps she feared that the family would be unable to support so many young persons in school at once, or as an educated African American woman she may have concluded that college-educated African Americans still felt the sting of discrimination. Alexander lived in his aunt's home until he graduated from college, but he may have mentioned his aunt's statements to demonstrate the challenges he encountered as an adolescent. Throughout his high school and college years, he earned money to support himself and his family.

Alexander attended the prestigious all-boys Central High School, the second oldest high school in America, and took college preparatory courses. When Alexander entered Central, the curriculum was divided into an academic track for college-bound students and a commercial track for those preparing for business careers. Central's academic curriculum was divided into four sections: Classical, Latin Scientific, Modern Languages, and Commerce. Alexander took the Latin Scientific course, coupling classical languages with modern sciences. Central's new curriculum was part of a trend in American education toward professionalization. In addition to his academic work, Alexander joined the track team, and his classmates elected him as the first black editor of the school newspaper, *The Mirror*.[13]

One afternoon, Alexander was delivering his newspapers near the Metropolitan Opera House in North Philadelphia when Jack Beresin, the owner of the Metropolitan Opera, called to him. Alexander was sixteen years old and a second-year student at Central High School. He told Beresin about his mother's death and explained that he had to work to help his family. After their talk, Beresin offered Alexander a job. Alexander later acknowledged that Beresin "opened a new world for me," and that environment, Alexander recalled, gave him "some of the smoothness and culture which characterizes my later years." After the meeting, Alexander recalled asking himself, "who in our families in the lower economic and social group had ever heard of opera?" This job served as his training ground in the rules and culture of the white elite. It provided a rare interracial space for Alexander to come in contact with wealthy whites. At the Met, he held a myriad of positions; he sold librettos and worked in the coat room, smoking room, and ticket booth. His colleagues at the Met called him Ray, and he became their friend. As a result, Alexander attended rehearsals and met opera singers from around the world. Since a large number of patrons were Europeans, Alexander's proficiency in German, French, and Italian improved. A number of his teachers attended the opera, which Alexander thought made his relationships with them "more intimate and more enjoyable." He worked at the Met for six years and maintained that his employment there prepared him for honors work at college. This experience stood Alexander in good stead after he entered the legal profession. His association with opera stars and elite whites gave him his stage presence. Throughout his legal career, Alexander recalled that people thought "he was acting while he was orating" in the court.[14]

Working at the Met and attending Central High School exposed Alexander to the upper-class white world. At the same time, the church provided him with a social and intellectual foundation in the black community and access to the black professional elite. E. W. Moore, the minister of Zion Baptist Church, had a great influence on Alexander. Alexander vividly remembered that it was "a rarity in those days (1905–1920)" for a church to have a "well educated and highly motivated Baptist clergyman." Moore represented a New Negro minister who concentrated on the religious, social, and intellectual needs of black Philadelphians. Complimenting Alexander on his college graduation, Moore told Alexander that his "success more than justifies my long stay in PHILA" and that religious teaching made him "a man of GOD and the RACE." Alexander recalled that Moore invited a number of influential African Americans to Zion Baptist because he wanted the church to serve as a meeting place for younger African Americans, regardless of denomination. During Alexander's sophomore year, he met the two most influential men in his life at the church's Annual Men's Day Forum: historian Carter G. Woodson and attorney William H. Lewis.[15]

In 1912, Carter G. Woodson became the second African American to earn a Ph.D. in history from Harvard University. (The first was W. E. B. DuBois in 1895.) Later that year, Moore invited Woodson to Zion Baptist. Alexander, who was fifteen years old, attended Woodson's lecture, and he discussed the lifelong impact of Woodson's address at the 1968 conference of the Association for the Study of Negro Life and History (ASNLH). According to Alexander, Woodson declared to his black audience that Africans were not "barbaric tribesman" but had built major civilizations; they were skilled artisans, especially ironsmiths. Alexander recalled that during Woodson's presentation, he said to himself, "I got the message I saw the image." Alexander realized that he "should be proud of his race, but I need to know more." Alexander admitted to himself that before hearing Woodson speak, he "knew nothing of myself, and the white man knew nothing about me. I was a total 'Stranger in the House,' and the house America was as much my house as that of my white schoolmate." Woodson's speech reaffirmed Alexander's American citizenship as well as his African identity. In order to understand American history, Alexander had to understand his African past and his people's contributions to American history. According to Woodson's biographer Jacqueline Goggin, whenever Woodson gave a speech, he presented a plethora of information on African and African American history, and "he frequently electrified them with his oratorical skills." Woodson's breadth of knowledge and passion for history inspired Alexander and laid the ideological foundation for Alexander's civil rights struggle, because it represented the New Negro's race pride and it influenced them to demand justice in America.[16]

The study of African and African American history was a vital ingredient in eradicating racism. Regardless of what whites professed about blacks' innate inferiority, Alexander knew that African Americans contributed to American history and that people of African descent were not inferior to whites. African Americans had the same rights and privileges as any white American did, at least in principle, and should be able to enjoy them in practice. Before Woodson's visit, Alexander contemplated dropping out of high school, although he never explained why. He might have felt alien in Central High's social environment. A number of black leaders of Alexander's generation were educated in all-black high schools in the South. The most famous was M Street High School in Washington, D.C., which attorneys Charles Hamilton Houston and William Hastie both attended. M Street's nurturing environment and challenging curriculum prepared black students for elite white northern colleges. Northern cities did not have an M Street High School, so gifted black students attended the predominantly white high school for middle-class whites. Although he was becoming acculturated at the Met and comfortable around white people, that environment constantly reinforced overt and covert reminders of race. While he never commented on the uncomfortable aspects of his social life at Central, it is possible that some white students ostracized Alexander. The majority of students in the academic track were from white, middle-class families. The only other black student who graduated with Alexander was in the commercial course. Woodson's speech inspired Alexander to complete high school, and the two remained lifelong friends. Although Alexander was not a professional historian, he, like most New Negroes in the 1920s, became an active member of Woodson's Association for the Study of Negro Life and History. Alexander embraced Woodson's view of black history as a tool to build race pride and combat racism. With Woodson, Alexander believed that if all Americans studied African American history race relations would improve.[17]

The individual who motivated Alexander to choose law as a profession was William H. Lewis, appointed by Theodore Roosevelt as the first black Assistant Attorney General in the United States. "Lewis's appearance at Zion Baptist Church was an outstanding occasion and created a lasting impression upon me," Alexander recalled. Lewis came from a background similar to Alexander's: his father was born a slave in the Tidewater section of Virginia. Lewis attended a prestigious white college, Amherst, where he was co-captain of the football team. In 1895, Lewis was the fourth black man to graduate from Harvard Law School. At the time, he held the highest-level appointment of any African American in the federal government. Alexander described his relationship with Lewis as like father and son because Lewis mentored him as a black professional and their relationship continued after Alexander graduated from law school.[18]

Together, Woodson and Lewis provided Alexander with inspiration, intellectual foundations, and an opportunity for a working-class black student to associate with black professionals. Woodson offered him historical consciousness and race pride, secure ground for his high aspirations: Lewis opened to him a legal avenue for personal achievement and the pursuit of civil rights. While Central High provided Alexander the information necessary to achieve in white society, Zion Baptist Church furnished him with the social and intellectual foundation for advocacy on behalf of his race. This was the defining moment of Alexander's young adult years, and Alexander combined racial consciousness and the law to create a template for obtaining black equality and eradicating racism.

In 1916, during Alexander's junior year, Central's president, Robert Ellis Thompson, visited Alexander's shoeshine stand and presented him with some excellent news: Alexander had been nominated for senior honors and had received a four-year scholarship to attend the University of Pennsylvania. Alexander described this as "the happiest moment of my life and a thrill of a lifetime." Winning a college scholarship was a remarkable feat for a working-class African American. The highly educated black faculty at all-black M Street High School in Washington, D.C., encouraged students' aspirations. In Philadelphia, by contrast, Alexander was isolated among white students in an environment that was more demanding than supportive. Raymond graduated from Central in February 1917, at twenty years of age. His senior yearbook praised "'Aleck,' whose ready wit and humor helps us pass many weary lecture hour."[19]

At commencement, Alexander delivered a speech entitled "The Future of the American Negro," which the *Philadelphia Tribune* published on the front page. Alexander reflected on the devastating impact of racism in America. Highlighting the progress of a people only sixty-two years removed from slavery, Alexander argued that "the Negro race is richly endowed with qualities that the white man cannot afford to leave undeveloped." He mentioned black people who had contributed to American history, including several Africans who had sailed with Columbus; Matthew Henson, the first American to see the North Pole; and Crispus Attucks, the first person shot in the Boston Massacre, and extolled the courage of black soldiers fighting for the Union during the Civil War. The second half of his address emphasized the national significance of southern racism. Alexander viewed the "Negro Problem" as a national rather than a sectional issue. Americans needed to shift the "Negro Problem to a Human Problem" and recognize that "when the South commits a crime the North commits a crime." By 1917, the North had abandoned blacks and allowed the white South to have its way on racial issues. Alexander cautioned, "If whites continue to treat blacks as second class citizens whites themselves will suffer."[20]

In 1917, Alexander enrolled in the University of Pennsylvania's Wharton School of Finance. During the first two decades of the twentieth century, the majority of African Americans obtained their bachelor's degree from black colleges and universities in the South. According to sociologist Charles S. Johnson, 146 African Americans graduated from northern colleges in 1920, and 439 graduated in 1933. This shift came about primarily because of black migration. World War I created more opportunities for African Americans in the north; as a result, a growing number of African Americans attended prestigious institutions in the North that prepared them for successful careers. These institutions exposed Alexander and many other black college students to the white elite. But social life remained segregated. Sadie Tanner Mossell, Alexander's girlfriend at Penn, recalled that the school prohibited black students from eating in the cafeteria, so "they brought their lunch and ate in the library." White universities rarely hired black professors, and the majority of black employees performed low-paid labor. By 1920, the University of Pennsylvania had approximately 35 black students, including undergraduate, professional, and graduate students.[21]

While taking a full load of courses at the University of Pennsylvania, Alexander worked not only at the Met but also as a waiter at the Broad Street Station Restaurant and in the Bellevue Stratford Hotel. Alexander recalled that World War I gave blacks an opportunity to work in the "greatest hotels in Philadelphia." Black labor was needed to fill in for white men who had gone into the armed forces and to compensate for the decline of European immigration labor resulting from the war. The majority of black students at Penn worked at service jobs to support themselves. For example, Herbert Millen, a law student at Penn, worked in the post office in the evenings. Alexander recalled they were both "involved with the problem of earning enough money to pay for food, rent, clothing and books." Few African American students at Ivy League colleges had much time to socialize and discuss social issues. During the summers, Alexander worked in Atlantic City and at a Murray Hill hotel. In his junior year, he worked as a red cap at Grand Central Station and later as a Pullman porter. He worked the New York-to-Boston run, the Manhattan Merchant Limited, and the famous Bar Harbor Express from Boston. In these service positions, Alexander interacted frequently with middle- and upper-class white customers. Other New Negro lawyers had similar experiences. For instance, when Thurgood Marshall was an undergraduate at Lincoln University in Pennsylvania, he spent the summers working with his father at Gibson Island, a resort located fifteen miles from Baltimore. Like Alexander, Marshall worked for wealthy whites and learned how to talk and negotiate for tips. These jobs provided Alexander with valuable social skills.[22]

Alexander attended college during the worst period of racism and violence in American history. Lynching and race riots were the most notorious methods of violence that whites used to maintain white supremacy. Competition between white and black workers exacerbated racial strife. White unions refused to allow African American to join, so employers hired black laborers at a lower wage. Working-class whites blamed black laborers instead of white capitalists. During the summer before Alexander entered college, in 1917, white strikers attacking black replacement workers triggered the East St. Louis riot. At the end of the violence, thirty-five blacks and eight whites had died. During Alexander's sophomore year, a race riot occurred in Philadelphia. In the "red summer" of 1919, race riots occurred in Chicago and twenty-three other cities. The race riots were a national phenomenon. In spite of the lawlessness, Alexander was not contemplating a career in law; he had excelled in economics.[23]

Most African Americans viewed World War I as an opportunity to demonstrate loyalty to their country. In July 1918, DuBois wrote a controversial editorial in *The Crisis* advocating that African Americans "forget our special grievances and close our ranks" to fight for democracy. DuBois believed that in order to demonstrate their patriotism, citizenship, and courage; fulfill the duties and earn the privileges of citizenship; and avoid white backlash, it would be best for African Americans to support the war despite the segregation of the armed forces and the violence that black people encountered across the nation. During Alexander's sophomore year, the War Department created the Student's Army Training Corps (SATC), a predecessor of the ROTC, which allowed college men to volunteer and become "uniformed and subject to military discipline and with the pay of a private." On October 16, 1918, Alexander answered DuBois's call and was inducted into the SATC. Like the rest of the U.S. military, the University of Pennsylvania chapter of the SATC was segregated. Just another example of hypocrisy: black students demonstrating patriotism in a segregated unit. Alexander received an honorable discharge on December 18, 1918, six months after the Versailles Peace Treaty. Ironically, the same month Alexander received his honorable discharge from the SATC, a white manager at the Shubert Theater prohibited Alexander and his three friends from entering.[24]

During his senior year, Alexander carried twenty-six hours both semesters. In his final semester, he enrolled in nine classes and earned eight marks of "Distinguished," equivalent to an A. He received the highest grades in banking, economics, finance, sociology, and corporate law. Alexander completed the University of Pennsylvania in three and a half years with honors and received a Bachelor of Science degree in economics from Wharton, the second African American to do so. Although he qualified for Phi Beta Kappa, the national academic honor society, and Beta Gamma Sigma, an honor society for "finance and business" students, he was not elected to either one of these prestigious organizations. D. Heubner and P. Kelsy, professors and Phi Beta Kappa members, tried to get Alexander inducted into the chapter, warning the committee that if Alexander were not elected they would "never attend another meeting of this society." They failed, and Alexander waited fifty years before he became a member. Not all chapters of Phi Beta Kappa at predominantly white institutions excluded African Americans; the chapter at Amherst inducted Charles Hamilton Houston and William Hastie. Henry Louis Taylor Jr. and Song-Ho Ha describe the "roaring twenties as a watershed decade in black higher education," when 80,602 African Americans earned a bachelor's degree. Obtaining a college degree granted status and placed Alexander in the new black elite.[25]

In 1970, on the fiftieth anniversary of his college graduation, Alexander had these wrongs put right. He wrote to John R. C. Wheller, president of the University of Pennsylvania chapter of Beta Gamma Sigma, and Professor Henry J. Abraham, president of Delta Chapter of Phi Beta Kappa at the University of Pennsylvania, asking them to check his record to see if he had qualified for the honors. Wheeler wrote to Alexander: "after thoroughly researching your case in the University archives, we were able to substantiate clearly your allegations." Alexander wrote Eustace Gay, editor of the *Philadelphia Tribune*, that he had graduated "Magna Cum Laude" but had not been elected to the two honor societies for which he had qualified. He said he would not "go into the question of why," but added in parentheses his allegations "(Of denial of membership because of race)." The changed climate that allowed Alexander to be belatedly inducted into these honor societies in 1970 was due, in part, to his own achievements as a civil rights advocate.[26]

Alexander's experience at the University of Pennsylvania was similar to that of Rayford Logan, who became an African American historian, at Williams College. Logan's biographer Kenneth Janken notes that for black students attending white northern schools, "the college experience was a relatively painless one; while they were never allowed fully to shed the disabilities of racism, they were generally spared the rudeness and brutality that lay beyond the college gates."[27] After graduation, Alexander wanted to work in a famous Philadelphia bank, but the best offer he received was an opportunity to work at the bank's "foreign branch in Rio De Janeiro," Brazil. Since the rudeness of racism prevented Alexander from pursuing his dream of working in business, Alexander's professors encouraged him to pursue a doctorate in economics. Instead, taking the advice of Harvard Law School graduate William H. Lewis, he decided to attend law school at Harvard because it was clear to him that the best way to address segregation was by becoming a lawyer.[28]

Harvard University had accepted black students since 1865, and Boston, home to many black and white radicals, was one of the most liberal cities in the nation. In 1920, Boston's black residents numbered 16,530, only 2.2 percent of the city's population; the black population in Philadelphia was 134,229, 7.4 percent of the population.[29] The relatively small number of black people may have been a culture shock for Alexander; in Boston, as in Philadelphia, the majority of the black population resided in a segregated community. Since the city had a smaller black population, white Bostonians did not feel as threatened by African Americans; therefore, Boston's racial climate was less racist than Philadelphia, but black Bostonians encountered the same structural disadvantages as black Philadelphians. Boston's small black elite consisted of professionals and businessmen, such as William Monroe Trotter, a Harvard graduate, editor of the *Boston Guardian*, and one of the first militants to denounce Booker T. Washington's strategy of accommodation. In addition to attending one of the top law schools in America, Alexander attended a university with a history of successful black graduates and resided in a city with a black protest tradition.[30]

By the 1920s, the learned professions, including the law, had raised their standards and prestige by demanding formal credentials from accredited law schools and conducting their own licensing examinations. Charles Hamilton Houston arrived at Harvard in 1919 and became the first African American to receive honors. Unlike Houston and Hastie, Alexander worked to support himself while in law school. From September 1920 to February 1923, he served as a teaching assistant for Edmund E. Day and B. Burbank of the Economics Department, grading papers and conducting research. When he entered Harvard, there were approximately thirty black students in the graduate and professional schools, and, according to Alexander, half of the black Harvard students "enrolled under the Veterans College Aid Program," a post-World War I version of the GI Bill. Of the eight black students in his first-year law class, six had graduated from black colleges, but they were "not too well prepared" because their institutions lacked the resources to equip students for success or they had difficulty adjusting to the all-white environment. Alexander was the only African American in his class to graduate in 1923.[31]

Alexander recalled that at Harvard, as at the University of Pennsylvania, "social life between the white law student body and the blacks was totally non-existent." The Ivy League schools accepted just enough qualified black students in order not to upset southern white students and their parents. African American students at Harvard socialized with one another. Charles Hamilton Houston recalled meeting Alexander, "a tall lanky, but handsome and outgoing" first-year student. Genna Rae McNeil notes that Alexander kept to a strict weekday study schedule; on weekends he attended socials at the Cosmopolitan Club, where he met other black students from Boston. Black graduate and professional students preferred to drink tea instead of liquor at the parties, and Alexander had earned the nickname "TP" for "Tea Party" because he served tea at socials. During Alexander's first year of law school, half of the four hundred law students were white southerners, and whites from both North and South "said a quiet hello and no more." White law clubs excluded black and Jewish law students; therefore, black students organized the Dunbar Law Club, which they allowed a "few friendly Northern Jews" to join. He continued to value the black-Jewish alliance for civil rights through the 1960s, when it was called into question by a growing number of African Americans. Alexander had close relationships with educated Jews throughout his life, but during the sixties, when tensions developed between working and low-income blacks and working-class Jews, Alexander could not understand why younger African Americans had a problem with the Jewish community.[32]

During the summers after his first and second years at Harvard Law, Alexander enrolled in the master's program in political science at Columbia University, but he never finished his degree. Columbia University was located in Harlem, the black Mecca where many professionals and artists resided, and a new attitude emerged that shaped Alexander's generation. In spite of the courage black soldiers had shown during World War I, whites lynched black soldiers in uniform. In northern states, whites continued to segregate and discriminate against blacks in public accommodations. Alexander's two years in New York City exposed him to the power of black culture and racial pride.

While living in New York, he worked at the Delaware, Lackawanna & Western Railroad in New Jersey as a porter and red cap. Instead of a salary, he received tips. One summer, Alexander recalled, he made a thousand dollars in tips to take back to Harvard. While in law school, Alexander continued his relationship with Sadie Mossell, who had earned a Ph.D. in economics from the University of Pennsylvania in 1921. He recalled later that she initially studied economics "so she could talk on his level of knowledge." A black woman completing an advanced degree in a field dominated by white men became a national news story. Sadie exclaimed to Raymond: "Can you imagine such publicity being attached to a little thing like me?" A photographer from the International Press Film Service came to Philadelphia and took her picture for the New York papers. She paid for Alexander's train ticket to come from New York to attend her graduation. After graduation, racism and sexism prevented Dr. Mossell from obtaining a teaching position in a black or white university. She did not apply to any of the elite black high schools, which often hired faculty with Ph.D.s, nor did they recruit her. She accepted a position at the North Carolina Mutual Insurance Company in Durham, North Carolina, a large black-owned life insurance company.[33]

While he was at Harvard studying law and living among a cohort of black students who wanted to improve the status of African Americans, Alexander recounted, his "sense of injustice to Negroes other than myself spilled to the point of public protest." Alexander had encountered discrimination as an undergraduate, but after his first year of law school he decided to do something about it. Alexander brought his first discrimination suit on July 19, 1921. Alexander went to Madison Square Garden to use its public facilities, which at that time included a bathhouse and swimming pool, but when he presented his ticket, the worker refused him entry. This act violated the 1918 New York State Equal Rights law prohibiting discrimination in public accommodations. Violators were subject to a fine of "not less than one hundred dollars nor more than five hundred dollars" and could be imprisoned between thirty and ninety days. Alexander hired an attorney, James D. McLendon, to represent him. The summons stated that the Garden refused to admit Alexander "because of the plaintiff's race and color." Although the outcome of the case is unknown, during the same month *The Crisis* reported that four African Americans "were awarded $100" in a discrimination case against a Manhattan coffee house. In the city that represented American freedom and equality, white immigrants just off the boat could be served in a downtown coffee house or swim at the Garden, while native-born African Americans could not. Alexander demanded justice through the courts and concluded that using the law was the best strategy to combat racism. Alexander's lawsuit was a culmination of personal experiences with racism as well as educational and personal development in his church.[34]

When he returned to Cambridge in September 1921, Harvard University had constructed five new freshman dormitories but refused to allow black students to live in them. After their freshman year, black students were allowed to live on campus. Harvard's former president Charles Eliot sought to diversify the student body, so Harvard had admitted more white students from public schools and from the South. In 1921, "the ultra conservative Brahmin" Abbot Lawrence Lowell initiated the segregationist policy and imposed a "racial" quota limiting the number of Jewish students at Harvard. Lowell maintained that he supported equal educational opportunity for blacks but that the university should not force white students into "social relations that are not mutually congenial." During the 1920s, African Americans and Jews "invaded" higher education and the professions. In the view of white Anglo-Saxon Protestant male aristocrats, the influx of black and Jewish students illustrated "outsiders" challenging their status and trespassing on their territory. Following in the tradition of blaming blacks and Jews for racism, Lowell opined that he was protecting black and Jewish students by not provoking white southern students. After class and on campus, Harvard University was entirely segregated. One of the students denied dormitory housing was Roscoe Conkling Bruce Jr., the son of Roscoe Conkling Bruce Sr., a 1902 Harvard graduate. Alexander's impassioned essay on the issue, "Voices from Harvard's Own Negroes," was later published in *Opportunity*, the National Urban League journal.[35]

Alexander asserted that the younger Bruce represented a "new element of Negroes" entering college. This second generation was academically better prepared than their fathers, but the "pernicious policy of discrimination" still existed. Harvard freshmen needed to live in the dormitories because middle-class black families in Boston "do not make a practice of taking lodgers." Working-class black families in Boston allowed students to live with them to increase their income. Alexander asked, "Will Harvard next adopt the Yale policy" that prohibited African Americans from living in the dormitories to "preserve race relations"? At the end of the essay, Alexander praised the tradition of excellence established by black Harvard graduates. Harvard can "look with pride at the list of America's outstanding Negroes such as W. E. B. DuBois and Carter G. Woodson, men who by their deeds have gained the respect and admiration of an entire race." Alexander's letter received support from members of the Black Harvard Alumni Association. White Harvard alumni such as Franklin Delano Roosevelt despised the racist policy. The president of the organization proclaimed that a black historical tradition existed at Harvard. In 1923, Harvard's Board of Trustees overturned Lowell's racist policy.[36]

Alexander and other black students organized the "Nile Club" to protest the university's discriminatory policy. The name signified the race consciousness and agitation that characterized the New Negro. A major component of the New Negro movement was the study of African and African American history, and the Nile River symbolized African American's identification with this ancient African civilization. The first president of the Nile Club was Charles Hamilton Houston, who obtained his law degree in 1921 and was completing his Juris Doctorate at Harvard in 1923. Hamilton mentored Alexander and other black law students. Genna Rae McNeil notes that in 1921 Hamilton invited Marcus Garvey, the Jamaica-born president of the Universal Negro Improvement Association (UNIA), to speak to the Nile Club. Twenty-two African American men, including Alexander, paid two dollars each to host the event. Theodore Kornweibel contends that this black nationalist leader was "an undesirable, and indeed a very dangerous, alien" and was J. Edgar Hoover's and the U.S. government's number one public enemy. Alexander and the Nile Club were not aware of the government's dealings with Garvey, but inviting Garvey to speak at Harvard illustrates the racial radicalism of the Nile Club and New Negroes. Expressing racial pride and solidarity in a racist society was a radical act. Members of the Nile Club used their racial consciousness to develop confidence, which enabled Alexander to succeed in an all-white environment. According to biographer Jacqueline

Goggin, Carter G. Woodson "admired Garvey and supported him," and at that time Alexander, like Woodson, appreciated Garvey's emphasis on history, race pride, and economic self-help.[37]

During the last semester of his senior year at Harvard, and for the first time in his life, Alexander did not have to work as well as study. He graduated from Harvard Law in 1923, one of 275 African Americans who earned law degrees between 1921 and 1925. Between 1920 and 1930, only nine black students graduated from Harvard Law School. While Harvard students tolerated black law students such as Alexander, Houston, and Hastie, Gilbert Ware suggests that Harvard Law "unwillingly planted the seeds of destruction—at least in a legal sense—of the racist order."[38] New Negroes of Alexander's generation became pioneers in their professions. In the twenties, the law was not the most highly sought-after profession in the black community. When Alexander graduated from law school, the total number of black lawyers trailed the total number of dentists and doctors. Black Ph.D.s were a "Talented but a Trapped Tenth"; they could teach only in historically black colleges or high schools. Racism deterred black people from entering the legal profession because there is only one system of justice and black lawyers met the judicial system head on and had to face all-white juries and judges.[39]

Alexander took the Pennsylvania Bar examination on July 2 and 3, 1923, and passed it on the first try. Geraldine Segal maintains that between 1908 and 1920, not one African American passed the Pennsylvania Bar exam, and this situation reoccurred between 1933 and 1943. In fact, between 1920 and 1933, only thirteen black attorneys in Philadelphia were admitted to the Pennsylvania Bar. In 1970, the Philadelphia Bar Association created a special committee to study discrimination in the admission to the bar. The Liacouras committee reported that the reason that a lower percentage of African Americans than whites passed the exam was pure and simple racism. All test candidates had to submit a photograph with their application, and the test graders received some personal information before they graded the exam. By 1930, Philadelphia had 219,599 black residents, making it the country's third-largest urban black population, but there were only twenty black attorneys. Chicago had 175 black attorneys, and New York had 106. When Alexander returned to Philadelphia, he represented a new generation of black attorneys, trained in elite law schools and primed to dismantle discrimination.[40]

Alexander made a number of connections with influential people at Harvard, such as Dean Roscoe Pound and Professor Samuel Williston. Both men tried to get Alexander a job at a prestigious white law firm in Philadelphia, their recommendations intentionally leaving out Alexander's race. Based on his Harvard education, the members of the Philadelphia firm assumed that he was a "white Anglo-Saxon Protestant of scholarship and character," but when Alexander arrived at the firm, he recalled that "Mr. X" read and complimented his letters of recommendation but stated simply "I am very sorry, we can't use you," and escorted him to the elevator. Following the exchange, Alexander "burst out in a flush of tears," and as the rejections mounted, Alexander became more determined to end segregation in Philadelphia and the nation. After his rejection, Alexander worked for attorney John R. K. Scott, a white Republican and state representative who defended famous black criminals. Scott was a customer of Alexander's father's riding academy, and the two had met at a restaurant where Alexander worked right before he left for law school. Alexander's exceptional work induced Scott to ask him to continue working for him, but Alexander refused and, just three months after passing the bar, opened his own law firm on the third floor of the Brown and Stevens Bank Building located on Lombard Street in the Seventh Ward. Knowing the difficulties that black attorneys faced, Alexander took a risk starting out on his own, but he knew the black community needed black attorneys, and with a great deal of hard work and, more important, victories in the court, Alexander believed he could be successful.[41]

The city of brotherly love and sisterly affection was an ideal location for Alexander to start his career because Philadelphia was a northern city with southern racial patterns. The city was de facto segregated but some white businesses posted signs reading "No Negroes allowed." Whites denied blacks equal opportunity in employment, housing, education, and the courts. On January 26, 1924, *Philadelphia Tribune*, a biweekly black newspaper, printed an editorial titled "What Is Segregation?" The writer explained that segregation "is the enforced separation of one group from another by law or with the sanction of the law." The "separate but equal" doctrine allowed whites to distribute funds to "their particular institution first," but African Americans had "a right to fight against" any institution that discriminated against them. During the twenties, a number of black businessmen had benefited from segregation, but the black economy could not end black underemployment, and the white power structure denied black voters and taxpayers equal access to resources. The editorial expressed an important rationale of the northern civil rights struggle as equal access to public funds. White citizens voted for white public officials whose first priority was providing public resources for whites. African Americans paid taxes and voted but still did not receive the amount of resources that reflected the proportion of their votes.[42]

Louise Thomas Case, 1924

The Louise Thomas case made Alexander a race hero. Criminal cases comprised the bulk of African American attorneys' business and attracted a great deal of attention in local newspapers. In 1923, Louise Thomas, an African American woman, was accused of murdering a male African American police officer in her home. The first trial occurred in May 1924. Thomas hired two attorneys, Thomas J. Minnick Jr., who was white, and the neophyte Raymond Pace Alexander. After the first trial, the jury found Thomas guilty and sentenced her to death. Women's groups in Pennsylvania protested this decision and demanded a retrial. Black churches and welfare organizations hired Alexander as the lead attorney for the appeal, which was heard by the Pennsylvania Supreme Court in November. The Supreme Court "reversed the verdict and reordered a new trial." Following that decision, Minnick resigned, and the Thomas family tried to hire another white attorney, but they all refused because they thought that Thomas was guilty. Reluctantly, the Thomases rehired Alexander for the new trial.[43]

The retrial commenced in October 1925 with Judge William C. Ferguson, who had heard the first trial, presiding. After the all-white jury was selected, Alexander meticulously questioned the coroner and demonstrated to the jury that the evidence indicated that Thomas acted in self-defense against attempted murder. Alexander's legendary savvy and demeanor was already apparent. The *Philadelphia Tribune* described Alexander's "opening address" as "clear and forceful." Alexander questioned "twenty character witnesses," and his closing statement lasted "an hour and twenty minutes." According to the courtroom journalist, Alexander described the crime scene so vividly that "fainting women had to be carried from the room, and even jurors wept." After two hours of deliberation, the jury found Thomas not guilty.[44]

This case was a landmark in Pennsylvania legal history because an attorney secured a retrial for a defendant who had been declared guilty and sentenced to death, reargued the case against the same district attorney before the same judge, and won an acquittal. Fortunately, because both parties were black, racism was not an issue, but the jurors were all white. Significantly for the African American community, a black attorney had replaced a losing white attorney and won. The *Pittsburgh Courier*, which covered the trial, concluded that this case "undoubtedly has established the fact that the Negro lawyer has ability," and a week after the decision, a *Philadelphia Tribune* editorial titled "Our Lawyers Are Competent" declared: "Alexander not only saved the life of an unfortunate woman but he saved the lawyers of his race from further aspersion cast upon them by ignorant and uninformed Negroes." The Thomas case proved that "our lawyers are as competent, qualified and as resourceful as white attorneys" and in bold print, he declared, "NEGRO BUSINESS MEN EMPLOYING WHITE LAWYERS, TAKE NOTICE!" This short editorial summed up the precarious position occupied by Alexander and black attorneys across America. Most African Americans did not hire black attorneys and may have internalized the racist stereotype that black lawyers were incompetent or accepted the reality that a black attorney does not have a chance in an all-white judicial system. The judicial system excluded African Americans from juries, so many African Americans believed that only white attorneys had the power, influence, and complexion required to win cases. Alexander had to convince both whites and African Americans that he could get the job done.[45]

Personal Injury Suits

Alexander, like most attorneys, made a substantial portion of his income from personal injury law suits. As the number of black attorneys in the city and state increased, their status in the courts rose. African Americans now had an opportunity to obtain equal justice in negligence cases. Across the country a dual compensation system existed in negligence cases. For example, Carter G. Woodson mentioned that African Americans in Cleveland received on average only half as much as whites in financial settlements, since white juries were "not inclined to award large damages" to African Americans. In Philadelphia a number of people were injured or killed each year by streetcars in accidents resulting from negligence on the part of the Philadelphia Rapid Transit Corporation (PRTC). African Americans had a difficult time taking the PRTC to court and receiving appropriate compensation. When Alexander began to litigate negligence cases, his clients were awarded more substantial sums. The larger the amount he won, the more press Alexander received in the *Philadelphia Tribune*. His first major negligence case involved Mrs. W. R. Henry, an African American pharmacist. According to the *Philadelphia Tribune*, Henry fell "boarding a trolley car and the door prematurely closed on her foot." The trial occurred in Common Pleas Court, with no witnesses except her husband and friend to collaborate her testimony. After deliberating for an hour and a half, the jury returned with a verdict in favor of Mrs. Henry, and she received

$5,000 and her husband received $500. This award set a precedent because the trial occurred "within the space of seven months" after the accident.[46]

Another well-publicized negligence case involved William Chew, a city employee who was struck by a trolley car on September 24, 1924, in North Philadelphia. Chew hired Alexander right after the accident. According to the *Philadelphia Tribune*, the PRTC "refused to pay a single cent" because Chew, a city employee, should have been cognizant of the danger of trolley cars. When the case was tried in 1926 in Common Pleas Court, both judges ruled in favor of PRTC. On appeal, a jury ruled in favor of Chew and awarded him $2,500. In October 1926, the PRTC appealed to the seven judges of the Superior Court. Alexander and John Williams, Alexander's colleague, represented Chew, and the Superior Court ruled in favor of Chew, for the first time holding the PRTC responsible for the safety of public employees. The entire settlement amounted to $8,000. The editorial stated that "Mr. Chew's patience, endurance and perseverance" made this victory possible. As in the Louis Thomas case, what mattered most to the black community was that a black lawyer defeated a white attorney in front of white judges and juries. Alexander's star as a New Negro lawyer was rising.

Desegregation Cases, 1924

Alexander filed his first civil rights suits in Philadelphia against Charles Starkosh, the manager of the Aldine Theatre located on 19th and Chestnut streets in downtown Philadelphia. In March 1924, Edward T. Green purchased two tickets "six days" in advance to see the film "The Ten Commandments." Josephine Williams accompanied Green to the theater. According to the *Philadelphia Tribune*, when Green handed the tickets to Starkosh, he informed Green that he could not enter because his tickets were "two stubs from an old date." Green told Starkosh that was a mistake, but Starkosh became verbally "abusive" and "ousted the couple from the theatre." Green hired Alexander. The case reached trial in April 1925, eleven months after the incident. The *Pittsburgh Courier* states that during the trial, Green and Williams argued that Starkosh was "insulting" when he forced the two to leave. Starkosh "denied any foul language and denied attempting to force them out." Theater employees supported Starkosh's testimony, although "there were noticeable discrepancies in their statements." The jury deliberated for thirty minutes and returned with a not guilty verdict. Starkosh had also used the switch ticket trick on Earl Groce and "his three companions," who "refused to be intimidated." Groce told Starkosh, "We bought our tickets and presented them." Starkosh did not resist and allowed Groce and his friends to enter the theater. In April 1924, Starkosh told some African American teachers that they arrived at the theater "too late" and could not enter. Alexander served as the lawyer for the teachers, and during the trial twelve African Americans testified on their behalf. Starkosh was held on "$500 bail" for violating the 1887 Pennsylvania Equal Rights Law. All twelve stated that Starkosh had violated their civil rights. In spite of the 1887 Pennsylvania's Equal Rights law, white managers such as Starkosh had the power to discriminate. On other occasions, such as the Groce incident, black people attending the theater in Philadelphia resisted and turned a potentially humiliating experience into a liberating one. In spite of Alexander's defeat in the Green case, African Americans continued to use his services. They must have realized that Alexander's defeat had nothing to do with his competency but rather reflected racism in the judicial system.[47]

Like most black lawyers, Alexander depended on the black community for most of his clientele. Since black lawyers were cheaper than white ones, immigrant whites hired them as well. In the early 1920s, black leaders such as Marcus Garvey, A. Philip Randolph, and W. E. B. DuBois all used white lawyers. They argued that black attorneys lacked experience, but how could an African American attorney get experience if black leaders refused to hire them? Alexander was determined to convince African Americans that he was competent. During his first month in business, Alexander grossed $456.50, and by the end of the year he had grossed $11,000. This income assured him that financial success was possible. Two months after opening the firm, Alexander asked Sadie Mossell Tanner to marry him. Alexander married into Philadelphia's black elite, but Alexander himself was becoming part of the modern black professional elite. After their marriage, Sadie Alexander decided to get a law degree from the University of Pennsylvania and, in 1927, became the first black woman to pass the Pennsylvania Bar exam. Alexander then hired his wife. The Alexanders had fulfilled the vow they made after the theater incident: they had both graduated from law school and were prepared to break down barriers in Philadelphia and participate in the national struggle for civil rights.[48]

The New Negro lawyer emerged from the collision between racial discrimination and the emerging race consciousness of a growing urban black community. Alexander benefited from the solidarity and resolve of black organizations. Alpha Phi Alpha, Zion Baptist Church, and the Nile Club exemplified the black community's strength, race consciousness, and protest. In May 1924, Alpha Phi Alpha invited the young lawyer to speak during its educational week. Alexander gave an address at the Dunbar Theatre titled "On to College." His comments were similar to the speeches Carter G. Woodson had made at Alexander's church a dozen years earlier. Alexander declared that "every colored boy and girl should know all there is to be known about those men and women of Negro of African descent." He lamented that black "boys and girls in our schools . . . know nothing of the Negro except what some sarcastic white man has written about his inferiority and his childlessness." Alexander was infuriated that two prominent scholars who spoke at the meeting, Mr. Watson and Dr. Barnes, two white men, concluded "the colored boy and girl should only be taught certain things, enough to make them good ordinary workers." Alexander used history to build race consciousness and to demand respect and equality for African Americans.[49]

August Meier suggests that New Negroes advocated self-help, race pride, and protest. Alexander experienced the impact of racism and segregation throughout his formative years. He faced discrimination at the University of Pennsylvania and Harvard, and exclusion from a Philadelphia theater and Madison Square Garden. These incidents induced Alexander to challenge segregation in the courts and create his own firm to aid other black attorneys. Alexander confronted the political, social, and economic as well as legal problems that plagued the black community, including housing, education, employment, and police brutality. In 1950, Alexander recalled that in 1923 whites treated blacks as second-class citizens. Black Philadelphians were refused service in white-owned restaurants; in white-owned theaters "the most uninviting side" was reserved for black patrons. Alexander was especially annoyed that a white criminal "just discharged from twenty years in prison for murder" received first-class service. African Americans struck by a trolley car received lower settlements than whites for similar injuries. Immediately after Alexander started to litigate personal injury suits, blacks received record settlements. By the 1920s, New Negro lawyers such as Alexander were in the forefront of local civil rights struggles across the nation.[50]

Chapter Two

USING THE LEFT TO FIGHT
FOR WHAT IS RIGHT

Civil Rights Law and Radicalism, 1925–1935

In 1934, Raymond Pace Alexander delivered a speech to a group of African American youth in Baltimore, Maryland, titled "The New Negro Fights For Justice." He declared that "this subject will be approached from the angle of the young, militant, Negro Lawyer and his efforts to obtain justice" for his people. Alexander's speech reviewed a number of significant national, state, and local cases that black attorneys litigated, with the "militant spirit exemplified by the new Negro attorney, both young and old, but principally the younger men that make up the Negro Bar in America." Alexander categorized the cases by their central issues: the right to serve on grand juries, the right to counsel, the right to vote, the right to free speech and assembly, the right to attend state-supported universities, the right to use public recreational facilities, and the right to picket and boycott for "race jobs." His address emphasized the major role that New Negro attorneys, like Alexander and others, played in obtaining civil rights for African Americans. The "young, militant, Negro Lawyer" Alexander was referring to was the New Negro Lawyer, and the eight central issues they litigated encompassed the civil rights struggle.[1]

According to law professor Kenneth Mack, New Negro attorneys advocated "racial uplift" that synthesized "a voluntarist strand that emphasized intraracial progress, and a legalist strand that centered on moral and legal claims directed to the larger white majority." The concern for race progress included developing successful black institutions and attaining economic gains, and Alexander's public accommodation desegregation cases used plaintiffs' class status in order to claim racial equality. Mack argues that New Negro attorneys, such as Alexander, used "respectable plaintiffs" with "appeals to common bonds of class . . . that turned intraracial identity into an effective claim for inclusion in civic life." Alexander and other black elites believed that their education, values, status, and light skin color entitled them to first-class citizenship, but racism and the Great Depression demonstrated the limits of only using legal and moral claims for equality. By the early thirties, working-class and left-wing activism increased, forcing black elites to adopt new tactics in the civil rights struggle. The political pressure from the left and working-class organizations persuaded Alexander to endorse a radical tactic, mass protests, and from 1925 to 1935, Alexander's New Negro radicalism consisted of litigation, black organizational and institution building, coalitions with liberal and leftist whites, and mass demonstrations. Alexander combined these strategies with civil rights law into a successful campaign that led to the passing of the 1935 Pennsylvania Equal Rights Law.[2]

Prior to the rise of the New Negro Lawyer, the black bar in America had embraced Booker T. Washington's strategy of accommodation. In 1909, the same year the NAACP was formed, black lawyers organized the National Negro Bar Association (NNBA) as an outgrowth of Washington's National Negro Business League (NNBL). Southern black attorneys, including Mississippi's Perry Howard, a close friend of Alexander, dominated the NNBA. The NNBA and the NNBL met every year from 1909 through 1919, but, according to law professor J. Clay Smith, the black lawyers left because the businessmen did not want to "rock the boat." The NNBA adopted Washington's racial ideologies, but after World War I, African American lawyers rejected his acceptance of second-class citizenship. They continued to embrace Washington's self-help philosophy because black lawyers relied upon the black community for their success.[3]

After World War I, black lawyers espoused the civil rights agitation advocated by W. E. B. DuBois. The majority had graduated from prestigious white law schools. According to J. Clay Smith, in 1920 there were 946 black male and 4 black female attorneys; a decade later those numbers had increased to 1,223 men and 24 women. In 1925, George Woodson, a black lawyer who had formed the Iowa Colored Bar Association in 1895, founded the National Bar Association (NBA). Black attorneys with the "New Negro" outlook controlled the NBA; its constitution states that the organization assisted black attorneys to perfect their craft and "protect the civil and political rights of all citizens." The NBA represents the shift toward New Negro activism among lawyers. According to Darlene Clark Hine, the NBA "proved to be far more radical, far more capable of nurturing resistance, than anyone could have anticipated" during the 1920s. Hine contends that the NBA was a "parallel institution" that "offered black Americans not only private space to buttress battered dignity, nurture positive self-images, sharpen skills, and demonstrate expertise" but also "safe havens" that allowed black attorneys to develop "networks across communities served."[4]

Black lawyers formed local bar associations that mirrored the NBA. New Negro lawyers created such radical bar associations as the Mound City Bar Association in St. Louis, Missouri, and the John Mercer Langston Law Club in Philadelphia. Alexander joined the NBA and the John Mercer Langston Law Club in 1925. These "parallel institutions" provided him the resources and connections he needed to fight for civil rights. Alexander recalled that when he started practicing law, two generations of black attorneys lived in Philadelphia: the "older Negro bar," including men like John C. Asbury who passed the bar before 1920, and the thirteen lawyers who passed the bar between 1920 and 1933 and "had been trained at the larger and more prominent schools and universities of the North." The John M. Langston Bar Association brought the two groups together and provided "a means of closer association among its members." Alexander's views and activities exemplify the New Negro lawyer.[5]

Walter Rounds Case, 1925

As an active member of the NBA and his local bar association, Alexander was more than adequately prepared to fight for equality in Philadelphia. On the local level, he joined a legal struggle initiated by the NAACP. By the 1920s, the NAACP was successful in defending the rights of African Americans. The NAACP strategy consisted of using test cases the NAACP legal team could win in order to build support for the organization. The test case strategy was problematic on a local level. If the NAACP's national office did not believe that they could win a case, they refused to provide any financial or media support to the local attorney. Black attorneys had to use their own resources to fight cases the national office deemed unpromising. The tension between Alexander and the national office of the NAACP was visible in the 1925 Walter Lee Rounds assault case.

Walter Lee Rounds was a twenty-one-year-old African American elevator operator in Jacquert's department store in Philadelphia. On February 13, 1925, eighteen-year-old Margaret McPherson Stoddard, an upper-middle-class white woman from Savannah, Georgia, boarded Round's elevator. The elevator suddenly stopped between the fourth and fifth floors. According to court testimony, Stoddard "screamed, [Y]ou nigger, you hit me" and ran out of the elevator. The police arrested Rounds and took him to jail.[6] In February 1925, Joseph B. Bowser, a friend of Walter Rounds, sent a letter to Robert Bagnall, NAACP's director of branches, explaining that the police had "framed" Rounds and held him without bail. According to Bowser, the two detectives placed "guns to his head," "threatened to kill him," and gave him the infamous "3rd degree" when Rounds refused to sign a confession. Bowser maintained that Rounds's father was poor but belonged to the NAACP. All NAACP members regardless of class were entitled to the privileges of the organization. Bagnall forwarded the letter to Walter White, the assistant secretary of the NAACP. White immediately informed Isadore M. Martin, president of the Philadelphia NAACP branch, that the Rounds case "may be a good case" for the local group to take up. The branch was responsible for raising funds and getting publicity for the defense. White promised Bowser that the NAACP would investigate the case and "prevent injustice being done to Mr. Rounds." The Rounds case provided an excellent opportunity for the Philadelphia branch to increase its membership.[7]

The trial occurred on March 4, 1925, three weeks after the alleged crime. Alexander represented Rounds pro bono because Rounds's parents could not afford to pay legal fees but attended Alexander's church. A number of black attorneys felt obligated to assist fellow church members. Alexander had only practiced law for two years, and a successful criminal lawyer needed to develop "proper relationships" in the court. During the trial, Assistant District Attorney John B. Kelly called Stoddard to testify. She stated that Rounds stopped the elevator on the third floor and told her that the car was not working. She claimed that Rounds left the elevator, preceded to a small room, picked up an iron bar, returned to the elevator, and "struck her twice in the head." Then Rounds threw her on floor with his hand in her mouth. She screamed, bit

Rounds's hand, and ran out of the elevator. Alexander stated to White that Rounds recalled when the elevator reached the third floor "the car gave a sudden larch" and Stoddard hit her head and received two cuts. Following the incident, Rounds's manager accepted his story, and he remained at work. Four white women heard the incident and one testified that Rounds said, "Don't worry lady, you are not hurt." While the evidence supported Rounds, the fact that the case involved a black man allegedly assaulting a white woman stacked the odds against him.[8]

The police treated Rounds with the brutality they reserved for black Philadelphians. According to Rounds's testimony, the police placed the "handcuffs on him extra tight" and threatened, "We will finish you today." Another detective declared, "dirty nigger, if we had him in the South we would tear him to pieces." Living in Philadelphia saved Rounds from a lynch mob but did not protect him from its northern equivalent, a forced confession. Rounds testified that the police had forced him to sign a confession. When the event occurred, Stoddard had accused Rounds only of hitting her, but the police had charged Rounds with "aggravated assault and battery, assault and battery with intent to rape, and carrying a concealed weapon." During the trial, judicial racism made it difficult for Alexander to argue the case. Judge James Gordon instructed the jury to "ignore the testimony of the four white girls," who were the same color, gender, and age of the accuser but believed that Rounds was not guilty. After Gordon's charge, the jury deliberated for "forty five minutes" and found Rounds guilty on three counts. Gordon sentenced Rounds to "13½ to 27 years." During the trial Alexander charged Judge Gordon with "prejudice and bias, citing at least four grounds of error." A *Philadelphia Tribune* editorial reported that the Rounds verdict "assured strangers protection" for the next year's sesquicentennial celebration. Given the expanding black population and the criminalization of the race in white newspapers, Judge Gordon wanted to assure the city and its white visitors that the city was safe from black male criminals. According to Alexander, the judge's biases and interpretation of the law prevented him from successfully defending his client. After Walter White read the testimony in the case, he and Isadore Martin concurred that something had gone wrong during the trial.[9]

Immediately following the case, Alexander, White, and Martin reviewed the testimony and developed a new strategy. White told Alexander that a black man attempting to assault a white woman in an elevator during the day "seems to us preposterous" and assured Alexander that they were "not attempting to interfere." In some cases, the national NAACP provided legal and financial assistance, but Alexander insisted that he handle the case alone. Although he was inexperienced, Alexander might have rejected the NAACP's offer in order to demonstrate his skills. Most likely, he thought that if the NAACP's white-controlled Legal Committee intervened, he would appear incompetent and the white lawyers would get the credit. Martin, who was not an attorney but attended the trial, secretly told White that both Alexander and Stoddard's attorney had failed to present the facts. The local branch of the NAACP believed that they had a better chance during the second trial because Judge Gordon had made a financial contribution to the Philadelphia chapter.[10]

Two weeks after the verdict, Alexander appealed the case to Pennsylvania's Superior Court. Alexander informed White that the first trial "was wrapped in a blanket of the most vile sort of race prejudice." The day after the police arrested Rounds, Alexander visited Rounds in jail, heard his story, and was convinced that he was "absolutely telling the truth." Alexander thought Rounds's confession was "preposterous" and "unbelievable." All the detectives were "liars of the worse sort." The "English in the statement is that of any college graduate would be proud of," but Rounds had completed only the fourth grade. He even sounded uneducated. Alexander hired a white detective agency that he believed was "not tinged with race prejudice" in order to prove Rounds's innocence. Rounds did not attempt to leave work after the alleged assault. Two white women willingly testified to Rounds's "excellent character." Rounds worked during the summer with "two young white girls taking stock at night" and never made an advance.[11]

Alexander had litigated the first Rounds trial pro bono, but for the new trial he requested financial support from the NAACP. The Rounds family was poor, and no local organization had contributed to his defense. Alexander hoped that White could "influence" the national and local NAACP "to help in the appeal." After Alexander appealed the case on March 25, he sent White a bill for $535.50 but collected only $31.00. White believed that the Rounds case was an excellent test case for the NAACP to address the issue of forced confessions. White law enforcement officials used forced confessions to convict black men, especially in alleged assaults against white women. White decided that the Rounds case was worth the time and money and that Alexander would remain as his lawyer, but Alexander's ego may have hurt his client in the long run.[12]

The NAACP agreed to provide financial aid, but White and Martin's confidence in Alexander wavered as he prepared for the second trial. Martin maintained that he was "reasonably sure of our grounds" for the case, but the NAACP should not fully commit to the case until Martin obtained a copy of the transcript of the first trial. On reviewing the testimony, White opined that Alexander had made a number of mistakes during the trial. Martin told White that Alexander "did not want us in the case" and that he felt apprehensive about supporting it. Martin suggested to White that it was "a very nasty case and we want to be sure we were right before going ahead." What made the case nasty was a black man assaulting a white woman. Martin believed that Rounds might be guilty, and the NAACP could not afford to lose this case. In spite of Martin's caution, White concurred with Alexander that Rounds's confession was "couched in phrases" that were too complex for a functional illiterate. White sent his summary to Martin and Arthur Spingarn, chairman of the NAACP's Legal Committee, a white lawyer who was extremely interested in the case.[13]

White's letter questioned Alexander's strategy during the first trial. According to White, Alexander never called Herbert Denby, a black elevator operator who saw the incident, or Herman Eisner, Rounds's white male boss, as defense witnesses. Alexander might have decided not to call Denby because he mistakenly assumed that a black witness testifying in defense of a black man accused of assaulting a white woman to a white jury and a white judge would not be credible. In a racist society, most whites assumed that all African Americans sided with one another. Alexander may have feared playing the race card, but the Rounds case was a racial matter. Alexander might have outsmarted himself in this instance. Alternatively, his decision may have reflected his assumptions about the racist character of the judicial system. The all-white jury might have believed Denby's testimony, but Alexander was unwilling to take that chance.[14]

At the end of April, in a letter marked "Personal and Confidential," White informed Martin of the Legal Committee's response to the case. According to White, "the appeal is going to be decided not upon facts but only upon record," and he believed that the second trial would be a repetition of the first trial. White prefaced the letter with the parenthetical remark, "Here I am speaking confidentially for I would not like to go on record as transmitting a criticism of Raymond Pace Alexander's legal ability." The Legal Committee concluded that Alexander "made a serious mistake in not summing up." This decision could have been "construed by the jury and the court" as Alexander believing that Rounds was guilty. Alexander's theatrical summaries had contributed to his previous successes in court. White was also surprised that

Alexander did not ask Rounds to show the "marks on his wrists" that demonstrated the "third degree" treatment he received from the police. Alexander believed that he had enough evidence to prove that the detectives beat the confession out of Rounds. White told Martin confidentially, "all of these and other points I have already gone over with you are not a criticism of Alexander's ability as a lawyer nor his intelligence. It is simply that, through his inexperience he committed these grave fatal mistakes." White argued that they needed the best criminal lawyer to overturn the jury's decision. The Legal Committee suggested "the case ought to be quietly investigated," and they would not talk to Rounds unless Alexander agreed. White was unsure if Alexander would "consent to associating counsel with him" and suggested to Martin that if Alexander rejected the idea, the branch should "refrain from going into the case at all." From the NAACP's perspective, the evidence was not conclusive and too much doubt weakened the case.[15]

Alexander was unable to introduce new evidence in the second trial, and, more important, the white judge and white jury were unwilling to convict the police of brutality and falsifying evidence and other forms of misconduct. The Rounds case did not damage the local black community's opinion of Alexander. Inexperience was the major reason the NAACP Legal Committee avoided hiring black attorneys. Conversely, the NAACP's use of white attorneys might have been the major reason that Alexander rejected its assistance. How could Alexander gain experience if the NAACP did not hire black attorneys? This self-defeating strategy was the dilemma that Alexander encountered during the twenties. The NAACP's use of white attorneys infuriated black attorneys, but the NAACP was concerned with winning cases and obtaining more credibility for the organization. By the 1930s, black lawyers had started to play a leading role in civil rights law.

Building a New Negro Institution

Institution building was an important component of the northern civil rights struggle, providing the resources and social networks needed to uplift the race and fight for civil rights. In 1923, Alexander transformed two rooms in the Brown and Stevens Bank building in the Seventh Ward into a law office. The following year, he relocated to the Commonwealth Trust Building, but the landlord did not renew his lease because the white tenants complained "too many Negroes were in the vicinity." The practice was certainly thriving.

In 1925, Alexander hired John Francis Williams, a graduate of Yale University Law and an editor of the *Yale Law Review*. Born in New Haven, Connecticut, Williams had worked in the Claims Division of the New York, New Haven, & Hartford Railroad after he completed law school. He passed the Philadelphia bar in 1924 and started practicing law in August 1925. Like Alexander, Williams was northern-born, had attended an Ivy League university, and was a member of Alpha Phi Alpha Fraternity, Inc., and the Prince Hall Masons, a black fraternal service organization.[16]

In October 1926, Alexander relocated to 19th and Chestnut Streets downtown. In order to lease the "entire second floor" of the building, he had to get a white person to sign the lease. This modern, 1,800-square-foot facility had air conditioning and a room for a law library. Ironically, it was adjacent to the Aldine Theatre where Alexander had first vowed to combat racial discrimination. The new office provided Alexander with a number of advantages. He was closer to city hall; not only did the location have greater prestige, but he could shower and change his suit in between trials. To meet the needs of African Americans who worked late, Alexander allowed clients to come to his home in the evenings. In 1926, Alexander added a real estate department that was managed by Lewis Tanner Moore, a Bates College graduate and grandnephew of Sadie Alexander's uncle Henry O. Tanner, a famous artist. Moore had dropped out of Harvard Law after two years, but he graduated from Temple Law. Alexander's secretarial staff increased from one to three. All were high school graduates, and one had graduated from Temple University. The Raymond Pace Alexander Law Office provided white-collar jobs for a small number of African Americans. In an era of segregation, whites denied black professionals employment opportunities, but Alexander enabled more black attorneys to practice and he created an institution that became symbolic of the civil rights struggle in Philadelphia. Churches, schools, funeral parlors, and black law firms have all been at the foundation of the civil rights struggle.[17]

In 1927, Alexander hired two attorneys, Maceo Hubbard and Sadie Tanner Mossell Alexander. The twenty-six-year-old Hubbard became the twenty-sixth black lawyer in Philadelphia. Born in Georgia, Hubbard graduated from Lincoln University, a historically black college, located in Oxford, Pennsylvania, and from Harvard Law. During his senior year in law school, he worked in the Harvard Legal Aid Bureau, where he practiced law in Boston courts. He passed the Pennsylvania Bar in December 1926. Sadie Alexander, Raymond's wife, passed the Pennsylvania Bar in 1927 and became the first black woman lawyer in Pennsylvania. When Alexander hired her, she recalled, one of the male lawyers in the practice stated that he "didn't want a woman in the place." Raymond Pace Alexander responded. "then I guess you would like to resign." Alexander hired his wife, and the lawyer remained at the practice. In spite of Alexander's intention to treat male and female attorneys equally, Mrs. Alexander stated that her husband assigned her the cases that "the other men didn't want." Like many pioneering women lawyers, she specialized in estate and family law. Alexander's practice was exceptional for its time. It contained four Ivy League-trained lawyers and was located in downtown Philadelphia. Woodson's 1934 study of the 1,230 black lawyers in the nation revealed that "45 percent practiced individually" and a minute percentage worked in a practice with four lawyers. Alexander's thriving practice was unusual among black attorneys.[18]

National Bar Association, 1930–1932

From its founding in 1925, the NBA held an annual convention. Lawyers and other black professionals attended the meetings, and the black press covered the proceedings. Resolutions passed at these conventions provide insight into the pressing civil rights issues of the period. Alexander attended the NBA's fifth annual convention in Detroit, Michigan, and gave a speech outlining the economic impact of the black migration on northern cities and the new specialties of black lawyers. Prior to World War I, African American lawyers had specialized in criminal law; however, after the Great Migration, black real estate firms, insurance agencies, and grocery stores developed, which created a need for African American lawyers to specialize in property law. Alexander argued that the "colored lawyer must change his provincial methods in the practice of law or forever be a second or third-rate factor in our public life." According to Woodson, some African American businessmen argued that black attorneys were not properly trained and did not understand modern "economic theories." Black attorneys protested that they needed an opportunity. The problem for African Americans attorneys was the lack of experience and training. To address new modern business techniques, Alexander suggested black attorneys form "partnerships or associations" in which each lawyer specialized in one area. Alexander viewed the law firm as a corporation that needed large amounts of capital, and the only way black attorneys could accumulate working capital was through reinvesting the proceeds from personal injury suits. Black lawyers "should also be the forerunners in breaking down race prejudice in business . . . by forcing white businesses to hire Negro brains." Alexander's practice served as a model for a modern African American law firm. At the convention, C. Francis Stradford stressed that black attorneys should focus on getting states to pass a "comprehensive civil rights law." Although it remained difficult to induce northern states to strengthen their equal rights laws, it was easier to amend existing laws and get them enforced than to overturn Jim Crow in the South or in the federal courts.[19]

At the end of the 1929 convention, the NBA elected Alexander, who was only thirty-two years old, to serve as the organization's third president. Alexander gave numerous speeches about developing a successful practice, fighting for civil rights, and improving the relationship between the NBA and black local bar associations. During his two terms, he expanded the organization and encouraged it to work with radical organizations to advance the cause of civil rights.

Two hundred twenty-one members convened for the NBA's 1930 convention at the recently accredited Howard University Law School in Washington, D.C. Alexander voiced his concern over the relationship between the NBA and local bar associations. According to Alexander, some attorneys suggested that the NBA should work through the local black bar associations, while others suggested that the NBA only work as "a national organization with individual members."[20] The national tension is the same issue that plagued the NAACP. Black lawyers who advocated working with their local bar association probably appreciated the autonomy it provided from the NBA. If an issue emerged on the local level that the NBA did not support, the black attorney could still provide the services that African Americans sought. Alexander's presidential address, "The Negro Lawyer: His Duty in a Rapidly Changing Social, Economic and Political World," summarized three major goals for black attorneys: securing civil rights, advancing economic equality, and facilitating participation in politics. In many northern states, African Americans had to force courts "to grant even the most ordinary social rights, such as the right of recreation and amusement in public places." Alexander noted that sixty years after Emancipation, after "absorbing knowledge and the habits and customs of the American people" and obtaining an education in the best schools "equal to, indeed, if not with greater facility than his white brother," African Americans were still treated as second-class citizens. Alexander recalled when he "was refused service as a soda fountain of the United Cigar Stores"; the manager of the store told the clerk "not to serve colored people at the fountain." Alexander stressed to the black attorneys that they should not practice for money alone but that they should "guard against further and more dangerous encroachments of the rights of the Negro." He described civil rights litigation as a noble service to the race and said attorneys should pursue these cases pro bono or for reduced fees.[21]

While civil rights dominated the discourse of black America in 1930, economic inequality was an increasingly visible consequence of racism and segregation that forced Alexander and other black lawyers to broaden their civil rights ideology and tactics. The civil rights model argued for equal opportunity, but if African Americans could not earn a living, inequality remained. The Great Depression illustrated the devastating impact of economic inequality on the black community. Alexander asserted that job discrimination was the most "dangerous and far-reaching in effect than any kind we have heretofore experienced and which, unless checked, will bring the most disastrous results." Alexander warned black attorneys that economic inequality would affect African American attorneys' "right to work, free from race influences," which was "the very root of our existence." Black attorneys, like other black professionals, relied on the black community for clients. The unemployed could not pay for their services, so they lost their financial independence. In the political arena, the Republican Party no longer gave African Americans patronage as they had done in the past. As a consequence, Alexander insisted that African Americans "should cast a ballot not by virtue of traditional allegiance" or because the Republican Party was "the party of Lincoln." African Americans must vote for the party "that offers opportunities in the affairs of government" to black supporters. Alexander recognized the political and economic benefits of patronage, and it was imperative that black lawyers receive their fair share. Finally, Alexander reminded his colleagues that, although black lawyers faced different problems than white attorneys, they could still make a larger impact on American jurisprudence. Alexander reminded the audience that white lawyers received "public offices molding public opinion" and they were not "faced with all the popular distrust of laymen." The only way to change common perception of black attorneys was through improved training and work with the NBA. After the convention, law schools and law students "requested information on the colored lawyer," and in 1931, the National Urban League's journal *Opportunity* published a shorter version of his address titled "The Negro Lawyer."[22]

During the summer of 1931, when the Scottsboro case was in the news, Alexander invited "attorneys for many of the big radical movements, such as Theodore Dreiser and Joseph Brodsky," to attend the NBA convention.

Unlike Walter White and the NAACP, Alexander and other members of the NBA welcomed their presence. Alexander invited William L. Patterson, executive secretary of the ILD and a member of New York's Communist Party, attorney Clarence Darrow, and Dean Roscoe Pound of Harvard University. Later that summer, Alexander made a financial contribution to the Emergency Scottsboro Defense (ESD) through the National Committee For the Defense of Political Prisoners (NCFDPP). Walter White, the acting secretary of the NCFDPP, wanted Alexander to "make a personal appeal to" the NBA on behalf of the ESD. Alexander sent him a copy of the NBA's program and congratulated him for the work that the NBA did for the "members of the lower strata of Negro society, the poorly adjusted members of our group." He promised White that he would send him more money and allow White to make "an appeal to the membership." Alexander was not a Communist, but the ILD used the law to protect African American citizens. A progressive pragmatist, Alexander was convinced that the radicals' ideology had little impact on the outcome of the case.[23]

Kenneth Mack argues that from 1931 to 1941, Alexander and the NBA combined "legalism and mass politics . . . into a new civil rights paradigm," and Alexander used his professional success to build a coalition with white liberals in Philadelphia. As the labor movement was gaining strength during the 1930s, black working-class activists started "Don't Buy Where You Can't Work" campaigns, using boycotts and protests to increase the number of black employees in white-owned businesses and encourage African Americans to shop at black-owned businesses. Rather than disparaging the new radicalism in the civil rights struggle, Alexander merged litigation and mass protests.[24]

Alexander's 1931 presidential address covered a variety of issues and themes he had discussed in the past, such as improving the status of black lawyers. Alexander noted that the NBA needed a forum to publish articles and the convention minutes as the American Bar Association did. The convention ended with a controversial debate over the Scottsboro trial, as some lawyers supported the ILD and others refused to do so. The anti-ILD factions won by a slim, five-vote margin. Alexander likely voted in favor of working with the ILD; he supported any organization that used the legal process to get justice for African Americans. Alexander's radicalism understood the necessity of working with the left. The left provided publicity for many civil rights cases, such as the Willie Brown murder case that Alexander later litigated.[25]

The close vote over the Scottsboro case forced Walter White of the NAACP to attend the NBA convention in 1932. White knew that black attorneys were divided over the ILD question. Moreover, influential African American journalists, such as Robert S. Abbott of the *Chicago Defender* and Carl Murphy of the *Baltimore Afro-American*, encouraged African Americans to support the ILD. Tensions had also developed between members of the NBA and White over the NAACP's refusal to employ black attorneys. On a local level, however, the NAACP branches hired black attorneys at a lower rate to assist the national office of the NAACP. African American attorneys complained about their second-class treatment by the NAACP. After 1931, the number of black attorneys on the NAACP's Legal Committee increased, and they made their presence known to White. The growing radicalism of the black bar and African Americans demanding that they should be in the forefront of the civil rights struggle had forced this shift.[26]

In his final presidential address, at the 1932 NBA convention in Indianapolis, Indiana, Alexander summarized the cooperative work of the NBA and the NAACP on economic justice. First he reviewed the NBA and NAACP's role in the Hoover Dam Project. Although this project was federally funded, white contractors did not hire black workers. The NBA collected testimony from black job seekers. In March, the NAACP and the NBA met with the Hoover Dam officials. Three months later, according to Alexander, "eight of our race went to work on the Hoover Dam." Alexander did not specify the type of jobs that the eight men received. During the Depression, having any sort of job was a blessing. For Alexander, civil rights included economic opportunity. Racial discrimination in employment was woefully evident in 1932. Alexander pointed out that African Americans were "eliminated from almost all work," even the unskilled jobs they had previously held. During the Depression, as competition for jobs increased, white workers replaced black workers. Black labor confronted white mobs and racist unions that denied African American access to employment opportunities. According to Alexander, to combat "white men's . . . selfishness and intolerance—the forerunners of racial prejudice," African American must place their "legal rights in the learned hand of a Negro lawyer." He insisted that the most effective way to combat job discrimination was through the courts, neglecting to mention that "Don't Buy Where You Can't Work" campaigns forced department stores to hire black women to work as salespersons.[27]

Alexander concluded his speech with a scathing critique of police brutality and American "lawlessness." He denounced lynching as "barbarous and inhumane." Although both African Americans and whites had been subjected to vigilante "justice," by 1932, white people were rarely lynched. African Americans and their white liberal allies had tried to force Congress to pass an ant-lynching bill, but Southern Democrats stonewalled, and Roosevelt needed their assistance to pass legislation. Alexander observed that most whites "decry lynch law and admitted that it was a horrible sin"; however, "those same white people believe in and sanction segregation and discrimination against the Negro" and sit on juries that deny African Americans equal justice. Alexander highlighted the contradictions in white America. Northern whites despised lynching but were not outraged over the police brutality that ran rampant throughout the nation. Alexander mentioned the cities that had a history of police brutality and in the fact that each city they had a special name for the treatment reserved for African Americans. In Dallas, Texas, police employed the "Electric Monkey"; Chicago had "its celebrated 'Goldfish Room'"; Detroit used the "Loop System"; and such "forms of direct police action as the 'Third Degree'" were nearly universal. Police departments used illegal interrogation techniques to intimidate African Americans to admit to crimes they may have not committed. Alexander noted that "white judges" sanctioned the "police lawlessness" that was extremely common in large cities. "The injustices imposed upon the Negro of Mississippi can and will be imposed upon the Negro of Massachusetts and in Maine in due time. So closely related is every section of America that each section is affected by the customs of every other. Usually men take their prejudices with them, seldom their virtues."[28]

Alexander concluded that the NBA was one of the best organizations to end "the violence of lawless and enforcement of law" and to provide African Americans with "equal economic opportunity." Alexander's civil rights strategy embraced the political, social, and economic concerns of the black community. The NAACP concentrated on civil rights and equality, but the Depression forced local NAACP chapters to address economic issues as well. Alexander's presidential addressed synthesized litigation and mass protests and demonstrated the nexus between civil rights and economic opportunity. Over the next few years, Alexander reached the apogee of his radicalism.[29]

Willie Brown Case, 1932–1933

In February 1932, Dorothy Lutz, a white seven-year-old, was found dead, "ravished and bloomers tied around her mouth and throat," five days after her mother reported her missing. Blanche Lee, mother of sixteen-year-old William E. "Willie" Brown, reported her son missing around the time of the murder. After the police located Brown, they arrested him and "grilled" him

for over thirty-six hours until he signed a confession stating he had committed the murder. This case made headline news in Philadelphia, a black male
allegedly murdering a young white girl. In the South, this type of allegation
was followed by lynching, but in Philadelphia, Brown at least had a trial. In
the Willie Brown case, Alexander used left-wing organizations to provide
support and publicity for the defense.[30]

The defendant Brown hired Alexander and Robert C. Nix Sr., another
black attorney (who in 1964 became Philadelphia's first black congressman).
As they prepared for trial, Alexander wrote a letter to Walter White stating the facts of the case. Dorothy Lutz had "disappeared from her home
in a very bad section of the city where foreigners, low class Americans and
poor class of colored people live." After Lutz disappeared, the police arrested
twelve white men, who were most likely poor immigrants or ethnics. The
police released the men without charge. Alexander concluded the crime "was
a white man's act," because "several strands of long brown hair were clasped in
the child's hand." He insisted that foreigners of "a very low and unruly class"
had attacked white girls several times during the last year. Intraracial sex
crimes committed in poor neighborhoods are not as newsworthy as a black
man allegedly raping and murdering a little white girl. This sort of crime was
not unusual and was typically committed by adult males. Most crimes are
committed intraracially. For a black male to murder a white child was insane,
and this was part of Alexander's rationale.[31]

According to Alexander, Willie Brown came from a lower-class family. His "reputation was not any too good" and he "fought and stole." But he
never committed a "sexual offense." Brown often "stayed out all night," which
Alexander maintained was not an anomaly because the Brown family had a
"very loose living" arrangement. Brown was not a rapist or murderer; he was
a victim of racism, poverty, and neglect. At the police station, Brown received
neither food nor water during "44 hours of questioning." This "broke Brown,"
and he signed a thirty-five-page confession. Alexander emphasized that the
police officers forced Brown to "DRAW PICTURES OF HOW HE DID IT AND
EVERYTHING ELSE TO MAKE A COMPLETE CASE." Alexander volunteered to
take the case "without any compensation because of the reflection cast upon
the race and my manifest duty to protect this youth, whether guilty or not,
from further police intimidation." Forced confessions amounted to northern-
style lynching. Alexander viewed this case as a typical "third degree" Philadelphia police brutality.[32]

He could not comprehend the lack of interest shown by the local NAACP
branch in this and other criminal cases involving African Americans. Nelson

contends that during the 1920s and 1930s, the local NAACP was primarily a social organization for the black middle class. The group avoided getting involved with criminal cases because poor black men with questionable character had committed the majority of crimes. Alexander reminded White that his civil rights cases received "his attention without the slightest bit of compensation." He litigated desegregation cases pro bono but charged for his criminal cases. Alexander asked the NAACP to pay for the Rounds defense. By 1932, Alexander believed that he had made a larger contribution to black civil rights in Philadelphia than the NAACP and "other agencies organized to protect the rights of the colored citizens."[33]

During the thirties the Communist Party competed with the NAACP for civil rights cases and for members. In addition to pursuing litigation, the ILD held rallies, demonstrations, fund-raisers, and letter-writing campaigns to attract public attention to the cause. White believed that their protest tactics would only hurt Brown and other African Americans on trial, but in his defense of Willie Brown, Alexander worked with the ILD instead of the NAACP. White advised Herbert Millen, president of the Philadelphia branch of the NAACP, to "prevent the Communists from gripping cases for their own purposes" and criticized the local chapter for not doing their work. Millen informed White that he was familiar with the case and did not want to "refer it to the home office." White believed that the Willie Brown case sounded like an excellent test case for the NAACP. He wrote to Arthur Spingarn and Roy Wilkins, assistant secretary of the NAACP, that the local branch wanted to handle this case without any aid from the national organization. Referring to the Philadelphia's branch's successful fund-raising drives, he warned "we don't want to antagonize a reasonably good branch" because "it would do us irreparable harm." Still, White concurred with Alexander, who referred to the local branch as "timid and inactive." White decided that, "although Raymond Pace Alexander is most avid for publicity, and though he has been . . . working with the ILD," he should handle the case. White informed Spingarn, Wilkins, and Herbert J. Seligmann, director of branches for the NAACP, that Millen should "go sit on a tack" and the local branch "should cooperate with Alexander." Spingarn reviewed the case and submitted it to the sixteen-member legal committee. The committee agreed with Millen that it was "not a cause for the NAACP to enter." White was convinced that Brown was innocent and informed Spingarn that Philadelphia's police brutality was "most flagrant." In March, the jury found Brown guilty of first-degree murder and sentenced him to death. The grounds for appeal were numerous; primarily, Alexander argued that the police forced Brown to sign the confession. In November, Alexander successfully appealed to the Pennsylvania Supreme Court, which ordered a new trial.[34]

During the first trial, Judge Harry S. McDevitt referred to Alexander's defense as "an attempt to throw sand in the eyes of the jury" and a "smoke screen." McDevitt called Alexander's critique of the death sentence a "harangue." Pennsylvania Supreme Court Judge George W. Maxey reversed the lower court's decision and stated that McDevitt had violated judicial procedure. Referring to the Scottsboro case, Maxey stated that everyone is entitled to a fair trial. Maxey did not comment on Brown's third-degree treatment by the police; he was more concerned with Judge McDevitt's violation of judicial procedures. Maxey commented on Alexander's use of a sociological argument to explain Brown's behavior. Maxey agreed with Alexander and declared Brown's "upbringing . . . his poor adjustment to the community and 'bandbox' back alley" existence may have contributed to his behavior. Maxey's ruling saved Brown from the death penalty. After the trial, Alexander asked White to inform W. E. B. DuBois, editor of *The Crisis*. "I do not mind how much you mention my name as counsel," but, Alexander cautioned, "do not publish my critique of Judge McDevitt." Alexander's effort to build positive relationships with white judges depended upon their having a positive attitude toward him. The new trial, before the same judge, was set for February. The *Philadelphia Tribune* reported that the ILD sent Judge McDevitt a letter insisting that "Negro jurymen be included." ILD chapters from Baltimore, Maryland, and Wilmington, Delaware, came to Philadelphia "to start a vigorous campaign for the release of Brown."[35]

The Commonwealth of Pennsylvania introduced additional evidence at the new trial. According to Robert C. Nix Sr., Brown's attorney, a ring that Alexander thought belonged to Lutz's mother was "in Brown's possession two weeks before." Two witnesses saw Brown near the crime scene. The prosecution maintained that the hair in Lutz's hand "came from the pubic region of a highly pigmented person." Although defense witnesses claimed Brown was nowhere near the crime scene, Nix thought the new evidence against Brown was overwhelming. He believed that a jury would find Brown guilty and that Brown stood a better chance if he pleaded guilty. The jury sentenced Brown to life imprisonment, but Nix stated that as long as he was alive he would search for "proof of his client's innocence." Nix regarded averting the death sentence as a minor victory.[36]

After the Brown decision, White wrote to Alexander and Millen that the "Communists are trying to blame us for the guilty plea. By telling a deliberate lie the ILD is working in every possible way to try and mess up NAACP cases." White assumed that Alexander was going to defend Brown again, but White forgot that Alexander had resigned in April, eight months before Brown's sentencing. In April, in a letter marked "confidential and personal," Alexander told White that there were "so many complications in connection with my withdrawal" but offered no further details. Alexander insisted that he was "squeezed out of the case" because he suggested that the defense team "do the right thing toward this boy in order to maintain his self-respect." White tried to convince Alexander to remain on Brown's defense team and "fight for him as you have fought and can fight." White accused the ILD of tampering with the case and influencing Alexander's decision to withdraw from the case even though the ILD had not participated in the legal process. William L. Patterson, national secretary of the ILD, heard of the controversy and wrote a letter to Charles Hamilton Houston, a black attorney who was sympathetic to the ILD. Patterson declared that the ILD did not make statements "to incriminate the NAACP." Houston visited Patterson in Harlem and found out that Alexander's colleague Nix had blamed the local chapter of the NAACP for failing to support the case. Members from the local chapter of the NAACP, like White, believed in Brown's innocence, while Alexander believed Brown was guilty. This tension between Alexander and the local and national office of the NAACP occurred on numbers occasions.[37]

The Willie Brown case benefited from the Scottsboro case. In the 1930s, the left used mass protests to obtain publicity for defendants in cases of injustice. The Rounds and Brown cases demonstrate the difficulty of exonerating black men accused of assaulting white women. Remarkably, Alexander won an appeal in both cases. The trials enhanced his status in the legal profession. Viewed from a professional and political perspective, Alexander's resignation made sense, even though the ILD deplored Alexander's withdrawal from the case and questioned his commitment to racial justice. The ILD had its own agenda, as Walter White and others pointed out, but getting as many black members as possible was grounds for competition between the ILD and the NAACP. In the 1930s, in spite of the ideological differences, the left and right complemented one another, and this coalition increased political, social, and economic opportunities for African Americans.

Berwyn, Pennsylvania, School Desegregation Case, 1932–1934

Like most northern cities, Philadelphia had a long history of institutionalized segregation. New schools were generally constructed for white students in growing neighborhoods on the urban periphery, while African American students were crowded into run-down buildings in older areas near the city center. In some places, the influx of black migrants required new black schools as well. The imposition of segregation often met with protest; according to Meier and Rudwick, there were fifteen school boycotts in northern cities between 1920 and 1944.[38] Alexander became involved in the issue as it arose in Berwyn, Pennsylvania.

On July 13, 1933, Alexander wrote to Walter White, the executive secretary of the NAACP, seeking the organization's support for the school desegregation suit brought by black parents in Berwyn, Pennsylvania. "The National Association has given to other cases involving lynchings and the defense of men accused of murder and other crimes and nothing has been given for the litigation of a case involving human rights and a fight to save the self-respect of our race of people." Berwyn was a predominantly but not exclusively white upper-middle-class suburb near Philadelphia. As suburbanization took hold, African Americans established small communities in some suburbs. According to Andrew Wiese, by 1920, Chester County's 7,125 African American inhabitants comprised the largest black suburban population in the country. The majority of black men worked as unskilled laborers, and most black women worked as domestics. Prior to the 1930s, most suburban northern schools had integrated school districts, but when the black population increased, many school districts segregated. In 1930, the black population in Chester County reached 13,153, a 90 percent increase over the previous decade.[39]

In March 1932, the Eastown Township school district built a new $250,000 elementary school in Berwyn. The adjacent Tredyffrin school district closed its old school and decided to send its white students to the new school in Eastown. The districts agreed to keep the old Eastown elementary school open "for the instruction of certain people"—code words for black children. An editorial in the *Philadelphia Tribune* stated that Norman J. Green, a southerner who had recently been elected president of the school board, had excluded Negro students from attending the new school in order to "maintain the high standards." "Six grades of Negro children in one room!" Green exclaimed. Upholding academic standards was used as a justification for racial segregation. Previously, black children had attended all of the elementary schools in Chester County, so the board's decision to segregate them infuriated the black community. In June 1932, 212 African American students boycotted the schools in Eastown and Tredyffrin townships.[40]

African Americans from the two townships met at the Mount Zion A.M.E. Church in Tredyffrin, and Essie Brock recalled that her father, Primus Crosby, declared: "I came from a segregated school in the South. I'll not stand for it."[41] O. B. Cobb, African American president of the Bryn Mawr chapter of the NAACP, filed a suit against the Chester County school board and then hired Alexander as its prosecuting attorney. In August, Alexander asked Robert Bagnall of the NAACP to obtain information about "school cases of this sort" and to provide "any opinions or citations in your own office covering these cases." A month later, in a letter marked "SPECIAL DELIVERY," Roy Wilkins, the assistant secretary of the NAACP, provided information about nine school desegregation cases being filed outside the South.[42]

When the school opened in September, African American parents brought their children to the new school, but the "district officials refused to enroll all of the children." The few allowed into the classroom "were given no books, paper, or pencils."[43] In September 1932, Alexander filed petitions representing plaintiffs in each township. According to the *Main Line Daily Times*, Alexander's petition stated that, in March 1932, Priscilla Temple and other African American students had tried to enroll in the white school but were refused despite the fact that the white school was closer to Temple's home than the black school. The plaintiffs argued that "mixed schools have been maintained for 50 years;" and since the new school was financed by their taxes, the children had a right to attend it. Alexander obtained a writ of mandamus that required the townships to justify why they prohibited black students from attending the new school. In September 1932, 212 African American students boycotted the schools.[44]

In October 1932, Judge J. Frank E. Hause filed the writ of mandamus and gave the school boards two months to come up with a reason that justified segregation. According to Alexander, the school boards "filed motions to quash the mandamus writs." Since the plaintiffs had accused the school boards of discrimination, Pennsylvania's attorney general, William Schnader, had to add his name to Alexander's petition. But Schnader sided with the school boards, stating that this was a local decision. School board members tried to persuade other white people of the merits of segregation, and even met with the Committee on Race Relations (CORR).[45]

Members of the Society of Friends (Quakers) had formed CORR in 1929 to expose "white Friends to educated Negroes," and they held monthly meetings in Philadelphia addressing such issues as race relations, anti-Semitism, and discrimination in housing. In December 1932, W. T. Vandevere and Mr.

Wetzel, two Tredyffrin school board members, attended the CORR meeting and "explained in detail the reasons why the school board felt justified in their recent action of segregation." The notes of the meeting provide no details, but according to CORR's secretary, Pauline Cheney, Wetzel wanted CORR members to "act as mediators to help get the children back into school." However, the committee "refused to be used as a means of getting the children back first." CORR wanted to organize a meeting with Schnader, a few members from the school board, and black parents in order to find "an interracial aid in helping to heal the bitterness of both groups."[46]

Alexander maintained that after Schander refused to add his name to the suit, the school board proposed a compromise, "to admit to the schools . . . the two children of the two petitioners." "The school board would entertain applications on behalf of individual children for admission to the white schools" and decide which students qualified. Alexander and the parents vehemently rejected this proposal. During the boycott, Alexander remained in contact with the national office of the NAACP. Walter White suggested that all the NAACP branches in Pennsylvania should send letters telling Schnader to "stop postponing the Berwyn School case, and try it at once." In spite of the letter-writing campaign, however, Schnader refused to add his name to the suit. In March 1933, Assistant Secretary Roy Wilkins told W. W. Hines, the secretary of the Bryn Mawr branch of the NAACP, that "the school board members whom you are fighting are probably the meanest and most vicious enemies that we have run across in many months. I do not feel that it is any longer necessary to be polite. If they want war, let's have war." By June 1933, the school boycott was a year old.[47]

As the defendants continued to delay the trial, legal fees increased, and the national office of the NAACP became concerned about whether Alexander and the Bryn Mawr branch had the resources to continue the fight. In June, White asked Alexander, "What in your opinion, is the next step to be taken?" During the first year of the boycott, Alexander and the local chapter of the NAACP raised all of the funds for the legal fees, but Schnader's actions forced White to consider using the NAACP's legal committee, which was responsible for litigating the organization's nationally known civil rights cases during the 1920s and 1930s. According to Alexander, "This is a direct blow at mixed schools in the North. The case should really be given more publicity." Alexander's letter to White highlights the significance of this case; if they lost, other northern towns and cities might segregate black students. Segregation was a national issue, but the national NAACP office did not have the resources to fund every single lawsuit. As Alexander put it wryly, if they lose the case, his firm would "have given thousands of dollars worth of time, but I am afraid we will have to charge this to our racial interest."[48]

By September 1933, an array of radical organizations offered their support, including the International Labor Defense (ILD), American Civil Liberties Union (ACLU), Philadelphia Committee for the Defense of Political Prisoners (PCDPP), and The League of Struggle for Negro Rights (LSNR). Liberal organizations such as the Educational Equality League (EEL) also decided to assist Alexander and his clients. Founded in 1932 by Floyd Logan, the EEL was designed to eliminate segregation and racist textbooks in Philadelphia public schools.[49] On September 20, the ILD and PCDPP held a meeting at the Bellevue-Stratford Hotel downtown. According to Reverend W. L. Johnson, a NAACP executive committee member, "five hundred or more Negroes and perhaps two hundred whites" attended the meeting and formed a "joint action committee." The committee was designed "to create public sentiment, by holding monster mass meetings, and to give the greatest and most far-reaching publicity about this case," using "parades and such other peaceful demonstrations as was employed in the interest of the Scottsboro case." Saul Carson, white secretary of the PCDPP, reported: "Fifty or sixty armed men turned out to break up that meeting; (at the Bellevue-Stratford Hotel) vigilantes and the Ku Kluxers were busy." Carson "was stoned and narrowly escaped a probable attempt at a lynching."[50] These radical groups provided the publicity that this case needed. After the joint committee was formed, Roy Wilkins informed Cobb that "these organizations are affiliated, some loosely and some closely, with the Communist Party." In spite of Wilkins's concerns about communist influence, the Bryn Mawr branch joined the joint action committee. Since Alexander was not associated with the national office of the NAACP, he had the autonomy to associate with left-wing organizations. The NAACP was concerned about the branch's ability to fight this case alone. Cobb replied to Wilkins that the branch and Alexander had handled the case for the past year and a half, but the mounting financial costs forced Cobb "to ask the national office NAACP to kindly take charge of the Berwyn school case at once."[51]

On October 20, Alexander informed White that Schander had "ordered the prosecution of the parents and yesterday four of them were sent to jail for failure to send their children to a segregated school." Four parents participated in a jail-in, refusing bail and remaining in jail in order to protest Jim Crow education in Pennsylvania. Against Alexander's wishes, the NAACP paid the fines of the parents who did not want to participate in the jail-in. According to the *Philadelphia Tribune* editorial, Alexander believed that paying bail sanctioned segregation. The NAACP's moderate position illustrated its concern with respectability. The NAACP's strategy was based on convincing moderate whites and blacks that these parents were law-abiding citizens who deserved to be treated fairly. If they remained in jail, NAACP leaders feared, the court of public opinion would view the parents as criminals who were not concerned about their children's education. The NAACP insisted that this stereotype should be avoided. After the police arrested the parents, Roy Wilkins called an emergency meeting at Cobb's home and invited Alexander and other major figures in the NAACP, including Isadore Martin, member of the national board of directors, and E. Washington Rhodes, attorney and editor of the *Philadelphia Tribune*.[52]

Debate at the meeting turned on the relationship between the NAACP branch and the joint action committee. Wilkins's four-page summary of the meeting captured the mounting tensions between the parents and leaders. In spite of White's and Wilkins's concern about the joint action committee, most of the parents agreed that the Bryn Mawr branch of the NAACP "should not have withdrawn from the Joint Committee." One parent mentioned the "constant pressure from white public opinion because of their stand on the school question." These parents were "at the mercy of their employers," but, in spite of economic repercussions, they had "whispered and grumbled affirmation" of the joint action committee. In August 1932, Wilkins reported that Reverend W. L. Johnson, a member of the NAACP's executive committee, had asked NAACP members "to recruit new groups to stir up the masses." Despite seven hundred people in attendance at the September 20 meeting at the Bellevue Stratford Hotel, only thirty-five dollars was raised for the case, not even enough to pay the sixty-five-dollar fee to rent the hall. Johnson and Alexander wanted the joint committee to raise funds for the case, but Cobb vehemently denounced the Bryn Mawr chapter for joining it. Wilkins noted that Cobb stated that the joint action committee "was a racket of cheap, unemployed white agitators, who had no jobs and nothing to do but stir up trouble and try to make a few dollars out of it." At the end of the meeting, Cobb officially withdrew the Bryn Mawr branch from the joint committee, but Alexander had convinced the other men at the meeting that the joint action committee would serve as "a contributing and supporting agency in the fight."[53]

While Alexander had encouraged support from the left, some African Americans on the left were convinced that Alexander's legal approach was not effective. James Watson, a journalist for the radical *Harlem Liberator*, wrote an editorial on the Berwyn case. Watson's critique of Alexander and the NAACP presented the black left's dissatisfaction with relying only upon the legal approach to seeking equality. The first portion of his essay provides a history of the Berwyn case. Watson mentions the social and economic reprisals participating parents endured; "unemployed Negroes were arbitrarily stricken from the relief rolls, Negro domestics and other workers were fired from jobs." The ILD and the LSNR had written a letter to parents that criticized the Bryn Mawr branch of the NAACP for resigning from the joint action committee. The editorial ended by voicing frustration with Alexander: "Experience should convince the parents of Berwyn that neither the pussyfooting and kneebending leadership of the NAACP or EEL, nor the clever legalism of Attorney Raymond Pace Alexander will win victory." Watson believed that "militant united action" was the only way to end segregation.[54]

Watson's criticism of Alexander was inaccurate. Alexander would not have joined the LSNR, but he supported "militant united action." In January 1934, two months before Watson's diatribe, Helen Bryan of the Committee on Race Relations was planning a "Seminar on Segregation" in Philadelphia. Bryan's letter stated, "recently various members of our committee have heard the policy of segregation defended by certain outstanding Negroes." Bryan sent a survey to a list of distinguished black Americans, including Alain Locke, a philosophy professor at Howard University, attorney Sadie Alexander, and Max Yeargan, the first black professor hired at New York City's public colleges. Bryan asked them to list "those aspects of segregation which you think are in need of careful analysis at this time." Charles Hamilton Houston and Ralph Bunche listed segregation in education, pubic employment, and housing in the same order. In January 1934, W. E. B. DuBois wrote the controversial editorial in *The Crisis* titled "Segregation." DuBois maintained that "the thinking colored people of the United States must stop being stampeded by the word segregation." African Americans must not be opposed to working together and "there should never be an opposition to segregation . . . unless that segregation does involve discrimination." DuBois is recognized for initiating the national debate over segregation, but Bryan organized a conference about the same issue and, surprisingly, did not invite DuBois. The CORR "Seminar on Segregation" demonstrates that DuBois was not the only black thinker reconsidering the term "segregation."

Alexander attended the seminar, which was held on January 26, 1934, during the school boycott's nineteenth month. During the afternoon session, Alexander declared, "Some kind of resistance is necessary as the opposition put up by the parents against segregated schools in Berwyn. We need more active resistance, the use of political force, demonstrations to embarrass public officials, the resources of the law. We need more than a discussion of ills and resolutions; we need a more belligerent plan of action, such as newspaper publicity, the support of prominent citizens, effective demonstrations."[55] Alexander's comments did not sound like the "pussyfooting and kneebending" that Watson mentioned in his editorial. Alexander's radical comments illustrate his frustration with white backlash and resistance to school desegregation, and he advocated both using the law and holding mass demonstrations.[56]

By 1934, the school boycott had entered its twentieth month with no victory in sight. In February 1934, the EEL decided to have a protest march in Philadelphia. EEL secretary Lania Davis mailed letters to all of the Berwyn supporters and declared March 11, 1934, "Berwyn School Segregation Protest Day," encouraging everyone to sign a petition addressed to Governor Pinchot. According to EEL's president, Floyd Logan, "It is our purpose thorough silent public demonstration . . . to resolve the situation." The EEL requested a "police escort" so as "not to be molested by any radical group"; Logan feared that racist whites might harass demonstrators. Police commissioner Joseph LeStrange had "no objection to the proposed parade" as long as there was no music or interference with traffic. The police also had to approve the demonstrators' signs before they marched. Some of the slogans stated, "Keep Scottsboro out of Pennsylvania," "Down with Jim Crow Schools," "Schnader, Will you be the King of Right," "Slave of Segregation," and "Segregation is Un-American." The police permit stipulated that "no personal names and No red lettering" could be used (red connoted communism). The protesters proclaimed they were anti-segregation, pro-democracy, 100 percent American, and anti-communist.[57] Some organizers did not want the ILD to participate in the protest march, but Alexander welcomed the ILD's support in order to obtain more publicity. The *Philadelphia Tribune* reported that more than five thousand people were expected to participate. The prediction of a huge crowd prompted LeStrange not to issue the permit.

In April, Wilkins informed attorney Herbert Millen that since "Mr. Schnader is a candidate for Governor, it would seem that this is an opportune time to effect a settlement" of the case. In November 1933, African Methodist Episcopal minister W. L. Johnson had written an editorial in the *Philadelphia Tribune* warning Schnader that if he failed to side with the parents, he would lose "500,000 votes" in the upcoming election. Johnson reminded Schnader that the NAACP had prevented Judge John Parker from becoming a United States Supreme Court Justice.[58]

In March 1934, gubernatorial candidate Schnader promised Alexander that he would add his name to the suit. Alexander advised the children to go to school, but the all-white schools still denied them admission. The following month, Schnader appointed Herbert Millen and Harry Cheatham, two black attorneys from Philadelphia, as special deputy attorneys general and finally added his name to the suit. Schnader declared in the *Philadelphia Tribune* that he always advocated "equal opportunities for all people, regardless of wealth, creed or race" and proclaimed that all children deserved an equal education.[59] Schnader's newfound enlightenment was a direct result of the growing political power of African Americans in Pennsylvania and the Berwyn movement.

On May 1, 1934, the *Philadelphia Record* stated that Alexander had met with the special deputy attorneys general and they had settled the Berwyn case outside of court, after a boycott lasting "two years and one month." The national office of the NAACP congratulated Alexander and his staff, but Alexander extolled the commitment of the parents. In a letter to Wilkins, Alexander wrote: "This case has been the best example of fortitude, courage, willingness to sacrifice against all odds on the part of colored people, especially the ordinary class of working people who are willing to undergo the greatest hardships and the imprisonment of mothers and fathers of young children in order to stand up for the deep-seated principle of equality educational opportunity in the same buildings and through the same methods of teaching along with white children."[60] According to Davison, during the 1920s and 1930s, black parents and lawyers who fought segregation in northern schools encountered three major obstacles: inability to find an attorney, fear of economic retaliation by whites, and white resistance to "compliance with court orders requiring integration." In spite of these difficulties, Alexander and the Berwyn parents were victorious. Most of Alexander's public accommodation cases involved the black middle class, but the Berwyn case, like the postwar civil rights movement, involved "ordinary people doing extraordinary things." In spite of their lack of economic resources, these working-class African Americans had sustained a two-year boycott. In November 1934, Schnader, a Republican, lost the election to the Democratic candidate, George Earle. Most African Americans were leaving the Republican Party; Schnader's late conversion to racial equality had lost him the black vote.[61]

After the victory, controversy continued in the black press. The settlement occurred near the end of the school term, and the new Berwyn school was overcrowded. Some African American students attended the new school, but, according to the *Philadelphia Record*, "the old Berwyn school will be used for about 80 backward white and Negro children." Isadore Martin complained to Walter White that the "settlement was a complete sell-out on the part of Raymond Alexander." Eustace Gay wrote in the *Philadelphia Tribune* that "no permanent settlement has arrived"; he believed that "the townships . . . may resegregate, AFTER the present official political campaign is over." The *Philadelphia Independent* described the settlement as a "partial victory for this little band of Negroes." The editorial recommended the two townships pass a "resolution prohibiting discrimination on the grounds of race or color." Alexander's critics correctly concluded that the only reason Schnader added his name to the suit was that it would assist his campaign for governor. Alexander, White, and others were cognizant of that fact as well, but Alexander had negotiated this deal in good faith with two African American lawyers.[62]

In 1932, working-class African Americans left the party of Lincoln and joined the Democrats led by Franklin Delano Roosevelt. Alexander remained a Republican for the time being, although he never stated whether he had voted for the Democrat, George Earle. Some black elites in Pennsylvania switched parties. For example, Robert Vann, a black Republican lawyer and editor of the influential *Pittsburgh Courier*, supported FDR in 1932 and was appointed as Special Assistant to the Attorney General of the United States, the highest position that the Democrats had given to an African American.[63]

In the Berwyn and Willie Brown cases, Alexander and the ILD worked side by side. Unlike Walter White and many other moderate black leaders, Alexander was not afraid to work with radical and left-wing organizations. In the spring of 1932, Alexander mentioned his work with the ILD in the Willie Brown case while speaking to the Washington Bar Association. Alexander declared that it was "not the radical side of the program in which the lawyer's services are used, but in the intelligent management and execution of the plans." Alexander did not define what the "radical side" meant. Did "radical" connote communism or illegal demonstrations? He informed the audience that he had used "intelligent management and execution of the plans," including litigation, mass protests, and alliances with radicals.[64]

Pennsylvania Equal Rights Law, 1935

During the 1930s, African American leaders in the North used their growing political power to force states to pass stronger Equal Rights Laws. In January 1935, Hobson Reynolds, an African American state representative from

Philadelphia, introduced House Bill No. 67, "An act to provide Civil Rights for all people regardless or race or color." According to Alexander, this law, unlike the 1887 law still on the books, had "some nasty, sharp-edged teeth" and included all public accommodations, such as libraries, theaters, schools, swimming pools, and ice cream parlors. The law was designed to "curb Honorable James Crow's activities in Pennsylvania." Any person who violated the law would receive a penalty from one hundred to five hundred dollars or ninety days in jail. Modeled on New York's 1918 law, the Pennsylvania bill allowed lawyers to sue businesses whose employees practiced segregation, even if the company policy prohibited it. In April, when Senator Samuel Salus introduced the Equal Rights Bill in the Senate, more than twenty branches of the NAACP offered their support. A month later, Governor George Earle promised to sign the bill. Hotel managers in the state sent Earle letters asking him not to sign it; they feared that black customers would ruin their business and stated that it violated their right to run their businesses as they wished. In May, the Democratic House and Senate passed the law, illustrating the impact of the black vote. Governor Earle signed the Equal Rights Bill in June 1935, although it was not effective until September. The *Philadelphia Tribune* reported that some whites referred to this as "special legislation," laws that benefited a particular group, in this case, African Americans.[65]

In August 1935, the *Philadelphia Tribune* printed a letter by the White Crusaders, a white supremacist group from Ellsworth, Pennsylvania, who had formed in reaction against the new Equal Rights Law. The White Crusaders passed out a leaflet declaring they were going "to chase the n_____ [nigger] out of Pennsylvania." The White Crusaders rhetoric sounded similar to the Ku Klux Klan's: "We were honest, law-abiding citizens until the n_____ used his influence To have a so-called Equal Rights bill passed by a group of selfish Politicians. We did not want to discriminate against the n_____ Every-One seemed to be satisfied, but we must have treated the n_____ too good. He wants the same privileges as the white man, especially with the white woman."[66] Although southern whites are most closely identified with white supremacy and violent hatred, many northern whites also maintained white supremacist attitudes. The Crusaders encouraged whites to join and "help move the Mason-Dixon line north of Pennsylvania." This organization, like the white hotel mangers, believed that the Equal Rights Bill provided unfair advantages for African Americans.[67]

In spite of Alexander's reputation and the new Equal Rights Law, Alexander's wife still encountered discrimination. In August 1935, J. V. Horn, president of Horn and Hardart, a popular chain restaurant, received a letter from

Alexander stating that after the Equal Rights bill was passed, he noticed a "change of service and attitude towards our patronage." In July and August, when the Alexanders went to the restaurant, they noticed "large quantities of salt in the food." The waitress who had served them the previous day apologized and exchanged the food. On August 8, Sadie Alexander's salad had too much salt and her corn fritter platter contained only "one fritter," a small amount of spinach, and "one slice of bacon." Horn stated that their policy prohibited discrimination against African Americans, but some franchises, managers, or employees intentionally made black customers miserable. The final two paragraphs of Alexander's letter summed up the black elite's attitude toward segregation. According to Alexander, "there is nothing more vexing than the ridiculous feeling of racial hatred, especially when other things, such as education, . . . training, ability, progress . . . are never taken into consideration." Alexander and the New Negro elite constantly reminded whites not to lump all African Americans together. The Alexanders did not take the manager to court; since they were longtime patrons, they gave the restaurant an opportunity to rectify the problem, but their diplomacy did not end Horn and Hardart's discriminatory behavior.[68]

Six days after the Equal Rights Bill went into effect, Alexander informed Charles Hamilton Houston of the NAACP that it was better to wait for a test case to develop than to play into the hands of the white press, which had predicted that immediately after midnight on September 1 African Americans would flood to the hotels and file frivolous law suits. Alexander told Houston that the black community should wait a month or two before testing the law, but a number of incidents occurred immediately after the new law took effect. In September 1935, the manager of the Doris Theatre, Charles Shields, refused to sell Catherine Belton a ticket unless she sat in the "Negro section." Six weeks later, Alexander informed Wilkins that he might have a test case. In October 1935, Mamie Davis and Ruth Jones went to Stouffer's Restaurant. According to Alexander, the clients were not met with "an outright refusal"; they were seated, but the waiter "deliberately adulterated the food with thick layers of salt." When Robert Smith, a reporter for the *Philadelphia Afro-American*, accompanied the women to the restaurant, they again received excessively salted food. In the November meeting of the Committee on Race Relations minutes, Helen Bryan had noted that the "two young colored women sat fifty minutes" before they were served. Alexander believed the judge would "interpret this as a positive refusal" to serve black customers. After two white secretaries received proper service, two black women entered the restaurant and were served food that was extremely salty and "unfit to eat."[69]

In October 1935, the *Philadelphia Tribune* reported that Jean Anders, a white waitress at Horn and Hadart, refused to serve Gladys Drayden, a clerical worker from the Athletic Commission, and Frances Rankin, daughter of Reverend Arthur E. Rankin. The women called Anders's manager, Daniel Hare, and he "told the women that they could not eat in the main cafeteria." In January 1936, Alexander took the Stouffer's, Horn and Hardart, and Doris Theatre cases to court to test the new 1935 Pennsylvania Equal Rights Bill. The *Philadelphia Tribune* reported that the all-white jury ruled in the Stouffers case that "giving too much salt was not a refusal to serve." However, Alexander's clients in the Horn and Hardart and Doris Theatre cases won, and both businesses paid the fine. In the CORR minutes, Helen Bryan noted the activism of the NAACP Youth Councils, an organization of young black and white students that was "an outgrowth of the Young People's Fellowship," a Quaker organization. Bryan remarked that the "action program" of the NAACP Youth Council consisted of students trying "out the bill in twelve restaurants, in nine of which satisfactory service had been accorded." These interracial demonstrations occurred in Philadelphia seven years before the creation of the Congress on Racial Equality.[70]

During his first twelve years in practice, Alexander became one of the nation's leading black attorneys. He won a majority of his civil rights cases, and, even though he did not win the Willie Brown or Walter Rounds case, both the black community and the white bar in Philadelphia admired Alexander's work. He had a direct impact on the lives of black Pennsylvanians with the passage of the 1935 Equal Rights Bill. The NBA was just as important as the NAACP during the civil rights litigation movement. Most black attorneys practiced in the North and fought civil rights cases with support from the community, devoting their own resources to the cause. Alexander's civil rights struggle in Philadelphia complemented the NAACP's campaign in the South and made the civil rights struggle a national rather than a southern phenomenon.

Part Two

FROM RACE RADICAL TO
RACIAL REFORMER, 1936–1953

Chapter Three

MAKING A NATIONAL MOVEMENT LOCAL

The Civil Rights Struggle in Philadelphia, 1936–1948

As Alexander's success and reputation gained local and national attention, he wanted to become a change agent in Philadelphia's racist judicial system. Judicial equity was an important civil rights issue in Philadelphia and the nation, as African Americans encountered all white judges and juries. Alexander's next major goal in Philadelphia was becoming a judge, and in 1933, Alexander had run for the Court of Common Pleas but became sick and withdrew from the race. On a national level, the Democrats wanted black voters, but, in Philadelphia, Democrats and Republicans did not want a black judge. In seeking the opportunity to become a judge, Alexander switched political parties three times, something that was not uncommon in Philadelphia among the black elite. Switching parties made both parties suspicious of his motives, Alexander had reiterated to the party leaders that his civil rights work and competency had qualified him for a judgeship.

World War I, the Great Depression, and World War II aided the twentieth-century civil rights struggle. All three events provided political and economic opportunities and obstacles for the black community and Raymond Pace Alexander. World War I produced the Great Migration that introduced southern black migrants to industry, but most men worked in unskilled jobs and most women worked as domestics. On the other hand, the black middle class, which had produced New Negro lawyers such as Alexander and other black businesspeople, benefited from the new black migrants. Black political and economic power had increased in northern cities, and that forced the white political structure to increase the amount of black patronage. However, white racial backlash that is often associated with the modern civil rights movement was evident during the twenties. Racial tensions intensified after World War I, and African Americans encountered rampant discrimination throughout the city and numerous race riots occurred.

The Great Depression forced the government to address poverty and the role of government. Historically, African Americans had a higher percentage of poverty than whites, but as the percentage of poor whites increased, poverty became a national problem. During the 1930s, the federal government created the New Deal to end the Depression. The New Deal used federal money to create employment, primarily for men. The Democratic Party relied upon the urban black vote; therefore, President Roosevelt created the Black Cabinet, a group of black leaders, such as educator Mary McLoud Bethune, to address racial issues. During the 1930s, local African American leaders had organized "Don't Buy Where You Can't Work Campaigns" that were designed to increase the number of black employees at white businesses. The Depression also forced black leaders such as W. E. B. DuBois and labor leader A. Philip Randolph to analyze the nexus between economic justice and civil rights. Eliminating segregation in public accommodations and schools did not end black poverty or provide jobs for the masses of African Americans. The New Deal sought to create a social safety net for all Americans; Southern Democrats prohibited the New Deal from creating equality between blacks and whites. According to Ira Katznelson, the New Deal was an "affirmative action" for whites because whites received a disproportionate amount of benefits. The New Deal did not end the Depression, but, as Harvard Sitkoff suggests, it mainstreamed the civil rights struggle and racial reform.[1]

Historians Nikhil Singh and Jacqueline Dowd Hall argue that the "long civil rights era" started during the 1930s, but the longer civil rights struggle began during the 1920s, as urban black professional class and labor leaders emerged in the United States as well as in other English colonized nations. The rise of Nazism and fascism in Europe forced the nation to see the contradiction between American racism and democracy. World War II ended the Great Depression, and it was nearly the exact political and economic replica of World War I. More black migrants moved into northern and western cities

for industrial jobs, inducing labor and hate strikes such as the 1944 Philadelphia Transit Strike, in which white workers went on strike because the
Philadelphia Rapid Transit (PRT) had to hire three black rail conductors.
This form of white backlash occurred during the war, as well as a few lynchings and the 1943 Detroit race riot. Similar to the New Negro, a new generation of black businesspeople and professionals emerged, and they benefited
from the political gains made by the New Negro as well as the influx of black
migrants.

In 1942, the *Pittsburgh Courier* started the Double V Campaign, noting
that African Americans fought two wars, one against fascism in Europe and
another against racism in America. Labor leader A. Philip Randolph's March
on Washington Movement forced President Roosevelt to sign Executive
Order #8802, which banned discrimination in hiring for government contracts and created the Fair Employment Practices Commissions. The federal
government did not enforce the FEPC, but northern states sought to do so.
Similar to passing stronger northern state Equal Rights laws during the late
nineteenth century and the first forty years of the twentieth, the post–New
Deal, World War II civil rights struggle fought to get states to enforce state
FEPC laws.[2]

Working in city hall, Alexander saw all white judges, juries, and police
officers. African Americans were rarely tried in front of a jury of peers. In
spite of their growing political power, African Americans remained politically marginalized in Philadelphia. Alexander enjoyed his legal victories and
the city's progress towards civil rights, but he had another goal: to become the
first black judge in Philadelphia. Unlike in Chicago and Harlem, in Philadelphia the black population was overly concentrated in three sections of the
city: the north, west, and south. This residential pattern was the major reason
for African Americans obtaining less political power than in Chicago and
New York, each of which contained one large voting bloc—the South Side
and Harlem.

Nationally, the 1948 presidential election was important, as the Democrats were in a close battle with the Republicans and were losing votes to the
Dixiecrats and to Henry Wallace's Progressive Party. In 1947, President Harry
S. Truman created the Committee on Civil Rights, appointing Alexander's
wife Sadie Alexander, one of only two African Americans (the other being
Dr. Channing Tobias of the National Urban League) on the fifteen-member
committee. The committee published a report titled *To Secure These Rights*,
outlining the impact of racial discrimination. This commission and report

demonstrated the Democratic Party's commitment to civil rights, but it also created white backlash in the party. Southern Democrats formed the Dixiecrat Party, supporting segregation and electing Strom Thurmond as their presidential candidate in 1948. Moreover, Sadie's appointment to the Committee on Civil Rights in 1947 allowed Alexander to rejoin the Democratic Party and campaign for Truman. Locally in 1948, the Pennsylvania state legislature passed the Home Rule Charter that promoted urban reform, business development, and an end to corruption. From 1936 to 1948, Alexander's professional status shifted from the margins as black lawyers started to gain national recognition. In Philadelphia, his political status as well as the civil rights struggle shifted from the margins to become prominent.

Entering City Politics

The Republican machine provided patronage to laborers but refused to appoint more middle-class African Americans to higher-level positions. As a result, when high positions became available, black lawyers fought among themselves for the few appointments. Many white members of Philadelphia mayor Bill Vare's machine were racist and did not want African Americans working at white-collar jobs in city government. For example, in 1926, Vare wanted to appoint a black man as assistant district attorney. G. Edward Dickerson, president of the John M. Langston Bar Association, had recommended Alexander; however, District Attorney Edward Fox refused to have any African American on his staff. In 1933, Alexander ran for the Court of Common Pleas, but the *Philadelphia Tribune* reported that he withdrew because of poor health. By 1937, he had fourteen years of experience, numerous court victories, a growing reputation in the black and legal communities, and years as a loyal Republican. Alexander believed it was time for him to become the first black judge in Philadelphia."[3]

By the 1930s, most working-class African Americans voted Democrat, and a growing number started to receive lower-paying city jobs. However, a number of black elites in Philadelphia, such as Alexander and E. Washington Rhodes, lawyer and editor of the *Philadelphia Tribune*, had remained Republicans. In spite of the New Deal and Democratic Party attempts to attract black voters, Alexander and many of the black elite had remained with the Party of Lincoln. Middle-class black Republicans such as Alexander believed that the growth of the Democratic Party would force the

Republican Party to reach out to black voters. Famous black Republicans, such as Robert S. Abbott, editor of the *Chicago Defender*, viewed the upcoming 1937 Philadelphia election as an opportunity to "bring the Negro vote back to the GOP." Abbott declared that he would put the "full force" of his newspaper behind Alexander's candidacy. In October 1936, a year before the election, Alexander spoke to the Philadelphia Chapter of the NNC about the need for an African American judge. According to Alexander, the *Philadelphia Tribune* reported that the high number of black criminals gave white "jurors and officials . . . the idea that Negroes are inherent criminals" and that African Americans seldom had adequate legal representation. A black common pleas judge would have "tremendous power" to improve the judicial process for African Americans. In November 1937, eighteen judicial seats were available in Philadelphia. Nationally and locally known colleagues in law, journalism, and politics, such as Philadelphia native Nannie H. Burroughs and black attorneys such as Thurgood Marshall, William L. Houston, and Perry W. Howard wrote letters of recommendation in support of Alexander to Jay Cooke, president of the Republican Central Campaign Committee. Howard's letter stated that he had followed Pennsylvania politics and that Alexander's "Republicanism is as regular as the multiplication table." Even some black Democrats such as Francis Ellis, a black judge in New York City, had supported Alexander.[4]

In order to ensure that a black judge was elected, black Republican organizations such as the John Mercer Langston Law Club, the Citizens Republican Club, and the Colored American Citizens Organization requested that the Republican Party nominate one black judge. African American city councilman James H. Irvin, a Democrat, also supported a black Republican for judge. Irvin told Alexander that whoever their organization nominated "would receive whole-hearted support of the other named candidates." During the Methodist Ministers Conference, African American Methodist and Baptist ministers endorsed Alexander in a 56-to-1 vote. Ed Henry, an African American Republican and magistrate and one of the most powerful black politicians in Philadelphia, attended the conference. Henry, talking about Alexander's civil rights litigation, stated Alexander "shouldered the responsibility of practically all litigation affecting the economic, political and civic rights of the Negro in Philadelphia during the last 14 years." Henry's comments echoed the view held by many African Americans in Philadelphia and attested to Alexander's major role in the civil rights struggle in Philadelphia. In spite of the black organizations' efforts to get the Republican Party to select one candidate, the Republican Party nominated two candidates, African American attorney Herbert Millen and Alexander.[5]

One month before the election, the National Bar Association held its fifteenth annual convention in Philadelphia at the University of Pennsylvania. Alexander used the convention to discuss his nomination and have his colleagues send supportive letters to Cooke. Alexander's campaign took a turn for the worst after Republican Party Committee chairman Jay Cooke, speaking to a group of black Republicans, boldly declared that "The Time is Not Ripe" for a black judge. The *Philadelphia Tribune* reported that Cooke stated "white voters will not vote for a colored candidate." Henry, chair of Citizens for Alexander, reminded Cooke that the Democratic Party had a "more generous and liberal attitude" toward African Americans and that all five black judges in the country were Democrats. Henry told Cooke that it was impossible to go out before people and urge them to vote Republican when the party consistently kept African Americans off the bench. Henry declared that Alexander "would add hundreds of thousands of the younger, forward thinking Negroes to the Republican ranks." Alexander Martin, a black attorney from Cleveland, heard of Cooke's remarks and wrote to Alexander, "of course that is the ordinary attitude of the lily white dough face republican of our day." According to Martin, the Republican Party shifted from "the chief protagonist of a representable democracy" to representing the "bourbon Democracy of the South." Martin abandoned the Republican Party in 1936 after Republican presidential candidate Alf Landon supported states rights. He warned Alexander not to "expect the Republicans to nominate you, nor to elect you if they do. They haven't got 'the guts.' P.S. You may substitute intestinal fortitude for guts." Martin's cynicism represented the sentiment of working-class African Americans who had abandoned the party in 1932, but, in spite of Martin's comments, Alexander remained cautiously optimistic that the Republicans would support a black candidate.[6]

After Cooke's speech, Republican candidate Herbert Millen left the party, obtained thirteen thousand signatures, and created an independent party called the Millen Judicial Party because the Republican Party would not support a black judge. Millen and his supporters were convinced that "both the Republicans and Democrats have formed a conspiracy to stop the rise of colored people." Millen's decision to start an independent party may have been questionable because it split the black vote, but Cooke's comments and the behavior of both parties justified Millen's stance. Two weeks before the primary election, Henry wrote to white Republicans about the need for the Republican Party to appoint a black judge. He reminded Judge Frank

Brown that Alexander was an ideal candidate who may have had up to fifteen thousand former client voters. In August, the *Philadelphia Tribune*, ran an ad: "HELP US ELECT A COLORED JUDGE IN PHILADELPHIA." The ad encouraged African Americans to register with the Republican Party in order to vote in the primary. Rhodes wanted registered black Democrats to vote for their race over their party because a black judge would improve the status of African Americans "in all the station houses of the City and all the courts of the state." An African American judge might be more understanding of the impact of social inequality and its relation to receiving a fair trial. Henry sent a letter to black Republican voters and encouraged them to "*VOTE THE STRAIGHT NEGRO TICKET.*" The primary election was held on September 14 and Alexander lost the election. Philadelphia, with the third largest African American population in the country, remained a city without a black judge. In spite of Rhodes's efforts, most African Americans remained Democrats, and Alexander and the independent Millen lost the election.[7]

Alexander won the majority in black wards, but, as Martin predicted, Alexander did not get enough support from white Republicans. After the primary, Alexander and Hobson Reynolds, an African American and former Republican state representative, joined the Democratic Party. This shift was not unprecedented in Philadelphia. Ed Henry was a Republican who joined the Democrats from 1925 to 1935 and returned then to the Republican Party from 1935 to 1939. Political scientist James Miller described the black voting patterns in Philadelphia between 1932 and 1944 as "fluid," and each party won six elections during those years. Comparing Philadelphia to Chicago, Detroit, and New York, Miller concluded that the Democratic Party in Philadelphia did not gain as it did in the other cities. In a statement to the *Philadelphia Tribune*, Alexander told the Democratic Party that he was "interested in doing all that I can to aid in a sweeping Democratic victory." Alexander boasted that the Democrats would receive an additional 60 percent of the black vote because he and Hobson Reynolds had shifted their party allegiance.

Alexander blamed his defeat on a Republican Party that was "not interested in policies of liberality or a square deal for minority groups," and his defection caused a major stir in Philadelphia. John B. Kelly, chair of the Democratic Committee Office in Philadelphia, received a barrage of support letters from local black Democrats such as Dr. Nathan Mossell, Alexander's father-in-law, and Luther Harr, a black Democrat and former Republican who was running for City Treasurer. Alexander's letter to Democratic judge Curtis Bok displayed his frustration with the Republican Party, a party that "would rather lose without us than win with us." He promised Bok and the

Democratic Party his full support in the upcoming November election.[8] Alexander voiced his frustration to Arthur H. Fauset, president of the National Negro Congress Philadelphia chapter, that he was "so thoroughly disgusted with the way our people neglect their opportunities especially political ones." Alexander blamed black voters for not supporting his candidacy, but most African American voters were Democrats, and, as he stated, the Republican Party did not support his nomination. Racism was the roadblock.[9]

Two weeks before the November election, Alexander gave a radio address that castigated Philadelphia's Republican machine and explained his defection to the Democratic Party. He referred to the party's "greed for control of all arms of the city government." Alexander was encouraged to switch parties. Since 1934, Democratic governor George Earle appointed thirty-four of the thirty-eight judges in Philadelphia. When Alexander was a Republican, he did not support sitting judges, but as a Democrat he endorsed sitting judges. A week after Alexander's radio address, an editorial in the *Philadelphia Tribune* commented on Alexander's hypocrisy and his criticism of Philadelphia's black elite. The editorial noted that when Alexander was a Republican, he "opposed sitting judges," but two months later he switched his position since most sitting judges were Democratic appointees. E. Washington Rhodes, owner of the *Philadelphia Tribune*, was a staunch Republican, and his paper warned the black community, "It will be a cold day in August before he or any other colored lawyers sits on the bench." While both parties competed for black vote and provided patronage for African Americans, they agreed not to have an African American judge.[10]

Alexander gave another radio address to Philadelphia's Democrats and referred to Philadelphia's Republican machine as "political overlords" who ran the city into massive debt. While the Republicans refused to appoint a black lawyer to any important position, since 1934, Democratic governor Earle had employed 146 African Americans "above the grade of janitors and porters." The state government increased the number of black skilled workers, and there were six black Democratic state representatives. Alexander told black voters that the Republicans have "betrayed you" and that Abraham Lincoln "would disown the Republican Party." Alexander mentioned a comment by David Watson, a white Republican candidate for city treasurer: "No colored man is deserving of a position paying over $1800.00 or $2000.00 a year." In closing, Alexander urged African Americans to "Vote for your own protection because party labels are not important," and by 1937, most African American voters were Democrats. Alexander may not have been as influential as he thought it was.[11]

Alexander and Reynolds chaired the City-Wide Colored Citizens Committee and ran an ad in the *Philadelphia Tribune* that maintained that the Democratic Party had provided more jobs to African Americans in the last three years than the Republican Party had done during the previous sixty years. As Clara Hardin notes, African Americans sought political patronage that provided "governmental positions in proportion to their numbers, and according to their ability as individuals." Alexander never stated that he supported a quota system; he advocated proportionality equality that used the percentage of the black population in Philadelphia in order to come up with a fair number of African American representation. In spite of Alexander's efforts for the Democrats, Governor Earle did not appoint Alexander or any other black attorney to the bench. Miller argues that Republicans and Democrats supported "sitting judges," a policy that stated "there is no vacancy on the slate." African Americans in Philadelphia believed that the sitting judges policy was a "gentlemen's agreement" between both parties in order not to appoint a black judge. Alexander's inability to become a judge reflects Philadelphia's southern-style race relations and the impact of the city's housing policies. By 1937, Philadelphia contained three separate black communities. Therefore, the African American vote in Philadelphia did not form a major geographic block as it did in New York and Chicago, two cities with African American judges. Despite the major setback, Alexander continued with his work in the NBA and in the civil rights struggle in Philadelphia.[12]

Alexander's defeat in the 1937 election and defection to the Democratic Party had no impact on his business. Former clients continued to express their gratitude in the *Philadelphia Tribune*. For instance, Ms. Cotton who suffered an injury by a trolley was encouraged by her black friends "to get a white attorney." Cotton stated, "I got so sick and tired of people advising me to go get a white man that I lost a lot of friends." Cotton attributed this condition to "habit and tradition." She thanked Alexander, who had obtained an out-of-court settlement for her. Cotton told others that if Alexander did not take the case "she would not be in the good condition that" she was in.

Alexander and the Black Bar, 1937–1945

During his political campaigns, Alexander remained active in the NBA, conducted a study on the status of black attorneys, and created the organizations journal, *The National Bar Journal*. The 1937 NBA convention addressed many of the pertinent political and economic concerns of the black community:

restrictive covenants, anti-lynching bills, desegregating higher education, and civil rights legislation. According to the *Philadelphia Tribune*, the majority of the panels "were characterized by the emphasis of the economic view point by most of the speakers." For example, C. Francis Stradford, an attorney of the Brotherhood of Sleeping Car Porters, maintained that the "Negro needs industrial democracy" and that black labor must join labor unions and refuse to be used as strikebreakers.[13] In spite of the emphasis on economic concern, the NBA voted 21 to 18 in a contested election against supporting the Congress of Industrial Organization (CIO), then a rival to the American Federation of Labor. The *Philadelphia Tribune* reported that initially the ballot favored the CIO, but supporters lost in an extremely loud recount in which some members "could not distinguish the voters voice." Philadelphia attorney G. Edward Dickerson explained that he voted against the CIO because he "could not back an organization which was starting out on a perilous journey and one which advocated such unlawful tactics as sit-down strikes." Dickerson assumed that all labor strikes resulted in violence, but Alexander supported the CIO and, "despite his vigorous efforts," the CIO "went down to defeat." Black labor needed an organization that represented its interests and that used the courts and mass protests. Labor had the right to demonstrate and bargain for their wages. Alexander used this same rationale during the Berwyn case when he supported the parents' jail-ins and permitted the local ILD chapters to participate. The members who voted against supporting the CIO wanted to improve the status of black labor but refused to support the CIO's radical tactics, such as sit-down strikes. By 1937, Alexander had remained committed to combining litigation and mass action in the form of labor strikes; however, most black attorneys continued to support a litigation campaign and they viewed the CIO and strikes as radicalism and counterproductive.[14]

Alexander presented a paper on the status of black attorneys and the challenges they faced. He noted that for attorneys in any minority groups to succeed, they needed support from a strong business elite, an industrial working class, and black professionals. Alexander urged his fellow attorneys to organize such partnerships. According to Alexander, "the most difficult problem is to create a greater interest on the part of the Negro himself in the Negro lawyer." In spite of the success of black attorneys like Alexander, most African Americans, regardless of class, remained reluctant to employ black attorneys. Alexander suggested that black professionals needed to work together, along with a black industrial class, because these groups had the finances to employ black attorneys. Alexander acknowledged that racism prevented black attorneys from succeeding by encouraging African Americans to use white attorneys and hampering black professionals' ability to form adequate partnerships.[15]

The NBA's convention was a huge success. During the convention, the first book on the history of black lawyers appeared, *Negroes and the Law* by Fitzhugh Lee Styles. The book, sold to "colleges, universities, Law schools, and Law libraries" around the nation, chronicled the training and legal work of black attorneys such as Alexander. Styles stated that Alexander's success was "but another example of the many successful, progressive and thoroughgoing lawyers of the race today practicing throughout the country." Attorney C. Francis Stradford referred to the convention as a success with great political implications for Alexander. Stradford wrote Alexander, "As a reward, I hope the Republican Committee will designate you as the choice of Judge of the Common Pleas Court."[16]

After the convention, Roger Butterfield, editor of *Time* magazine, wrote an editorial titled "Future Cloudy" that summarized the precarious situation of black attorneys, especially in the South. According to Butterfield, in 1930 there were 11.9 million African Americans and only 1,247 African American attorneys. Washington, D.C., had the largest number with 225 African American attorneys, but more than half were "sun downers," a euphemism for black attorneys who practiced law in the evening after they completed their daytime government jobs. New York City had 112 lawyers and Philadelphia a dismal 30, but 80 percent of African American attorneys practiced in the North, and there were only 200 black attorneys in the entire South. Austin Thomas Walden, a black attorney from Atlanta noted that, for black attorneys in the South, "the future is often cloudy and even ominous." The *Time* article referred to Alexander as the "most active Negro lawyer," who handled 200 cases and made $20,000 a year. Alexander was quoted as saying that he preferred being called mister to doctor or professor because "Mister sticks." Alexander stated that Butterfield portrayed him as a "conceited person with absolutely no judgment or sense of decorum." Alexander told Butterfield that while in City Hall in Philadelphia, one of his employee's overheard "four lawyers of the opposite race" discuss the editorial, and made an "uncomplimentary remark" about him. Alexander was concerned with his image because at the time he was "running for public office." He believed that the reporting of his salary might have alienated him from most white and even some black attorneys and that the editorial may have reinforced the stereotypes of black attorneys as arrogant and ostentatious.[17]

By the late thirties, Alexander was gaining a national reputation, even though all of civil rights work was in Philadelphia. In November 1939, *The Crisis* ran a front-page feature titled "The Philadelphia Lawyer" that reviewed Alexander's civil rights campaign in Philadelphia and applauded him on the numerous negligence settlements he won. In December 1939, the white-owned paper *Philadelphia Inquirer* conducted a poll on "the most prominent citizen of the Negro Race," and Alexander came in third behind opera singer Marian Anderson and scientist George Washington Carver. In January 1940, Elmer Carter, editor of *Opportunity,* congratulated black attorneys and main-tained that Alexander's victory in the Arsenic Widow Case (in which two Italian women were charged with murdering their husbands for insurance money) added to "an inspiring record by Negroes in the field of law. Insofar as we know, a Negro attorney defending white women accused of murder is without precedent in American history."[18]

By 1942, local and national civil rights victories piled up, but African American attorneys did not have a law journal to document their court vic-tories and discuss the legal ramifications of their work. The American Bar Association prohibited black lawyers from joining, and civil rights law was not taught in white law schools. In 1937, Alexander served as chair of the editorial board of the journal of the NBA. The first edition of the journal was supposed to be published that June, but the NBA did not have the funds until 1940 to start their journal. Alexander served as editor, and Freeman L. Martin, a black attorney from St. Louis was the editor in chief. Martin asked Alexan-der to write the foreword to the inaugural edition. Many African American attorneys considered Alexander an elder statesmen who contributed a great amount of energy to civil rights and to the development of the NBA. The first issue was scheduled for July 1941. During the summer, Martin and Alex-ander corresponded and worked feverishly to get the journal published and distributed across the nation. Martin viewed the journal as the voice of all black attorneys, and "when the NBJ speaks everyone should stand attention." According to Martin, the *National Bar Journal* was designed to address "all legal questions affecting the Negroes of America."[19]

The *National Bar Journal* debuted in July 1941 at the NBA convention in Little Rock, Arkansas. A plethora of black newspapers and a couple of white periodicals commented on the journal. Alexander's "Forward—Editorial" examined a wide range of issues. The first portion of the article explained the purpose of the National Bar Association and the difficulties of black attor-neys. Alexander compared the differences between black and white physicians.

Alexander noted that African American physicians practiced in private, at a home, or in a segregated hospital. According to Alexander, when a black doctor made a mistake, Alexander believed that the mistake remained within the office and in the black community. Whites may not find out and thus would not argue that black doctors were inferior and lose black patients. On the other hand, black attorneys practiced in public where white counsels, juries, spectators, and newspapers viewed any mistakes. Whites and blacks highlighted small mistakes that scared away potential black clients and reinforced stereotypes about black lawyers. According to Alexander, the NBA developed race pride and allowed the African American to "believe in himself."[20]

The journal was a huge success. Martin wrote to Alexander that the NBJ was "the greatest achievement of Negro lawyers in America and compared the . . . applause from Negroes attorney to bombs raining from the sky." Sixteen years after the start of the NBA, African American attorneys had a journal to inform all Americans on the civil rights work of black attorneys. Alexander, the guru of publicity, sent a free copy to as many individuals as possible. Historian Rayford Logan used the book in his history class. U.S. Supreme Court Justice Felix Frankfurter extolled the journal's "very high quality." George Maxey, Pennsylvania Supreme Court Justice, congratulated Alexander's thesis that the law "should not be affected by race or color." Attorney Alice Peppers enjoyed the journal's lack of "emotional hysteria." Unlike the *New Masses* or *Daily Worker's*, the journal did not "resort to blood and thunder and riot-inciting material for effect." The *American Bar Association Journal* stated "the most impressive feature of this creditable publication is its consciousness of race and color." Martin Popper of the National Lawyers Guild stated that the journal united "all lawyers in our common effort to defeat Hitlerism." Alexander printed all of the journal's accolades in the October 1941 issue. The NBJ provided a liberal, moderate, and scholarly analysis of civil rights and law.[21]

In 1939, Alexander presented a speech, "Let My People Live," to a group of black lawyers in Cleveland. Alexander talked about the number of public accommodation discrimination suits that he litigated but emphasized the "more fundamental, material and substantial rights." These rights included equal education, the right for African Americans to attend state-supported public but segregated universities, "the rights to bargain with our employers to work; the right to be employed in industry," and the right for equal pay. Alexander reiterated, *"Do not misunderstand me,"* public accommodation discrimination was important, but "we will agree right here between us, that if we don't eat on Euclid Avenue, we won't starve to death." African

Americans could go down to Cedar Avenue in the black community. In 1939, African American communities had their own theaters, hotels, and restaurants, and African Americans needed to support those businesses. Alexander also argued that African American children must be able to attend "modern, public schools" that were built with African American tax dollars. The major emphasis of Alexander's civil rights struggle was jobs and equal education. African Americans needed the education to obtain higher-paying skilled and professional employment. During World War II, African Americans organized the Double V campaign. Victory against racism in America included, as Drake and Cayton observed in Chicago, eradicating the "Job Ceiling."[22]

One year before the United States entered World War II, Alexander presented a speech to a group of African Americans titled "What about National Preparedness for the Negro?" The next to last paragraph summarized Alexander's stance on the role of the federal government and equal employment for African Americans. According to Alexander, "federal legislation demands that all industries working on defense contracts employ Negro workers" in skilled positions. He maintained that the federal government must continue to lobby for a "Negro judge in our Federal Supreme Court Circuit." In 1940, there were 316 federal judges, none of whom were black. Alexander saw World War II as an opportunity to expand opportunities for all African Americans. Working-class African Americans would obtain skilled jobs while Alexander and other black attorneys might receive judgeships. In February 1942, three months after Pearl Harbor, Alexander and the "old boys" Robert C. Nix and Joseph Rainey volunteered to selective service. During World War II, African Americans wanted to demonstrate their loyalty to the country and fight for democracy. Alexander also wanted to show his loyalty. Between 1942 and 1943, Alexander corresponded with white and black War Department officials and inquired about war-related positions. He corresponded with Major General J. A. Ulio, the adjutant general. Alexander applauded the number of African Americans who were inducted into the military but noted that his white lawyer colleagues had "been called to the service and commissioned direct from civilian life." Alexander suggested that there were a large number of African American professionals between ages thirty-six and forty-four who were "anxious to assist our war effort" but could not support a family on a private salary. For example, in 1943, R. C. Butts of the Office of Price Administration appointed Alexander to the Rationing Board "without compensation—and no reimbursement for travel or any other expenses." Ulio responded to Alexander that a number of lawyers applied for commissions but needed military training to serve.[23]

Alexander wrote letters to President Roosevelt and Supreme Court Justice Felix Frankfurter. Alexander informed Roosevelt that black soldiers were not involved in "active combat service' in fighting zones" and suggested that the War Department organize a meeting of "Negro men of national distinction" to study African Americans in the military. Alexander asked Roosevelt to grant him the "privilege" to tap this "rich manpower reservoir of Negro men." Roosevelt sent the letter to the war department with "no mention" of the civilian aide question. Alexander presented a list of black elites who were willing to serve a high military position, but he was concerned that the military commissioned too many physicians and not enough lawyers. According to Alexander, he knew a number of white attorneys in Philadelphia who obtained military positions, and he asked Frankfurter to consider him for one of these positions. In September, Alexander wrote Frankfurter a letter that highlighted his frustrations. Alexander was candid and he wrote that he "read in the local press" that white lawyers without military experience were commissioned. However, he softened his tone in the end because he did not want "to appear to be critical it may ruin whatever chances I may have for appointment." Alexander never obtained the civilian aide position that he desired, and this double standard annoyed Alexander. However, in September of 1942, the U.S. government leased Alexander's office for fifteen years for $225,000 to Bonschure and Holmes, an optical company, that converted his office to make bomb sights for U.S. planes. Alexander relocated his practice to 40 South 19th Street, and with the extra money created a scholarship for an African American law student to attend the University of Pennsylvania.[24]

The Thomas Mattox Case, 1942–1944

One major case that reflected the nation's racial tensions and contradictions during World War II was the Thomas Mattox Extradition Case. On July 11, 1942, Thomas Mattox, a sixteen-year-old black male who lived in Elberton, Georgia, his two sisters Emmy and Gussie, and four friends were returning home from a movie. While driving home, Mattox passed nineteen-year-old Wilbur Cornell who had two female friends in the car. Disgusted, Cornell sped up, passed Mattox's car, blocked his vehicle, and shouted that "a dirty black nigger had the temerity to pass a white man." Cornell approached their car and, when Gussie Mattox asked him to get out the way, picked up an "auto jack" and hit her twice and Mattox once. Mattox took out his penknife and cut Cornell. Cornell fled the scene and went to the police. As soon as whites heard what had happened, "mob crowds" gathered outside the jail. After hearing about the crowd, the sisters took Mattox to the train station, where he purchased a one-way train ticket to Philadelphia to stay with his brother Lester. When Mattox's sisters returned home from the train station, the sheriff was waiting for them. He arrested them for "conspiracy to assault and to commit murder." To find out Mattox's whereabouts, the sheriff arrested Mattox's older brother John, who was not even in the car, and "threatened" to turn him over to the "mob crowd." John Mattox told the sheriff that his brother was in Philadelphia. The sheriff telegraphed a message to the Philadelphia police about the fugitive. Mattox arrived in Philadelphia on July 13 and went to the hospital to take care of his bruises. Four days later, Mark Cleveland and Wilbur Dye, the sheriffs from Elberton, arrived in Harrisburg, Pennsylvania, to obtain the warrant and take Mattox back to Georgia, but the governor's office was closed. The next day, Lester Mattox, Mattox's brother in Philadelphia, hired Alexander. Alexander immediately "obtained a writ of habeas corpus" and gave it to Frederick Baldi, the superintendent of the county prison. This writ prevented the sheriff from taking Mattox back to Georgia until he received an extradition hearing. Alexander filed the writ, citing that Mattox could not obtain a fair trial in Elberton, Georgia, and would be lynched. In July, former Republican U.S. congressman and Court of Common Pleas judge Clare G. Fenerty honored Alexander's writ and scheduled the hearing for October.[25]

Between July and October, Alexander prepared for the hearing. His defense had to prove that if Mattox returned to Georgia he would be lynched. He argued that law enforcement officials in Elberton allowed Mattox's family to be abused. After Sheriff Cleveland arrested Mattox's two sisters and brother, their mother came to the jail to find out about bail but was unable to get her children from jail. On her way home, a car of whites ran in front of her car, shot at her, pulled her out of her car, and beat her with a black jack. The men asked her where her son was and, when she refused to tell them, "got a chain and put it around" her neck. They said that they would throw her "in the quarry" if she did not tell where her son was. She admitted that she sent him to Philadelphia.[26]

The extradition hearing was held on October 16, 1942, in the Quarter Sessions Court with Judge Clare G. Fenerty presiding. In November 1928, NAACP secretary James Weldon Johnson and Director of Publicity Herbert J. Seligmann mentioned that the NAACP had appealed to various governors to prevent extraditions. During extradition cases, the NAACP tried to prove that the defendant would not receive a fair trial, but the judge usually argued that the individual would receive a fair trial. Alexander used the entire Mattox family as witnesses. The Mattoxes recalled the incident and told the judge how the mob gathered outside of their home. After Mattox's mother admitted that her son was in Philadelphia, the sheriff kept her two daughters in jail as hostages to make Mattox return home from Philadelphia. Alexander collected evidence on the lack of African American rights in that part of Georgia.

In August 1942, William Henry Huff, chief counsel for the Abolishment of Peonage Committee of America, read about the Mattox case and wrote to Alexander about the death of Nathan Burton, whose body was tied "to the frame of an automobile and buried in the river," in Elberton, Georgia. Huff had sent word of Burton's death to Governor Eugene Talmadge of Georgia, who did not respond. According to Huff, in Elberton, African Americans did not have "any rights a white person thinks of respecting." Elbert County was one of many "counties where a continuous saternalia of hell rains upon the heads of Negroes." Huff maintained that sending Mattox back was "sending him to the lynching den." Alexander also used a brief filed by the National Lawyers Guild (NLG). The brief outlined the number of extradition cases in the country that illustrated racial violence in the South. The brief noted that "six lynchings occurred within the radius of thirty miles of Elberton." The NLG's brief also cited a 1942 report, "Negro Discrimination and the Need for Federal Action" by William Hastie and Thurgood Marshall, on lynching and mob violence. According to historian Fitzhugh Brundage, between 1919 and 1940, ninety-four African Americans were lynched in Georgia by burning at the stake, hanging, or shooting. Mississippi was the only state with more recorded lynchings.[27]

Philadelphia's District Attorney John H. Murer argued that Mattox had seriously wounded Cornell. After the fight, Cornell went to the hospital where he received twenty-five stitches. Murer's witness, Dr. W. A. Johnson, who treated Cornell, testified that he had "never heard of any threats of intimidation or threats of mob violence" in Elberton. L. C. Smith and Zelmon Smith, two African Americans who were in jail at the time of the incident, testified that "they never have been intimidated" and did not know anyone who had. Maurer argued that the "lynching statistics" were irrelevant because no one was ever lynched in Elberton and that the county officials had assured that Mattox would receive a fair trial. Nevertheless, the NLG brief asserted that "Elberton county mobsters" took their victims outside of county lines so that the county would not have any reported lynching.[28]

Another major piece of evidence that aided Mattox was a letter that R. Howard Gordon, the solicitor general of the Northern Judicial Circuit of Georgia, mailed to the District Attorney Maurer. Gordon warned, "we have noticed that this Judge has sponsored anti-lynch legislation" and therefore would "be biased in this case against the state of Georgia." Gordon recommended that Fenerty be "disqualified." Judge Fenerty was incensed over the letter. He denounced the state of Georgia for wanting a judge that did not want to aid all "lawless men to commit deliberate murder." Gordon's "tenor" in the letter "revealed to him that, in Georgia the crime of lynching is not of such seriousness that failure to prevent it on the part of the legal authorities should be punished." In 1935, as a U.S. member of Congress from Pennsylvania, Fenerty supported a modest anti-lynch law. In Fenerty's opinion, "We in Philadelphia considered lynching as exactly what it is murder-and the denial to the individual of the right of trial guaranteed by the Constitution." Fenerty ruled in favor of Mattox, but the state of Georgia appealed. The next hearing was scheduled in December in the Pennsylvania Superior Court. After the first hearing, Alexander received a letter from a disgruntled white Philadelphian. According to Fair Clay (Democrat), "Judge Fenerty is a Republican fake who always helped Niggers. Niggers have too many privileges now. Fennerty is a nigger lover." This letter shows the same virulent racism present in Elberton also present in Philadelphia, but it also illustrates the commitment to civil rights by a number of white liberals in Pennsylvania.[29]

For the December hearing, Alexander asked for research assistance from Roy Wilkins of the NAACP and Charles Hamilton Houston. Alexander wanted to know the number of lynchings in Georgia during the last thirty years, and if Thurgood Marshall could inquire if there was a case in which a judge from a lower court "overruled a governor's extradition warrant" and acquitted a defendant from another state. Alexander wanted Houston to send him a brief that would "sustain Judge Fenerty's lower Court opinion." In December the NAACP, the NBA, American Civil Liberties Union, and Civil Liberties Committee joined Alexander. Alexander filed a "petition for a re-hearing" with Governor James, and he asked Murer for a continuance. Pennsylvania Superior Court Judge William Keller was assigned to the Mattox trial, and Alexander suggested to him that the state should "adopt a broad and liberal view" of extradition cases and consider the lynching evidence. Alexander wanted the judge to use Georgia's lynching record as proof of mob violence. The December hearing was postponed until March 9, 1943.[30]

Alexander always connected his major legal cases to the political fortunes of others. Alexander wrote the new Pennsylvania governor, Edward Martin, and Lieutenant Governor John C. Ball. He reminded the two men of the political significance of the case. Judge Fenerty, Alexander, and Murer were Republicans. Alexander noted that the Democratic *Pittsburgh Courier*, "one of the most far reaching colored papers in America," criticized Murer for supporting the state of Georgia and not supporting the Republican judge. Alexander warned both men that if Mattox returned to Georgia, the Republican Party would face "unanswerable criticism on the part of 500,000 Negroes." In 1943, the black vote in Philadelphia had remained flexible, and if the Republican Party did not support Mattox, they could lose voters. Alexander came across an article in January on the "murder and lynching of Robert Hall in Newton, Georgia." After he read the article, he asked Walter White of the NAACP to mail him ten copies of the special bulletin. Alexander mailed a copy of the article to each superior court judge. On April 17 1943, William Keller decided to "sustain the habeas corpus," and Mattox remained in Pennsylvania. Keller stated that Fenerty had enough evidence to establish "reasonable grounds" that Mattox would not receive a fair trial in Elberton. Alexander called Keller's decision "one of the finest and fairest ever accorded a Colored American." Alexander waited for the state of Georgia to appeal, and in May, Alexander told Thomas Mattox that the "time has expired" for an appeal.[31]

Following the victory, Alexander received kudos from lawyers, academicians, and the black and white press. Howard Law professor Leon Ransom asked Alexander to leave his law practice, join Howard Law, and "make this an institution that could revolutionize the attitude of the courts towards the problems of our rights." Historian Rayford Logan maintained that Alexander had "made a great contribution to the history of American jurisprudence and to the cause of human justice." The *Philadelphia Inquirer* stated that this case was the first "in which a lower court had been sustained in examining evidence of what might occur in the courts of another state and in acting on that evidence." The *Pittsburgh Courier* journalist and lay historian Joel A. Rogers wrote a full three-page feature on the Philadelphia lawyer, calling Alexander "one of Americas best known lawyers." Although lawyers were not supposed to write to judges after a decision, Alexander wrote Keller that the decision was "the most liberal opinion ever handed down in history." The Mattox case appeared in *Temple Law Quarterly*, *Yale Law Journal*, and in the *National Bar Journal*.

After the trial, Alexander received some hate mail. One letter, from "Signed Democrat," referred to Alexander as a "Big shot" and called Keller a "nutty judge who saved a Georgia Nigger." The writer warned Alexander that when Harry S. Truman became president, "your kind will be just where the southern coon is—on the way to the back alley." Fortunately, for African Americans the "signed Democrat" was wrong, and the civil rights struggle and growing black political power in the North forced President Truman to give civil rights more attention.[32]

Another incident that demonstrated the legal impact was the lynching of Cleo Wright, a black male who assaulted a white woman in Sidekston, Missouri, and was lynched in January 1942. Historian Dominic Capeci convincingly argued that Wright's lynching started the *Pittsburgh Courier*'s Double V Campaign, and it forced the U.S. Justice Department to enforce the equal protection clause of the Fourteenth Amendment. The federal government needed to ensure black loyalty as well as assure their critics that America was not a fascist state and that racism would be eliminated. The Justice Department started to investigate racial violence, and the federal courts punished more whites for committing racial violence. The Thomas Mattox case was part of what Capeci referred to as a "constitutional revolution." Both judges allowed Alexander to use lynching statistics to prove that Mattox would have been lynched if he had returned to Georgia. During the hearing, both sides cited *Marbles v. Creecy*, 215 U.S. 63 (1909), in which an African American male accused of raping a white woman had fled from Mississippi to Missouri, but the U.S. Supreme Court ruled that Marbles must be returned to his state for trial. According to the NLG's brief, in the Mattox case, the plaintiff's attorney only "suggested" and "failed to prove" that Marbles would have been lynched in Mississippi. Alexander, with the help of the NAACP, NLG, and ACLU, convinced the judge that Mattox had an excellent chance of being lynched. Reflecting on the Mattox case, Alexander's statement symbolized the irony of the black experience during World War II. Alexander maintained that "the interesting paradox of it all is," in spite of "the unfair treatment" that the Mattox family received, when Mattox turned eighteen, four months after his hearing, he enlisted in the U.S. Navy. Mattox was a "first class seamen at Great Lakes Naval Training Base instead of perhaps buried in an unknown grave in the clay soil of Georgia if the liberal courts of Pennsylvania had not stepped in."[33] Alexander applauded the liberalism of the Pennsylvania Courts, but the state's judicial liberalism would again be put to the test. On December 9, 1944, Harry M. Wodlinger, a white real estate and insurance operator, came home for lunch and found his forty-five-year-old wife, Freeda Wodlinger, stabbed to death in their home; the suspect was Corrine Sykes, a twenty-three-year-old African American woman and domestic.

The Corrine Sykes Case 1944–1946

On Tuesday, December 7, 1944, Freeda Wodlinger hired Corrine Sykes, a twenty-three-year-old African American woman, as a live-in domestic at twenty dollars a week plus room and board. Sykes did not, however, give her employer her real name; she had obtained Heloise T. Parker's social security card. According to the *Philadelphia Bulletin*, in May, Sykes "was released from County Prison after serving 11 months" for stealing jewelry while working as a domestic. Two days after the Wodlingers hired Sykes, at 12:30 in the afternoon, Mr. Wodlinger came home for lunch and to pick up his golf clubs when he saw his wife's body in a pool of blood with three severe stab wounds to her left chest. Approximately twelve hundred dollars' worth of jewelry had also been stolen. Mr. Wodlinger called the employment agency and discovered that Sykes did not use the agency. The police found Sykes's fingerprints in the house and witnesses identified the "maroon Cadillac" that Sykes got into a few blocks from the scene of the crime. Jaycee Kelley, a known criminal and ex-convict, owned the car. As soon as the police identified the car, they gave the fugitives' description to eight states. The police went to Kelley's apartment and found Sykes's clothes with blood stains on them as well as "the stolen Social Security card and clipped advertisements of ten persons seeking servants," including Mrs. Wodlinger's name. The police captured both suspects in what the *Philadelphia Inquirer* reported as "one of the quickest clean-ups of a major crime in recent police history."[34]

When the police questioned Sykes that evening, she told them that she intended just to steal the jewelry but that when Mrs. Wodlinger saw her, she stabbed her and placed the knife in the piano. Sykes stated that she left the house and went to Kelley's house, where she "removed all the bloodshed clothes." After she cleaned up, she went to her mother's house and again changed her clothes and left to meet a friend to "give him the jewelry." Sykes gave the jewelry to Arthur Johnson, a thirty-one-year-old African American, who was charged with receiving stolen goods. Two days after her confession, Sykes changed her story and told the police that her boyfriend, James C. Kelley (Jaycee), planned the crime and had "wielded the knife." In fact, Kelley took the police to 17th and Oxford Streets, where they found one of the stolen items and arrested Kelley as an accessory to the crime. The depth of the stab wounds indicated that a strong person had to have committed the crime. Sykes was 5'5" and one hundred pounds, and Kelley was a larger man. Sykes had been convicted of robbery but had never committed a violent crime. During the December hearing, the judge charged Sykes with murder and robbery, and she was sent to Moyamensing Prison, located in Bellafonte, Pennsylvania. The grand jury charged Kelley with "being an accessory after the fact" and gave him a ten-thousand-dollar bail.

Two days after the murder, Alexander sent a condolence letter to Michael Saxe, an attorney and Mrs. Wodlinger's brother. Alexander was shocked and dismayed that "any human being could have acted so cruelly towards another woman." One of the Sykes family members asked Alexander to represent Sykes and Kelley, but initially he "declined because my heart could not be in such a case." The murder shocked the entire city, and for the next two years, the Corrine Sykes case was in the headlines.[35]

In January 1945, Judge Francis Schuck Brown appointed Alexander and John W. Lord Jr., a white attorney and "former assistant attorney general of Pennsylvania," to represent Sykes. Alexander informed Sykes that they were coming to prison to review the case and "she should not discuss the case with anyone but your attorneys." The trial was set for January 28, but her attorneys asked the judge to postpone the trial because Judge Vincent A. Carroll believed that Sykes was "not capable at present of comprehending the proceedings in which she is the chief actor." Two psychiatrists examined Sykes, one for the defendant and one for the prosecutor. Both doctors concurred that Sykes was "suffering from temporary hysteria," but Ephraim Lipschutz, the assistant district attorney, believed that Sykes's condition was temporary whereas Alexander believed that Sykes had "a definite mental condition." Sykes returned to prison, and the prison psychiatrists reevaluated her. In late February, the prison doctors stated that Sykes had recovered from her neurosis. Judge Carroll rescheduled the trial for March 12.[36]

Within months, the Corrine Sykes murder trial was in every local newspaper; therefore, it was going to be difficult to find "objective" jurors. Alexander and the prosecutor were interviewing potential jurors in a rambunctious courtroom where Judge Carroll had "threatened to sentence any demonstrators to 30 days for contempt of court." One potential juror interviewed by Lipschutz, D. Kulp, admitted "that he had followed the case so closely that he had a fixed opinion." When a black person murders a white upper-middle-class person, race becomes an important aspect of the trial. Wilda Robinson Smith, wrote an editorial in the *Philadelphia Tribune* to reassure her audience that "Psychiatry knows no race, creed, or color—and, no matter how clever and brilliant a lawyer is—regardless to his power of oratory—If white men[,] appointed to examine a Negro girl in America charged with murdering a WHITE woman, agree that she is suffering a mental condition which prevents her being interrogated, you may be sure it is true."[37] Smith was convinced that if white doctors concluded that Sykes was mentally incompetent, Sykes would at the very least not receive capital punishment. Smith reminds her readers that Alexander's brilliance and "power of oratory" were no match for white doctors. Most African Americans in Philadelphia knew that when a black person murdered a white person, even the most successful black attorney might not have a chance. This conclusion was aided by the fact that the judge and jury might be all white. Smith argued, however, that science is race-neutral, and when two white men concluded that Sykes was mentally ill, the black community should be hopeful that Sykes might not get the death penalty. Smith reported that in 1936 the Board of Education had recommended that Sykes "be committed to some institution because of her mental capacity" and she "had never passed the mental age of EIGHT YEARS." According to Smith, Sykes was a "SUBNORMAL CHILD and NOT A WOMAN." Smith portrayed Sykes as a young girl in woman's body. A week before the March 12 trial, Alexander wanted Carroll "to delay the start of the trial." Carroll denied the delay and decided to allow a "special jury" to see if Sykes was mentally fit for trial.[38]

The hysteria and racial aspects of the trial started immediately. Alexander received hate mail from disgruntled and racist white Philadelphians. One letter read: "A White Woman's Prayer. May God curse and plaque the negroe race. May God exterminate these vile creatures who bring only robbery and murder to the white people. May God kill every negroe in these United States. Amen." Another letter warned Alexander that he should not prevent "that *murderous, despicable negroes*" from death. Sykes "must be killed and we are going to kill you." This letter came from "The voice of one millions whites in Philadelphia." The letter stated that "Its going to be *'back to Africa'* for the niggers or kill them *All.*" This small sample of letters represented the racism that many whites felt toward Alexander and African Americans.[39]

Two days after Carroll allowed a special jury to rule on Sykes's mental capacity, the *Philadelphia Inquirer* reported that "in an 11th hour change of plans," Alexander "decided to forego a special jury sanity test in advance of the trial." Alexander had talked to Sykes a few days before the special jury and decided that she was mentally competent to stand trial, and Alexander informed Judge Carroll that "he would waive requests for additional neurological examinations." Carroll responded that "he had ordered the jury sanity test only out of an abundance of caution" and he "knew all along that this girl was perfectly able to stand trial." Carroll did not go into detail about the "abundance of caution," but African Americans and whites visited the courtroom and Carroll may have thought about the political and social ramifications if it looked as if he was not fair. Alexander's defense strategy was "the girl was under the complete domination of an admirer J. C. Kelly." Kelley, Sykes's boyfriend, owned a restaurant, was a bootlegger, and had been arrested nineteen times.[40]

The trial began on March 12, and Alexander's first defense witness was Corrine Sykes. Alexander's sought to prove to the jury that James C. Kelley had intimated Sykes and forced her to rob for him. Alexander asked Sykes about Kelley. Sykes stated that they met in June 1944, after her father died and she moved in with Kelley. Kelley owned a restaurant, but Sykes stated that "Whiskey was his racquet," "and the restaurant was a front." Sykes stated that Kelley had threatened to kill her and her family if she mentioned his name in the crime. Sykes cried on the stand and "threw her head on the witness box." The *Philadelphia Tribune* headline stated "All White Jury Selected to Weigh Corinne's Faith." The white papers avoided discussing the racial element of the case, but the *Tribune* made sure its readers were cognizant of the jurors' race. After Sykes's emotional testimony, Alexander stated to the all-white eight men and four women jurors that "we will not try to show that she did not do it." But he asked the jury to issue "a proper safe and intelligent verdict under which she will be placed in an institution for life."[41] During the Thomas Mattox case, Alexander praised the liberalism of Pennsylvania courts; however, during the Corrine Sykes trial, Alexander encountered a judge and prosecutor who were not liberal and made it difficult for Alexander to defend his client.

After Sykes's testimony, Alexander called Kelley to the stand. Alexander mentioned to the jurors his "record of 17 arrests and several convictions, mostly for bootlegging." In spite of his criminal background, Kelley was eager and took the stand. According to the *Philadelphia Inquirer*, "Alexander asked: What is your full name? Judge Carroll warned: Don't answer that." Carroll told Alexander: "You'll do this the right way or not at all" and "you just can't pull this out of a hat." Kelley was held under bail for accessory to the Wodlinger murder and if he testified, the judge concluded, he might incriminate himself. Carroll asked Alexander and Kelley's lawyer, Abraham Levinson, to his office, and when the men returned from the meeting, Alexander had agreed to "withdraw the witness."

Levinson called Kelley, who now was a witness for the Commonwealth. Kelley was on the stand, but the judge prevented Alexander from providing the jury with evidence of the stolen jewelry that was in Kelley's home. After Alexander's attempt to introduce the evidence, Carroll responded that Alexander had made "black indictments containing a charge without proof of anything, and the witness might well be acquitted upon them." Alexander questioned Kelley about his relationship with Sykes. Kelley testified that he paid Sykes thirty-five dollars per week and that ten dollars went to her mother because she was a widow. He said he had nothing to do with the murder. Alexander asked the judge to allow the three women from prison who had heard Sykes say that "she was afraid of Kelley" to testify, but Carroll refused, stating that these "questions would call for conclusions on the operation of the defendant's mental processes." Florence Sykes, Corrine's sister, testified that Corrine declared, "I swear I did not do it," but hours later she signed the confession. Carroll was determined to use his discretionary power to limit Alexander's strategy. In fact, the day after the trial, the first sentence in the Corrine Sykes article in the *Philadelphia Inquirer* stated, "Faced with a Commonwealth demand for the death penalty" it was clear that many in Philadelphia wanted Sykes to get the death penalty and Judge Carroll, an elected judge, was not going to settle for anything less.[42]

On the sixth day of the trial, Alexander summed with "if you give her life imprisonment we will never appeal to any board or tribunal for commutation of the sentence." The judge had instructed the jury that "it made no difference whether the defendant was under the domination of 'Jay-Cee' Kelly a self-admitted bootlegger." The judge mentioned Kelley's criminal background to convince the jury that Kelley had a criminal record but that had nothing to do with the murder. Alexander agreed with the jury that Sykes had committed the crime, but he wanted the jury to give Sykes a life sentence. In spite of the Commonwealth wanting the death penalty, only one woman had received the death penalty in Pennsylvania. In 1930, "Iron" Irene Schroder murdered a state police officer while leaving the scene of a crime. She was sentenced to death in 1931. "Six other women had been sentenced to the electric chair," including "Mrs. Tillie Irelan," who murdered her baby, but she received a life sentence. The Sykes case might have scared middle-class white women who had employed black maids; nevertheless, given the low numbers of women receiving the death penalty, Sykes had a chance to get life. The *Philadelphia Inquirer* reported that the jury deliberated for five hours and returned with the decision "Guilty in the first degree, with death as the penalty." After Sykes heard the decision, she fainted.

Alexander appealed the decision. The *Philadelphia Inquirer* reported that Kelley had confessed that "he had obtained a fur neckpiece stolen from Mrs. Wodinger, and he burned it at home." According to Alexander, Lipshutz, the district attorney, had intentionally "withheld the confesion [sic] from the jurors." Moreover, Alexander maintained that Judge Carroll had interrupted his summary and prohibited Alexander from proving to the jury that there was "a trend away from capital punishment.[43]

In April 1945, Alexander made an appeal in front of three judges, Carroll, Judge Brown, who had appointed Alexander to the case, and Judge Henry McDevitt. According to the *Philadelphia Tribune*, McDevitt stated in the hearing that if he was the judge, "the trial would have been held in January and she would have been executed in February." This judicial hostility was nothing new for Alexander; in fact, when Sykes entered the courtroom to get the decision, the *Philadelphia Tribune* stated that Sykes appeared optimistic, but Carroll did not grant the appeal and he informed Sykes: "the application of the current of electricity shall continue until you are dead." Kelley was tried by the same judges and was found guilty of "accessory and receiving stolen goods." The judge sentenced Kelley to five years in prison. From the start of the Sykes trial, Carroll and the Commonwealth were determined to give Sykes the chair, in spite of Kelley, Sykes's gender, and her mental condition. Carroll's callous statements to Alexander and his "joy" in the verdict highlight the racial overtones of the case.[44]

In December 1945, Alexander appealed Carroll's decision to the Pennsylvania State Supreme Court. Alexander argued that the jury was unaware of Kelley's confession and that Judge Carroll prohibited him from quoting a book by "former Warden Lawes, of Sing Sing Prison" that questioned the utility of the death penalty. On January 7, 1946, the Pennsylvania State Supreme Court denied Alexander a retrial, and Justice Howard Stern stated that Sykes "was the perpetrator of an extremely cruel, [sic] cold-blooded and atrocious murder." After the court's decision, Alexander stated in the *Philadelphia Tribune*, "The state failed to recognize and ignored the fact that Corrine Sykes is a mental derelict, a moron with a mentality of an eight-year old child." Alexander's harsh description of Sykes illustrated his frustration with the courts, but his argument for an appeal contained enough evidence without disparaging Sykes. Pennsylvania governor Edward Martin set Sykes's execution date for the week of April 29, but Alexander had three months to file an appeal. Alexander appealed the case to the United States Supreme Court.[45]

Alexander's appeal to the U.S. Supreme Court delayed Sykes's execution. Governor Martin granted Sykes a respite and moved her execution date to June 24, 1946. Alexander traveled to Washington, D.C. to plead his case to the Supreme Court. The *Philadelphia Tribune* reported that the U.S. Supreme Court denied Alexander his "petition for certiorari." Martin had to choose a new date of execution for Sykes. He picked the week of June 2 to give Alexander another opportunity to file an appeal to the U.S. Supreme Court, but the court denied Alexander's second appeal. In June 1946, Martin granted Sykes a three-month stay and scheduled her execution for the week of September 30. With one last opportunity to get Sykes off of death row, Alexander filed an appeal with the Pennsylvania State Board of Pardons. In September 1946, Alexander presented his case to the State Board of Pardons in Harrisburg. Black ministers attended the hearing in order to improve Sykes's chances of receiving life. Alexander informed the board that Sykes had the mind of an eight-year-old child and that the board needed "to consult the trial judge" before they made a decision. Unfortunately, Carroll was on vacation and could not be reached. In Pennsylvania, "the governor is without authority to commute the sentence to life imprisonment without a recommendation from the pardons board."[46]

Alexander was optimistic after the board took more than a day to make a decision. The delay may have been a sign that they were carefully examining Alexander's appeal, but, on September 17, the board did not delay Sykes execution. A week later, however, Governor Martin granted Sykes an unprecedented fourth respite and moved the date to October 14. Martin granted the stay because he wanted a "further study by the State Board of Pardons of the report of psychiatrists" and other evidence. The three white male psychiatrists at Moyamensing Prison examined Sykes but to no avail. Alexander continued trying to convince Martin and others that Jaycee Kelley was more involved in the murder. Three days before the execution date, Alexander made a final plea and wrote a letter to Martin, Lieutenant Governor John C. Bell, and the chair of the State Board of Pardons pleading for "understanding and tolerance." His letter documented Sykes's mental capacity. In spite of Alexander's plea, on October 12, the State Board of Pardons refused to grant Sykes a life sentence, and Martin scheduled her execution for October 14. The *Phila-delphia Inquirer* quoted Assistant District Attorney James W. Tracey Jr., who told the board that "this girl is not so stupid" and that no one proved that she did not know the difference between right and wrong. "There was no reason for clemency in the case," Tracey said. Alexander used all of his judicial and political acumen to get Sykes a life sentence, but the Commonwealth was committed to sending Sykes to the electric chair.[47]

Before Sykes's execution on Monday, October 14, her mother visited her for the last time and prayed with her. A female prison guard removed Sykes from her cell at eight in the morning. Both women, a prison guard, and two state policemen got into a sedan and drove to Rockview prison where the execution was going to occur. The car arrived late because of a tire blowout, but Sykes arrived at the prison and requested a chaplain to visit her. Next a prison doctor examined her and shaved a spot on her scalp to receive the elec-trical charge. At 6:30 in the evening, she had received her "last meal, a special menu, that consisted of 'roast chicken, candied sweet potatoes, lima beans, rolls and butter, vanilla ice cream and coffee.'" During her last six hours, "two prison matrons and a nurse" were at her side. At 12:31 A.M. the level was pulled, and four minutes later, Dr. R. E. Carrier, the prison doctor, "pronounced" her dead, applauding Sykes's "remarkable composure to the end." Sykes made no final remarks; she only left her mother a letter.[48]

After the execution, Sykes's mother took the body back to Philadel-phia for the funeral, which made the front page of the *Philadelphia Tri-bune:* "Thousands Watch Corrine's Funeral." Sykes was buried in a blue suit with a "yellow gold clasp." Sykes's mother did not attend the funeral; the *Baltimore Afro-American* stated that Sykes's mother wanted to "remem-ber Corrine as I saw her alive." In addition to the thousands of mourners, including Alexander, the *Philadelphia Inquirer* reported there was "a special squad of 60 uniformed Negro policemen. Sykes was buried in Mt. Lawn Cemetery. She remains the last woman executed in Pennsylvania. After the victorious Mattox case and, according to Alexander, the triumph of liberalism, the Corrine Sykes case demonstrated the racial hostility and complexity when a black person murders a white person. Moreover, since most live-in domestics were black women, the political pressure by whites to execute Sykes may have been a message to black women maids not to injure or murder their employers. In spite of the verdict and judicial hostil-ity, Alexander's commitment to this case demonstrated his commitment to civil rights and justice.[49]

Days after the murder, Arthur Huff Fauset, an African American principal and member of the National Negro Congress, wrote an editorial about recent crime waves in Philadelphia. According to Fauset, "The so called crime wave reflects not merely crime running rampant among the youth of our city, but crime in sinister places masterminded by we know not who." Fauset suggested that some Philadelphia police officers had allowed "a bootlegger here, a black market trafficker over there" to exist. The Corrine Sykes case demonstrates some of Fauset's concerns. The police arrested Sykes and Kelley, but Fauset states that there were "forces which are so anxious to see Jaycee Kelly released." After Sykes signed her confession, she told the police that her boyfriend, Jaycee Kelley, was at the crime. However, the local officials worked rapidly to convict Sykes and sentence her to death, in spite of her confession and the evidence that may have linked Kelley to the murder. Fauset may have been correct, but white Philadelphians wanted the police to solve the case quickly and Kelley may have made money for the police. White Philadelphians did not form a mob, but the hate letters they mailed to Alexander demonstrated a southern racist mentality that insists when an African American murders a white person the black suspect is guilty until proven innocent and justice (the death penalty) must be quickly served."[50]

In September 1937, Alexander joined the Democratic Party because the Republican Party did not endorse his candidacy for judge. He supported President Roosevelt's New Deal policies and extolled the number of African Americans who obtained government positions. By 1942, the majority of working-class African Americans and a growing number of African American professionals were Roosevelt Democrats. Still, a number of African American elites remained Republican. During Alexander's sojourn into the Democratic Party, from 1937 to 1940, he never became a judge nor did he obtain a federal position. In July 1940, the Republican Party held its convention in Philadelphia and nominated Wendell Willkie as the Republican candidate. Alexander congratulated Willkie and told him that he was a Republican but had switched parties in 1937 because he thought the New Deal would end the Depression. Alexander switched parties because white Republicans did not vote for him in 1937. In 1940, Alexander stated that "in recent years" the New Deal has stymied businesses and prohibited growth. Therefore, "I have returned to the Republican party." Alexander maintained that the Democratic Party failed to pass anti-lynching laws, desegregate the military, eradicate the poll taxes, and include domestic workers and farmers in the Social Security program.[51]

In October 1940, Francis E. Rivers, director of the Colored Division of the Republican Party, mailed a pamphlet titled "An Appeal to the Common Sense of Colored Citizens" to Alexander. The pamphlet proclaimed, "The New Deal treats the Negro so differently from all other Americans as to belie all of its social programs." It stated that the New Deal never passed any anti-lynching legislation and that many New Deal programs such as the Works Project Administration discriminated against African Americans. The pamphlet pointed out that southern African Americans remained disenfranchised and that Social Security benefits excluded domestic and farm workers, occupations in which African Americans were overrepresented. Rivers stated that, with Wilkie, "the Negro at least will have a chance." Ten days later, Alexander wrote a release for the newspapers: "New Deal Has Given Lip Service to Negro Aspirations." He presented this release in Washington, D.C., to the Republican National Committee. Alexander mentioned "his unwillingness to follow the New Deal." He was critical of the New Deal's "inadequate and unworkable housing programs" that left a shortage of affordable housing for low-income and "colored families particularly." Alexander stated that the Southern Democrats had too much control that forced the New Dealers to give "lip service to the constitutional principle of suffrage, equality, and the protection of liberty." While the Democratic Party accomplished a number of progressive legislations that aided African Americans, the New Deal operated under the political constraints. The New Deal only went as far as Southern Democrats and Republicans allowed it. Alexander's critique of the New Deal was correct; however African Americans had few other options. After Roosevelt's death in 1945, Harry S. Truman became president, and civil rights emerged as a national issue.[52]

During Truman's first year in office, all around the country postwar racial tensions worsened. African American World War II vets faced racial violence in the South. For instance, in 1946, African Americans prevented a lynching in Columbia, Tennessee. The wanton violence forced President Truman to act. In December 1946, Truman organized the Committee on Civil Rights (CCR), a group of moderate to liberal professionals given the task to "inquire into and to determine the law enforcement measure by the government to safeguard the civil rights of the people." The CCR was composed of fifteen members, two of whom were African Americans, Channing Tobias of the Urban League and Sadie Tanner Mossell Alexander. In October 1947, Truman's CCR met and published *To Secure These Rights*. The report presented thirty-three specific points on civil rights but aimed primarily at "dismantling de jure segregation." According to political scientist Charles Hamilton, Truman placed civil rights on the national political landscape. Truman provided African American attorneys some federal opportunities. In 1946, Truman appointed Irvin C. Mollison as a federal judge and William Hastie as the first African American governor of St. Thomas. Still, *To Secure These Rights* concentrated on the Jim Crow South and de jure segregation. The federal government's shift from an emphasis on the FEPC to *Secure These Rights* and the CCR represented a shift in civil rights discourse from a national New Deal emphasis on employment to a southern strategy of promoting voting rights and ending Jim Crow. Civil rights protection became a mantra for southern issues, and the federal government neglected to address the urban conditions in northern cities, like housing, education, police brutality, and employment until the riots of the late sixties. With Alexander's wife as a member of the Truman CCR, Alexander viewed this as another opportune time to become a federal judge. In 1947, he rejoined the Democratic Party.[53]

During the 1948 election, Alexander campaigned hard for Truman. After Truman won the election, Alexander wasted no time getting in position to become the first black federal judge. After the election, Alexander wrote Congressman William Dawson of Illinois, who aided Mollison's appointment in 1946. Dawson recommended that Alexander list Roosevelt's and Truman's judicial appointments since 1932. According to Alexander, since 1932, Roosevelt and Truman made twelve judicial appointments in the Third District Court, but not one was an African American. Alexander noted that Congress had passed the McCarran Bill, increasing the number of U.S. District Court judges. Philadelphia was the home of the Third District Court, and, according to Alexander, the judges were extremely busy and behind. He heard that another seat would be available and declared, "Under any and all circumstances, the Negro is entitled to this appointment without a shadow of a doubt." Philadelphia had a large African American population, and Alexander's appointment would aid the Democratic Party in the upcoming election. In December, talk surfaced about the position, and Alexander believed that white lawyers in Philadelphia would support a black judge.[54]

By 1948, African American attorneys continued to play a leading role in the northern civil rights struggle. The NBA's journal and conventions received notice in *Time* and in the ABA's journal, but in spite of all his success, Alexander never received the recognition from the white community that Houston, Marshall, and Hastie received for their civil rights work. Alexander was instrumental, however, in making the NBA an active organization, and in

Philadelphia his political status improved and he would be part of the reform movement in Philadelphia.

In Philadelphia, as in other northern cities, Alexander's civil rights struggle emphasized jobs, economics, and civil rights. During World War II, employment opportunities emerged as an important civil rights initiative. During the 1940s, Alexander mentioned the significance of skilled work and African Americans supporting their own businesses. After the second Great Migration, African American purchasing power increased and was much greater than in the 1920s, but, according to Alexander, African Americans threw away "valuable assets that any group of people in American can have for its own emancipation." During the late 1930s and early 1940s, Alexander linked black economic power to emancipation, but by 1947, the national civil rights discourse shifted to a greater emphasis on Jim Crow, suffrage, and civil rights protection in the South. By 1948, as public accommodation segregation declined, discrimination in employment, education, and housing took center stage. During the next ten years, Alexander's civil rights struggle focused on becoming a judge and on urban political reform.[55]

Virginia Pace Alexander, RPA's mother, ca. 1890s

Hillard Boone Alexander, RPA's father, between 1935 and 1938

Raymond Pace Alexander as an infant, 1899

Raymond Pace Alexander, first-year student at the University of Pennsylvania, 1920

Portrait of William H. Lewis, black attorney and mentor

Raymond Pace Alexander Law Office, 19th and Chestnut, 1935

The Old Brown and Stevens Building on Brown and Lombard located in the Seventh Ward. Alexander's office was located on the third floor.

Raymond Pace Alexander and
Saddie Tanner Mossell Alexander,
the New Negro power couple,
between 1921 and 1923

At Skywater Ranch, 1948. From left to right: Raymond Pace Alexander, Mrs. Marshall
Shepard, unknown, unknown, unknown, Hobson Reynolds, Reverend Marshall Shepard,
Saddie Tanner Mossell Alexander.

Trenton Six Trial: Mercer Burrell, Walter White, Executive Secretary, NAACP, Clifford Moore, Raymond Pace Alexander

Raymond Pace Alexander with Robert Felder at the steps of the Lincoln Memorial on May 17, 1957. Felder was one of the plaintiffs for the Girard College Case.

Judge Alexander's
swearing in, 1960

Raymond Pace
Alexander with Martin
Luther King Jr., 1965

An informal meeting with Vice President Hubert Humphrey, 1966. Pictured: Humphrey, Raymond Pace Alexander, unknown. Alexander was attending the Civil Rights Conference in Washington, D.C.

Raymond Pace Alexander with Thurgood Marshall, 1969

Chapter Four

THE COLD WAR, NORTHERN SCOTTSBORO, AND THE POLITICS OF CIVIL RIGHTS, 1949–1953

In March 1946, President Harry S. Truman invited Winston Churchill, the former prime minister of Great Britain, to Fulton, Missouri, to present a speech about the Soviet Union's expansion in Eastern Europe. Churchill's address, titled "From Stettin in the Baltic to Trieste in the Adriatic," declared that the Soviet Union had created an "Iron Curtain," denying fundamental freedoms to the people in nations under communist control. That phrase, which was rapidly propagated by the media, contrasted communism's denial of human rights with the "Free World" of the United States and Western Europe and configured Soviet communism as a major threat to America and Western Civilization. Truman should have asked Churchill to give a speech about the "Iron Curtain" created by the white supremacist violence that had escalated across the United States after World War II. In 1946, southern white racists had murdered three African American veterans, but the most vicious case of "savagery" occurred in Monroe, Georgia, where a white mob murdered two black couples; one of the female victims was seven months pregnant. Communist propaganda used southern violence to dismiss America's rhetoric about freedom and democracy.

In this war of words, the blatant contradiction between American's stated principles and its actual racial practice forced the U.S. State Department to repair the nation's image abroad by addressing virulent white racism at home. According to Mary Dudziak, "civil rights reform was *in part* a product of the Cold War." White liberal and black leaders took advantage of this new opportunity to advance the cause of civil rights; they also embraced Cold War politics as rhetoric and practice. Like many white leaders, especially labor activists, whose organizations had espoused progressive views in the 1930s, many black leaders supported the Democratic Party's foreign and domestic policy initiatives. They expelled suspected communists from their organizations, joined in red baiting, and dissolved their coalitions with left-wing organizations, whether they were primarily black, racially integrated, or predominantly white. Many black liberals deliberately stopped engaging mass-based political organizing, which was viewed as socially disruptive if not subversive. In their public statements, at least, they refrained from comparing the civil rights struggle in the South to anti-colonial movements in Africa and Asia, despite the parallels between the movements of oppressed peoples of color around the world in the wake of the war.[1]

From the late thirties to the mid-forties, black attorneys such as Alexander, Charles Hamilton Houston, and William Hastie were active in Popular Front politics, which united liberals and leftists in opposition to fascism abroad and in support of democratic change at home. All three attorneys belonged to the National Lawyers Guild, a professional bar organization of progressive black, white, and ethnic lawyers. Alexander was a member of the National Negro Congress, a leftist organization that included communists, liberals, and non-communists. According to Kenneth Mack, Alexander's, NNC activities had caused him to show up in the FBI's file as a "prominent negro communist front leader by 1945." Historian Kevin Gaines found that "liberals with prior radical associations, including Ralph Bunche and Murray, were investigated." (Pauli Murray was a black woman lawyer from Baltimore.) Although Alexander, Hastie, and Houston had associated with leftists in the Popular Front, they had never been affiliated with the Communist Party, and in the late 1940s, when association with communists became politically dangerous, they took an anti-communist stance. Some prominent black attorneys remained with the left, such as Ben Davis Jr., who served as a councilman in New York City, and William Patterson, president of the Civil Rights Congress (CRC). During the late forties and early fifties, the federal government carried out what Gerald Horne calls communist "front hunts," investigating any organization that they believed included communists without differentiating between a Communist Party organization and a non-communist organization with some communist members.[2]

The post–World War II Red Scare put severe pressures on black and white progressives who worked for social justice during the Depression and the war. A number of black lawyers, moved by various combinations of prudence, fear, and ideological conviction, participated in the anti-communist hysteria. These black leaders had to denounce communism as a violation of democratic rights and avoid linking the civil rights struggle in the United States to the global anti-colonial movement rather than denouncing racial discrimination as un-American as many had previously done. Splits over these issues ultimately divided black leadership and dismantled the 1930s progressive Popular Front coalition of labor and civil rights. As a result, Alexander and other civil rights leaders formed liberal interracial civil rights organizations and used the courts, black political power in northern cities, and moral suasion rather than mass-based organizing.

Cold War politics played out in Philadelphia reshaped Alexander's professional and organizational activities. From 1946 to 1951, a Popular Front coalition elected journalist Joseph Rainey president of the Philadelphia Branch of the NAACP. According to Matthew Countryman, after Rainey's election, "Alexander proposed to recruit a group of twenty to twenty-five leaders 'of both races' to vote against Rainey in the 1947 election." Alexander had belonged to the NNC, only two years before, and he was on the FBI's list of "fellow travelers" and suspected communists. By 1947, as political pressures mounted, Alexander found it important to remove visible progressives from the local NAACP leadership. Many members of the anti-Rainey group were black attorneys, such as William Coleman and Theodore Spaulding. Spaulding, the former Philadelphia NAACP Branch president, Coleman, and Alexander represented the postwar urban professional black leadership class that was embraced by the white power structure.[3]

In spite of the fact that the Democratic Party never enforced the Fair Employment Practices Act with an effective commission, passed any anti-lynching legislation, or eradicated racist hiring policies in New Deal agencies, black leaders such as Alexander were willing to work with the Truman administration. The Democratic Party used civil rights as a platform to increase the number of black voters, and the Cold War forced the federal government to respond to foreign countries' criticisms of America's lack of democracy. To do both, Truman rewarded a small number of black attorneys with high-level positions in the federal government and in foreign service. In 1946, Truman appointed attorney Irvin C. Mollison to the U.S. Customs Court, making him the first black judge with lifetime tenure of the federal bench. In 1948, Truman appointed attorney Edward Dudley as the first African American ambassador to Liberia. Throughout his career, Alexander believed that he did not receive the political opportunities that a Harvard-educated lawyer deserved. Alexander did not have enough political clout in Washington, D.C., to obtain a federal judgeship, and the State Department maintained that he lacked the experience required for a foreign service position.[4]

During the late 1940s, Alexander shifted from Popular Front politics to a Cold War perspective. He no longer advocated a coalition of African Americans with organized labor, mass protests, and association with the left in civil rights actions. Instead, he moved into an emerging coalition of black and white anti-communist leaders from the middle and upper classes. Countryman identifies three strategies that were central to this new approach: legally prohibiting discrimination, increasing the number of black city employees, and decreasing racial and ethnic tensions through social interaction. Alexander's activities during the early 1950s encompassed all three of these issues and demonstrate his shifting stance. The Trenton Six Case, the longest-running case in New Jersey's history, was a microcosm of Cold War politics. In 1951, Alexander was hired by the NAACP to defend two of the six black men who were accused of murdering a white man. While litigating this racially charged case, Alexander castigated the Civil Rights Congress (CRC), a left organization founded in 1947, whose lawyers had initially handled it. In the Girard College desegregation, Alexander enjoyed the support of the entire liberal civil rights coalition. Acting in concert with black and white liberals, he used the courts in an effort to open educational opportunities to black youth. The fact that this case was unsuccessful did not diminish Alexander's reputation; rather, it revealed the recalcitrance of the white racial establishment and residents of Philadelphia. During the 1950s, Alexander also promoted social interaction to fight discrimination. He and his wife, Sadie Tanner Mossell Alexander, joined the Fellowship Commission (FC), an interracial group of middle-class reformers, which became the main advocate of civil rights in Philadelphia. The FC managed to increase the number of black city employees and encouraged intergroup discussions among groups about improving race relations without inconveniencing or offending white Philadelphians. This was an effective strategy for years from the end of World War I to the late 1950s.

The Trenton Six Case, 1948–1951

Alexander's skills as a litigator and his shift from Popular Front to liberal Cold War politics became visible on the national stage when he served as a defense lawyer in the infamous Trenton Six murder case. *The Daily Compass*, a Trenton, New Jersey, newspaper, referred to the case as the "Northern Scottsboro." Both cases highlighted the denial of equal justice to black men accused of crimes against a white person, and in both cases left-wing attorneys and activists utilized the media and mobilized popular support by criticizing the failings of American democracy. But the Scottsboro and Trenton Six cases were litigated in strikingly different political contexts. The International Labor Defense, a left group, had defended the Scottsboro men and enjoyed wide support from moderate civil rights groups. The Civil Rights Congress, also a left organization, initially defended the six men accused in Trenton, but the defense was taken over by the NAACP, which discouraged left-wing advocates. During the 1930s and the Popular Front, Alexander welcomed support from the ILD in spite of the differences with the local and national NAACP in the Berwyn school boycott. During the Trenton Six trial, by contrast, the NAACP hired Alexander. He assured the organization's national leaders not only that he would win but also that he would prevent the left from using the case as propaganda. Alexander's success in this case demonstrated the skills of black attorneys and highlighted the racial inequalities that pervaded the criminal justice system. In Philadelphia and in other northern cities, police departments targeted and coerced African Americans, particularly the uneducated and poor, and extracted confessions by force. Accused African Americans were not tried before a jury of their peers and rarely had a black judge. In this case, Alexander worked alongside white attorneys; two white attorneys represented four of the men, while Alexander represented two of the accused and was assisted by two local black attorneys. In the Trenton Six case, Alexander demonstrated that black attorneys could effectively defend the civil rights of black defendants as well as or better than white attorneys and without the mass demonstrations and propaganda from the left.[5]

On January 27, 1948, at 11:30 A.M., a group of African American males entered the secondhand furniture shop of William Horner, a seventy-three-year-old white male. One of the men struck Horner's wife with a soda bottle, while the others robbed and murdered Horner. The crime occurred during an alarming crime wave in Trenton, so worried citizens wanted quick arrests. A February 3 *Trenton Times* editorial asserted ominously that the police should solve the crime "through one means or another." A pamphlet published by the Joint Committee to Secure a Fair Trial for the Trenton Six maintained that on January 30, the police organized a special squad equipped with "Tommy guns to arrest any suspicious looking person." From February 6 to 11, the police arrested six black men—Horace Wilson, Collis English, McKinley Forrest, Ralph Cooper, John MacKenzie, and James Thorpe—without any warrants. On February 12, Horner's "common law wife" visited the jail but "failed to identify any of the six suspects." When the men were in custody, the police obtained five signed confessions, but Horace Wilson adamantly refused to sign because he could prove that he was at work during the murder. The first trial occurred in August, with the all-white jury giving the six men guilty verdicts and the death penalty.[6]

The Civil Rights Congress, a Communist-affiliated group, represented the defendants in September 1948. The defense filed an appeal with the New Jersey Supreme Court on the grounds of numerous flagrant judicial errors, including withholding evidence and using "confessions obtained under duress." The "black radicals" of the CRC sought to gain public support for the defendants and even protested to the United Nations about the denial of human rights in the case. Earl Dickerson and William Patterson, black attorneys from the CRC, appealed the lower court's decision and managed to get the case to the New Jersey Supreme Court. In August 1949, one year after the six men were charged with murder, the New Jersey Supreme Court ruled in a unanimous decision to reverse the lower court's decision. According to Gerald Horne, the judge prohibited the CRC lawyers from handling the retrial because the CRC had "launched a mass campaign to win the case in the court of public opinion." The New Jersey judge argued that the CRC lawyers had violated New Jersey state laws by "publicly" discussing the case and terming it a "lynching" and "a Northern Scottsboro case." The CRC lawyers fought to prevent the judge from prohibiting them from taking the case, but by December 1950, the CRC lamented that "it become obvious that the strategy of the state of New Jersey was to refuse to let the case come to trial" and castigate "the alleged conduct of the lawyers and then blame the CRC." After the CRC withdrew, Alexander, the NAACP, and white liberal organizations took over. The New Jersey Supreme Court ordered a new trial, which began in March 1951.[7]

In December 1950, the NAACP Legal Defense and Educational Fund (LDEF) hired Alexander as the lead counsel for two of the defendants, Horace Wilson and John MacKenzie. Two black attorneys, J. Mercer Burrell of

Newark and Clifford R. Moore of Trenton, assisted Alexander. In March, the LDEF forwarded five thousand dollars to Alexander, who informed Thurgood Marshall that the trial would last "until sometime in June" and that the LDEF needed to raise an additional ten thousand dollars for the case. The NAACP printed a pamphlet outlining the facts of the Trenton Six case. The pamphlet asserted that if the case occurred in the South it would be called "outrageous but it happened in the enlightened North." The NAACP assured its contributors that their money would have a "careful accounting" and that "the NAACP will not, as have other organizations propagandize on the Trenton Six to raise money for other, unconnected, purposes." With this indirect reference to the CRC, the NAACP condemned radical organizations using race to exploit the black community. The NAACP handled the Trenton Six case in a way that it hoped would convince any left-leaning African Americans that the NAACP was a viable, nonopportunistic organization and demonstrated to white liberal allies that the civil rights struggle was not influenced by or connected to the communists.[8]

Three white attorneys represented the other four men: Frank Katzenbach III represented McKinley Forrest; Arthur Garfield Hays of New York and former Judge George Pellettieri of Trenton represented James Thorpe, Ellis Cooper, and Collis English. Hays and Pellettieri were members of the Princeton Committee for the Defense of the Trenton Six, a liberal nonpartisan group of New Jersey educators, ministers, and laymen that organized to get the men a fair trial. According to a Princeton Committee press release, the CRC chapter of New Jersey passed out "inflammatory handbills urging attendance at a Mass Meeting where inflammatory speeches were made," but, in spite of the propaganda, the group successfully "negotiated the withdrawal of the Civil Rights Congress attorney." In a letter to Trenton Six supporters, Edward S. Corwin, Professor Emeritus of Jurisprudence and Politics at Princeton, declared that it was "time for patriotic Americans" to defend these men instead of "those who too often exploit them for propaganda purposes." All of the defense attorneys, including Alexander, agreed that "public agitation" in the form of mass demonstrations and protest meetings was unnecessary and unwise because of its left-wing associations. The NAACP's statement that it did not employ propaganda was clearly disingenuous. The NAACP and other liberal organizations called their own dissemination of information about the case "publicity," while condemning as "propaganda" the similar efforts undertaken by radical organizations. During the trial, the CRC continued to wage its battle outside of the court; inside, Alexander assured the NAACP that neither the CRC nor the white attorneys from the Princeton Committee would outshine his own legal brilliance.[9]

The retrial started in April, pitting Alexander, Katzenbach, Hays, and Pellettieri against prosecutor Mario Volpe. The defense attorneys cross-examined Lieutenant Andrew F. Delate for three days. The defense tried to prove what the *Philadelphia Tribune* had reported: in searching for suspects, the Trenton police had conducted a "reign of terror" in the black community. The state called Henry Miller, the clerk who typed the confessions. He stated that after the arrests, doctors J. Minor Sullivan and George Corlo examined the defendants and did not complain about ill-treatment of the prisoners. Miller admitted in court that after "5000 previous statements the elaborate process for the 'Six' had no precedent." Alexander and the defense attorneys wanted to use psychiatrists as witnesses for the defense. *The Trentonian* reported that Alexander hired an "expert semanticist" to prove that his client's "alleged confession was beyond his mental and education level." In representing black defendants who were uneducated, Alexander sought to show that their supposed confessions were written in a formal styled they could not have possibly used and therefore must have been written by the police rather than by the accused.[10]

Alexander and the other defense lawyers cross-examined the state witness, J. Minor Sullivan, a black deputy county physician, in a way that benefited the defense. Four days after the police arrested the six defendants, Sullivan asked Peyton ("Scrappy") Manning, a black former Democratic leader and retired taproom operator, to accompany him to the police headquarters to witness the confessions. The state used these two African American men to prove that the police obtained the confessions legally. Manning testified that Alexander's client, Horace Wilson, had refused to sign the confession. According to a report in the *Philadelphia Inquirer*, Sullivan testified "that the defendants appeared dazed, nervous and controlled as a result of drugs and marijuana." Forrest was unaware of what was going on, Cooper was "drowsy and sleepy" as if he had smoked marijuana. Thorpe appeared depressed, and English was nervous. During the first trial, Sullivan testified that after he examined the defendants, he was not sure of what caused their conditions. After Sullivan's testimony during the retrial, the court found that Forrest, Cooper, and McKenzie's behavior "appeared abnormal" when they signed the confessions. The *Pittsburgh Courier* suggested that Sullivan's new testimony may have been intended to correct the injustice that African Americans faced in Trenton[11]

Prosecutor Volpe called Mario Corio, who had examined the defendants with Sullivan. He testified that Cooper was "slow moving" and had a "sluggish disposition" but was not drugged. Nevertheless, Sullivan's testimony had more weight with the judge than Corio's statement. The *Philadelphia Evening Bulletin* reported that Volpe told Judge Smalley that Sullivan's new testimony derived from "considerable pressure by the community." However, there is no indication that local African Americans had pressured Sullivan to change his story in favor of the accused.[12]

Next, the defense attacked the Trenton police. Alexander questioned Andrew Duch, the public safety director who was in command when the police searched for the suspects, "about a police machine-gun squad that allegedly had orders to shoot-to-kill." According to *The New York Post*, Alexander maintained that the Trenton police department was "over zealous" in their attempt to calm the white public's fears. However, Judge Smalley dismissed Alexander's "atmosphere of terror" argument. The *Philadelphia Inquirer* reported that Smalley asserted that Alexander's use of the term "crime crusher" and his disparaging statements about the Trenton police department were irrelevant. Smalley's rulings demonstrate the challenges Alexander faced when confronting coerced confessions. African Americans in Trenton and in other northern cities experienced numerous instances of wanton police brutality whenever a white person was alleged to have been murdered by an African American. The black community was convinced that when the Trenton police searched for the suspects they had used excessive force. Smalley, however, wanted to keep the case focused on the confessions and not on racism in the Trenton police department.[13]

During the third week of the trial, the defense attorneys received excellent news. According to the *New York Herald Tribune*, Smalley ruled out three of the typewritten confessions because the state "had failed to prove the statements were obtained legally." In addition, Smalley affirmed that it "was his duty to see to it that no illegal confessions be admitted as evidence." The *Philadelphia Inquirer* reported that Alexander was responsible for getting Sullivan to convince Smalley that three of the written confessions were not voluntary. According to the *New York Times*, Smalley ruled out the typewritten statements of Cooper, MacKenzie, and Thorpe. He allowed Cooper's oral testimony and the written confessions of English and Forrest. After Smalley's decision, the *Philadelphia Afro American* wrote approvingly about the progress of the case and observed that Alexander had "captured the admiration of all the newsmen covering the trial." During the hearing, the African American entertainer Josephine Baker made an "unannounced" visit to the courtroom. Alexander knew of the visit ahead of time and thought that Baker's presence brought more exposure to the case. According to Dudziak, the FBI considered Baker a communist and had investigated her, although she was "staunchly anticommunist." Baker was critical of U.S. race relations, and she stated her views boldly when she traveled and lived abroad. Her presence helped rather than hurt the case. Alexander understood the power of public opinion and utilized the media effectively.[14]

The *Trentonian* reported that the trial cost the state $3,000 per day, prompting Smalley to ask both counsels to "move along with all reasonable speed." Alexander asked Smalley to declare a mistrial. After this motion, Smalley asked the jury to leave the courtroom. The *Pittsburgh Courier* reported that the six defendants were accused of robbery, but Alexander argued that "there was, in fact no robbery" because, the state had failed to prove that the suspects robbed Horner. Horner had $1,632 in his pocket on the night of the crime, but the state never recovered the money. Smalley dismissed Alexander's mistrial motion. Volpe recalled Sullivan to the stand to "neutralize" his previous statements. Volpe challenged Sullivan's credibility and tried to convince the jury that Sullivan was an unreliable source. The *Trenton Evening Times* quoted Sullivan, who stated that "at the first trial I was asked about symptoms, Now I am asked for a diagnosis."[15]

Volpe brought in a surprise witness, George English, to testify against his own son, Collis English. In 1948, George English had been arrested for "carnal abuse" of a young lady and served two years in jail; therefore he could not testify during the first trial. The *Philadelphia Afro American* referred to Volpe's surprise witness as "a surprise of atomic bomb proportions." English testified that when he was in jail he overheard Ralph Cooper state that he had some "robbing to do," and while he was cleaning his home he believed that he found the bottle that Cooper may have used to strike Ms. McGuire and the articles of clothing that the defendants wore during the crime. After English's testimony, defense attorney Pellettieri was so livid that Smalley told him to stop shouting and banging his fist on the table. English's testimony shifted the momentum of the case back to the prosecutor. Volpe possessed the broken bottleneck that knocked out McGuire, and Smalley used English's confessions as evidence. When the defense questioned English, they wasted no time in questioning his character. According to the *Trentonian*, Alexander maintained that English's testimony was a "tainted source unworthy of belief" and was "highly conjectural, without the slightest relevancy, highly dangerous and prejudicial." The defense brought in David Graham, a barber from the state penitentiary, who declared that English said he was going to "fix Ralph Cooper." English claimed that Cooper had framed him on the morals charge. The *Pittsburgh Courier* noted that English's testimony was further undermined when Dr. Helen O. Dickens and Dr. Purvis Henderson, Alexander's friends, located English's former wife, Rube, in Hackendale, Georgia, twenty miles from Savannah. Alexander summoned Mrs. English to court, where she testified that her former husband had abused her.[16]

By the tenth week of the trial, the defense finally had the opportunity to present its case and witnesses, including the six defendants. Alexander's client Horace Wilson testified first. He claimed that during the murder, he was at work on a farm in Robbinsville, New Jersey. Wilson also maintained that when the police arrested him, they asked if his name was Buddy Wilson. Alexander's second client, John McKenzie, testified last. McKenzie stated that when the crime occurred he was at work cleaning chickens and the police arrested him without warrant. The *Pittsburgh Courier* reported that Alexander reiterated to Smalley "no case existed against Thorpe and McKenzie." In Alexander's view, the only evidence that the police had against McKenzie was the phrase he had allegedly uttered, "I was the lookout man."[17]

The end of May marked the twelfth week of the trial. Judge Smalley held night sessions on Tuesdays and Thursdays in order to speed up the case. Alexander and the other defense attorneys called in the alibis for the six defendants. One of the most important testimonies came from Roy Eisenhart, a plant foreman for Royal Crown Cola. According to the *Trenton Evening Times*, Eisenhart testified that the bottle used during the crime was made in Illinois and shipped to Allentown, Pennsylvania, in 1947 but not put into use until 1950. The prosecution used the bottle as evidence after George English's testimony. The defense countered that this evidence had been fabricated. The *Pittsburgh Courier* reported that Wilson's and Forest's alibis and the defendants' testimony shifted the case in favor of the defense. When English and Cooper, who were both only semiliterate, testified, they had difficulty articulating their stories, which made the jury question their credibility. Alexander hired "international handwriting expert J. Howard Haring," to see if McKenzie wrote his initial "McK" on the murder weapon. The *Trentonian* reported that the writing on the bottle was "a script of a trained person" and McKenzie's mark was writing from an "illiterate." Alexander and the defense team used their clients' ignorance and illiteracy to attempt to prove their innocence. Alexander allowed all six men to testify because he believed that there was insufficient evidence to convict them. In spite of English's and Cooper's disappointing testimony, Alexander still believed the jury would find them innocent.[18]

A week before Alexander's summation, he sent a seven-page "progress report" to Thurgood Marshall and Walter White of the NAACP. The report summarized the trial and listed the additional expenses that Alexander had accrued. Alexander expressed his gratitude to the NAACP for employing him as the lead counsel and lamented that more NAACP board members could not attend his summation. Originally, the NAACP paid Alexander $5,000 for the case and both parties assumed the case would last five weeks. The case lasted much longer, and by the end of the trial, Alexander had received an additional $7,250. "If I was employed by an organization able to pay a *fairly* substantial fee, I would not accept such an engagement for less than $25,000," Alexander explained. He concluded that he had lost six months' worth of business by devoting all his attention to the protracted trial. Alexander assured Marshall that he was not being "critical" of the NAACP and realized he would not be paid $25,000, but left "the matter entirely to" them. In other words, if the NAACP could pay at least $25,000, Alexander would be pleased. Alexander discovered that the Princeton Committee had raised $10,500 for the case and intimated to Marshall that this money may "enable you to meet my request for additional funds at this time." Alexander appreciated working the case because it advanced himself and improved the status of black attorneys. However, for handling a case of this magnitude, an attorney would ordinarily be paid more money. Alexander and all of the other civil rights attorneys of the era were underpaid, but their commitment to civil rights was worth it to all Americans, a point that they constantly reiterated.[19]

According to the *Nation*, "a hundred state and city police patrolled the courtroom" during the deliberations for a fear of racial violence. The trial took seventy-one court days, and the jury deliberated for nineteen hours. The jury acquitted four defendants, Alexander's clients Wilson and McKenzie, Forrest, and Thorpe, but they convicted English and Cooper and recommended life imprisonment. After the guilty verdicts, the CRC staged protests and ridiculed the NAACP attorneys. Although two men were convicted, the verdict was a huge victory for Alexander, the NAACP, anti-communism, and civil rights politics. The *Philadelphia Tribune* reported that the CRC "created and maintained hysteria" during the trial by accusing the courts of using "fascist tactics." Walter White, executive secretary of the NAACP, referred to the Trenton Six as the "Yankee Scottsboro" and asserted that, after the verdict, the CRC ran a "smear campaign" and tried to "crash the press conference." White quoted Trenton Six juror John J. Kelly, who revealed that the verdict was "a compromise." White maintained that the jury wanted to free all of the men, but he believed that the jury convicted two men to satisfy the large white crowd that stood outside the courtroom. The *Trenton Evening Times* editorial referred to the ruling as "Strange Justice" and maintained that the Horner case was not tainted with "subversive elements" although the "Communists and other agitators" disseminated misinformation about the trial. The *Newark Evening News* carried a favorable editorial on the Trenton Six. The editorial determined that the "result was not due to outside agencies or intervention." Criticizing the CRC, the editorial asserted that "neither protest rallies nor the intervention of the United Nations" was necessary to obtain justice. Carl Holderman, reporter for the The *New Jersey CIO News*, a labor newspaper, stated that the Trenton Six verdict illustrated equal justice and gave the "lie to communist propaganda that black men were electrocuted because of their color."[20]

Like the Thomas Mattox case, the Trenton Six case was a major victory for Alexander and black attorneys. Theodore Spaulding, Philadelphia attorney and NAACP board member, congratulated Alexander and declared, "You have done a magnificent job for the Association. I am just sorry that we are not in position to pay to you the $25,000" that Alexander had told Marshall that he deserved. Black judge Francis E. Rivers, compared Alexander's work in the Trenton Six case to the "work of (Clarence) Darrow in the Sweet Case." Clifford Moore informed Alexander that "Frank (Katzenbach) bluntly stated that the only reason" that Pellettieri's clients were alive was "because Ray saved them." Meanwhile, Katzenbach told Alexander that George Pellettieri was "miffed and jealous that you and Mercer and Clifford made out so much better than he did." Katzenbach intimated that Pellettieri's comments might have been sparked by racial bias. Alexander maintained that after the trial, Pellettieri passed out some "dirty digs" and "dirty lying statements" about Alexander. Pellettieri believed that Alexander was only concerned with his own clients and sacrificed Pellettieri's clients. Alexander reiterated to Moore that he always prefaced his defense with "I speak for all these boys." The NAACP attorneys proved that they were competent and dispelled the myth that they could not skillfully defend black clients in major cases before white judges and juries. J. Mercer Burrell, one of the NAACP attorneys, declared that the Trenton Six trial "should go far to blast the deep seated prejudiced opinion that . . . Negro Lawyers cannot successfully represent clients in important cases." Burrell noted that "while we deplore the conviction of English and Cooper, the fact that they were represented by 100% white counsel cannot be ignored." Burrell's comments reflected the other battle that the NAACP lawyers took on during the trial. Burrell believed that the NAACP attorneys should have represented all of the defendants, because if one white attorney worked with the black attorneys, the white attorney received most of the credit. Pellettieri's critique of Alexander illustrated that, in 1951, some white attorneys continued to question the competency of black attorneys.[21]

Alexander summarized the trial for the LDEF. He acknowledged to Marshall that he did not receive a "perfect verdict," but it was better than the first verdict. Alexander did not concur with the jury's verdict but admitted it "was impossible to expect six acquittals," no matter how strong the defense case, because the jury had to convict at least one defendant, in order to avoid a potential race riot. However, he reassured Marshall not to worry over the "communist yelpings about the verdict being a great miscarriage of justice, unfair, based on prejudice."[22]

Alexander's remarks represented the contraction of civil rights politics during the Cold War. Alexander, a liberal anti-communist, battled discrimination in the courts, but when the CRC stated that "bias" may have afflicted the jury, Alexander dismissed the group's claim because of its communist affiliation. Moreover, Alexander had admitted to Marshall that the all-white jury had to convict one defendant. After the trial, Cooper and English filed an appeal, and the NAACP, CRC, and ACLU competed to represent them. Burrell informed Alexander that the CRC tried "to take over all of the defendants." The CRC propagandized the two convictions to demonstrate the denial of equal rights to African Americans. Alexander informed Marshall that many people asked him to go on a publicity tour with the four freed men, but he "opposed, in making a carnival out of this." Attorneys Burrell and Moore met with Walter White to discuss the Trenton Six appeal. Burrell stated to Alexander that "the CRC invaded the National Offices and attempted to forcibly take charge of the defendants from Cliff and myself." Burrell suggested that the NAACP should "arrange some type of demonstrations featuring the defendants and counsel." Alexander believed that the NAACP should not use propaganda or demonstrations to fight the CRC because the organization could ill afford to employ tactics that white and black Americans would assume were communist. During the thirties, Alexander allowed the ILD to support the Berwyn school desegregation case, but during the Cold War era, Alexander realized that if the NAACP used radical tactics it could only damage the organization.[23]

The *Nation* and *New Republic* reported on the Trenton Six verdict and reviewed the history of the case. Neither publications mentioned Alexander nor the NAACP attorneys. *The Nation* editorial titled "Six Minus Four: Trenton's Way Out" mentioned the names of the Princeton Committee and ACLU attorneys and stated that "additional counsel were also provided by the NAACP." When Alexander read the editorial, he was furious and immediately wrote Moore, calling the editorial a "very nasty reference to the NAACP's contribution." He told Thurgood Marshall that Arthur Hays, the Princeton Committee attorney, only appeared in court "10 or 12 times" out of 75 court days. Three weeks later, the *Nation* published a letter to the editor from Henry Lee Moon, the NAACP's director of public relations, stating that the NAACP had "retained a battery of competent lawyers headed by Raymond Pace Alexander" and criticizing the original editorial for creating the misimpression that only the white lawyers "took an active part in the defense." The *New Republic* also named the Princeton Committee attorneys and referred to the NAACP attorneys as "various counsel for the NAACP." Bruce Bliven, a friend of Marshall and author of the editorial, maintained that "he was pressed for space" and would mention Alexander and the NAACP attorneys by name in the next issue. In spite of their support of civil rights, two liberal publications neglected to include Alexander's and the NAACP attorneys contributions to the case. Over the previous twenty-five years, black attorneys had developed a tradition of civil rights work that was now drawing white liberal supporters. The lack of recognition and respect for the work of black attorneys infuriated Alexander.[24]

The Trenton Six Case had a substantial impact in New Jersey and Pennsylvania. Alexander had saved the lives of his two clients and gained more visibility in the Democratic Party, which increased his visibility as he prepared for the November election. On a national level, the Trenton Six verdict, despite its positive outcomes, did not put Alexander in the spotlight. This combination of local prominence and national obscurity occurred throughout Alexander's career. His civil rights work profoundly affected the black community in Philadelphia and in other areas where he worked. While the NAACP won a number of U.S. Supreme Court decisions, Alexander was just one of many black attorneys who obtained civil rights for African Americans in local, state, and federal district courts.

Seeking a Federal Judgeship

Following the 1948 presidential election, Alexander wanted Truman to appoint him a federal judge to the U.S. Third District Court, which was located in Philadelphia. A year after Truman's inauguration, Alexander wrote to Philadelphia judge Louis E. Levinthall about the growing number of black judges across the nation and the continuing lack of black judges in Philadelphia. In 1948, Chicago had four and New York City had seven, while Philadelphia, whose black population was third-largest in the nation, had only one black judge, Herbert Millen, who served as a municipal court judge, the lowest-rank position in the judiciary. By World War II, black communities in New York and in Chicago formed powerful voting blocks that enabled them to elect black judges. In 1949, Congress passed the McCarran Bill, which added twenty-three federal judges. The U.S. Third District had two judicial vacancies, one in the district court. Alexander wrote William Dawson, black congressman from Illinois, about the possibility of obtaining a federal judgeship. Alexander noted that three federal positions were available in Philadelphia and that Truman had to appoint at least one African American. In a letter to Urban League president, Channing Tobias, Alexander stated that between 1932 and 1949, Roosevelt and Truman had appointed twelve federal judges in Philadelphia, but not one was African American. He wrote, "It is incredible and inconceivable that our distinguished President would appoint twenty-three new judges without at least two of them Negroes." Alexander believed that the appointment of a black federal judge in Philadelphia was overdue.[25]

One major obstacle that Alexander confronted in his quest for a judgeship was his party loyalty. Between 1937 and 1947, Alexander switched parties three times, in a search for reliable white allies who would advance the civil rights agenda rather than make promises to woo black voters and then renege after they were elected. His wife, Sadie Tanner Mossell Alexander, and other African American attorneys, such as J. Austin Norris, also switched parties. Reporting on the upcoming appointment for the federal bench, Walter A. Gay, Philadelphia native and Assistant U.S. District Attorney stated in the *Philadelphia Inquirer* that Alexander was an active New Deal Democrat and "well known in Democratic circles," although he "was a new comer to the New Deal following recent years as a fringe Republican." A week earlier, Alexander had defended his commitment to the Democratic Party to James A. Finnegan, chair of the Democratic City Committee of Philadelphia. Alexander wrote a four-page letter to Finnegan about his commitment to the

Democratic Party. He emphatically declared, "Let me categorically state that *I am a Democrat and I have burned my bridges behind me and I expect to be a Democrat the rest of my life.*" He reminded Finnegan about his role during the 1932–34 Berwyn school desegregation case and asserted that the case aided in the election of George Earle as the first Democratic governor of Pennsylvania in fifty years. Alexander also informed Finnegan that in 1938, as a "REGISTERED DEMOCRAT," he spent valuable time campaigning and lost some business but still did not receive a judgeship. Finally, Alexander mentioned Earl Harrison, a white Democratic lawyer who had supported Republican presidential candidate Thomas Dewey and still became a high ranking Democratic lawyer. Alexander pointed out that voting across party lines on the part of white political figures was tolerated. Why should the loyalties of black leaders be evaluated by a stricter standard?[26]

By mid-summer, as the race for the federal judgeship heated up, it became clear that in 1949, in contrast to 1937 and 1938, the local and national Democratic Party had to appoint at least one black federal judge. In the crucial 1948 presidential election, some black radicals such as W. E. B. DuBois and Paul Robeson had supported Henry Wallace of the Progressive Party, and a number of black Republicans supported Thomas Dewey. In a fairly transparent effort to retain black support for Truman, white liberals promised that black Democrats would be rewarded for their loyal service to the party. Walter Annenberg, editor of the *Philadelphia Inquirer*, wrote an editorial, "A Negro Federal Judge," declaring that "In all fairness, the exclusion of Negroes from the federal bench should end." Alexander hailed Annenberg's statement as "the strongest and most liberal pronouncement ever made by a great metropolitan newspaper." In spite of Annenberg's support, Alexander stated, Pennsylvania senator Francis Myers appeared to have "an extreme reluctance" to submit "the name of a Negro lawyer" for nomination to the federal bench. To ensure his nomination, Alexander asked Carl Murphy, editor of the *Baltimore Afro American* and a number of influential black Democrats such as Mary McLeod Bethune to write President Truman to recommend Alexander's appointment. By August the *Philadelphia Tribune* reported that three black attorneys from Philadelphia headed the list for a federal judgeship in the U.S. Third District Court: Alexander, Walter A. Gay Jr. and Maceo Hubbard, Alexander's former employee, who had recently served as a civil rights lawyer for the Department of Justice. The newspaper added that Channing Tobias of the Urban League had unofficially received word that Alexander would obtain the position.[27]

In August, Alexander traveled to Washington, D.C., to see Congressman Dawson. When he returned to Philadelphia, Alexander informed Annenberg about his trip and the rumors that he heard about the federal judicial appointment. Alexander stated to Annenberg that Senator Myers was "seeking to reach a compromise" by naming William Hastie, governor of the U.S. Virgin Islands, to the U.S. Circuit Court Bench. Alexander maintained that he had received the information from a very "reliable source" and declared that "There can be no excuse whatsoever for the naming of "Governor Hastie a non-resident of Pennsylvania." Hastie was born in Tennessee and lived in Washington, D.C., for thirty-years, so Alexander suggested that Truman should appoint Hastie to a federal judgeship in Washington instead. However, Truman knew that this would offend Southern Democrats.[28]

In September, the Democratic Party leaders of Philadelphia held a meeting to discuss the upcoming election. Alexander briefed Marshall Shepard, Democratic candidate for Recorder of Deeds candidate, on what points he needed to discuss in reference to the federal judgeship. Alexander stated that if the Democratic Party appointed Hastie it "would be a shocking insult against competent, outstanding" black Democrats in Philadelphia, and it would take twenty-five years before another black lawyer from Philadelphia would be appointed. According to Alexander, Hastie's appointment violated the law. The law stated that any judge appointed to the U.S. Circuit Court except in Washington, D.C., "must live within the circuit Court area at the time of his appointment." Alexander believed that the Democratic Party "would not insult any other minority race" and bring an Italian or Jewish judge from another city into Philadelphia. In an angry tone quite unlike his usual style, he declared, "It is time that the white man stop making appointments of Negroes without consulting the Negro leadership." Alexander's notion of racial representation was not based on particular bias against Jews and Italians but on the premise that each racial-ethnic group should be represented by its own leaders and not ruled over by members of other groups chosen by powerful politicians.[29]

Truman's decision was based on partisan politics rather than on an assessment of Alexander's legal acumen. The Democratic Party's commitment to civil rights gave Alexander hope. The Truman administration had appointed black leaders to high-level positions and even had staff members specifically responsible for addressing civil rights issues. For example, during his campaign for an appointment, Alexander contacted David Niles, Truman's secretary for "minority affairs." However, Carol Anderson argues that Niles "was a watchdog for the status quo" who did not advocate civil rights reform. Alexander noted that the black lawyers of the Philadelphia Bar were "very greatly disturbed over the rumors that persisted about the likely appointment of Governor Hastie," although Senator Myers had personally assured Alexander that he "should pay no attention to the public's report" and advised him not to believe the rumors. Alexander reminded Niles that his appointment to the U.S. District Court would have a greater meaning to the black community in Philadelphia. In relation to national politics, however, Hastie was an excellent choice for the Truman administration. He was a New Deal Democrat and active with the NAACP's civil rights campaign. In 1937, President Roosevelt had appointed him as the first black federal judge to the U.S. Virgin Islands. Over the years, Hastie developed a national reputation and accumulated more clout in Washington, D.C., than Alexander.[30]

On October 15, President Truman nominated William Hastie as the first black judge of the U.S. Circuit Court for the Third District, but Truman appointed Hastie as a "recess appointee."[31] Truman rewarded Hastie for his work in the 1948 election, when Hastie made speeches around the country to ward off Henry Wallace and the Progressive Party. Hastie's appointment received mixed reviews from black lawyers in Philadelphia. The day after Truman's announcement, the *Philadelphia Tribune* reported that the John Mercer Langston Bar Club would boycott Hastie's official welcome, although the local NAACP celebrated the appointment of a black judge. The *Baltimore Afro American* headline read "HASTIE CHOICE: IRKS BAR." The *Pittsburgh Courier* headline stated "HASTIE APPOINTED: RACE GYPED" and argued that President Truman had appointed Hastie as a political move to secure the reelection of Senator Myers in 1950. In addition, Truman's appointment made up for "the failure to pass any of the civil rights legislation" that he and the Democrats promised. Truman did not appoint Hastie to a federal judgeship in Washington, D.C., because he feared "Southern opposition" and Truman "never challenged the racial discrimination in the capital." In Philadelphia, the Hastie announcement annoyed some local black lawyers; however, the NAACP and the black community celebrated the appointment. Locally, and across Pennsylvania, Alexander's peers were cognizant of his work, but nationally, Hastie had more leverage in the party. Truman was neither willing to offend Southern Democrats by appointing Hastie to a court in the nation's capital nor compelled to appoint prominent local attorneys such as Alexander and other African Americans seeking to elevate the position of their race as well as their own status who sought posts in the foreign service.[32]

Seeking a Position in the Foreign Service

After World War II, a number of black leaders castigated the U.S. State Department's exclusion of African Americans from the diplomatic corps because a white male elite dominated the State Department and Foreign Service. According to a series of articles written in 1950 by historian Rayford Logan for the *Pittsburgh Courier*, in 1947 less than two hundred of the seven thousand employees of the State Department were African American, and the majority of them were janitors. Logan argued that many African Americans were qualified for high-level appointments to the foreign service. At that time, peoples of color across Africa and around the world were engaged in a liberation struggle against European colonialism and white domination. The small number of black diplomats worked in what Krenn refers to as the "Negro Circuit": Liberia, the Azores, Madagascar, and the Canary Islands. These countries contain people of African descent, and many whites believed that African American diplomats were better served in black nations. During Truman's administration, it became imperative for the government to increase the number of African Americans in high-ranking positions in the State Department. Krenn describes the decision to hire African Americans as a "diplomacy of desegregation" intended to improve the United States' image in the eyes of newly independent nations. In 1949, Truman appointed Edward R. Dudley, a lawyer from New York, as the first black ambassador to Liberia, a country with close historical ties to the United States. A number of prominent African Americans, seeking to elevate the position of their race as well as their own status, sought posts in the foreign service.[33]

Alexander was cognizant of efforts to appoint African Americans to position in the State Department and counted himself among those qualified to serve. Alexander said, "I always wanted to be an Ambassador to Haiti," but he did not express this aspiration to Senator Francis Myers at the time he was seeking an appointment to the federal bench. Alexander declared that the "dark Haitians" rule the county, and they prefer a "Negro ambassador." Alexander had an inside track because he had served as counselor of the Haitian government and as an honorary consul to Haiti in Philadelphia. Democrats and African Americans in the city and across the state would have supported his appointment, and nationally prominent black Democratic leaders might have done so as well.[34]

Alexander wanted to work in the State Department to increase the number of black diplomats, improve the status of black attorneys, inform other nations about racial progress being made in the United States, and counter Communist propaganda about America's racial problems. Dudziak argues that during the 1950s, the United States Information Agency (USIA) wanted middle-class African Americans "who would say the right thing. Talking about progress, and embodying black middle-class status." Alexander's education and professional success made him part of that group. Unlike Paul Robeson and W. E. B. DuBois, who were critical of U.S. foreign policy and the capitalist economy as well as racial injustice, Alexander's criticized racism while expressing optimism about the country's progress toward racial equality, integration, and harmony.[35]

From 1949 to 1951, Alexander tried to obtain a number of positions in the U.S. State Department. During that time, Democratic Party leaders such as Washington, D.C., attorney Roy Garvin suggested to Dawson and Democratic National Committee (DNC) leader William Boyle that the government should appoint an African American to "the middle east where white Americans are not in too great favor." Some black leaders believed that non-European nations, especially those in Africa, would prefer African American diplomats. However, Krenn suggests that a rumor developed in the State Department that black nations preferred white diplomats to black ones. Although he was not trained in diplomacy, Alexander told Illinois congressman William Dawson, that a number of his "classmates at Harvard had worked their way up to the highest bench." Throughout his career, Alexander observed that his white Harvard Law classmates had obtained federal positions with or without the credentials that were assumed to be necessary. If Alexander did not receive a State Department appointment, he informed Dawson that he wanted to work as an assistant solicitor general or as an assistant attorney general of the United States. Alexander contended, "There is no reason why an appointment as an Assistant Secretary of State should not be offered to a Negro." He was convinced that the Democratic Party and the nation owed African Americans higher-ranking positions.[36]

In 1950, Alexander demonstrated the valuable service he could render to the United States abroad by publishing an advisory report on black soldiers then stationed in Europe. In August, Alexander traveled to Germany "at his own expense to conduct an unofficial" study of the eight thousand black soldiers who comprised just 8 percent of the U.S. servicemen there. Alexander recommended that the military continue to increase the number of black soldiers in Germany to counteract the Communist propaganda that proclaimed that the United States does "not grant equality to people of all colors and races without restrictions." Alexander observed that when he was in Germany, Europeans often asked him about the hypocrisy of Americans who proclaim ideals of equality but practice racial segregation; he explained how difficult it was for him to tell the truth about how the United States treated African Americans. As Communist propaganda intensified during the Cold War, Alexander believed that black diplomats were ideal ambassadors to talk about race relations and democracy in the United States. The *Pittsburgh Courier* stated that Alexander's report received attention from the State Department and that officials there tried to get Alexander a diplomatic position.[37]

Pennsylvania Congressman Earl Chudoff became Alexander's most ardent supporter after his election in 1950. Chudoff informed DNC chair William Boyle that, "under great criticism," Alexander aided him in his campaign against Theodore Spaulding, a black Republican and Philadelphia attorney. A white congressman from a black majority district, Chudoff felt that Alexander "was one of the great contributing factors of my victory." During the campaign, E. Washington Rhodes of the *Philadelphia Tribune* derided Alexander as a "so called big-shot Negro Democrat" for supporting Chudoff against Spaulding. Rhodes alleged that Alexander and attorney Harvey Schmidt were "being paid in dollars, speech by speech, or paid in promises of jobs" to endorse Chudoff. This exchange between Rhodes and Alexander demonstrates the blurred lines between personal ambition, racial progress, and party loyalty.[38]

In a 1950 *Pittsburgh Courier* editorial, Ralph Bunche, United Nations secretary, maintained that Ethiopia was a "danger spot" with potential religious tensions among Christians, Muslims, and "pagans." Alexander asserted that he was a race relations expert who could help mediate the situation in Ethiopia. From January to April 1951, William Boyle of the DNC, James Finnegan, Senator Myers, and Congressman Earl Chudoff wrote recommendations for Alexander to serve as an ambassador to Ethiopia. Chudoff reminded President Truman that Alexander, a "good and personal friend," was a "great Democrat and campaigned day and night for your election," but white diplomats recognized Ralph Bunche as the most qualified black diplomat. During Alexander's campaign to become ambassador to Ethiopia, the *Philadelphia Afro American* ran a political cartoon titled "Why Not Share the Spotlight?" that pictured Ralph Bunche in the middle of a circle surrounded by six prominent African Americans. The opinion piece below, "Give Others a Chance," summarized a speech given by W. E. B. DuBois at

Yale University in which he asserted that Bunche was "not the only man of caliber in this country" and maintained that Alexander possessed the "suave manner and mental poise" to be an effective diplomat. Despite their political differences, DuBois recognized Alexander's professional skills and potential usefulness in the foreign service. Most white State Department officials assumed that African Americans were not intelligent enough to serve. Alexander wanted to join the State Department in part to eradicate the racist myth about black inferiority.[39]

In April, Chudoff received a telegram from Alexander that contained a *New York Times* article announcing the appointment of a career diplomat as the new U.S. ambassador to Ethiopia. Chudoff replied that he "Was very much surprised and hurt" because Alexander did not receive the position. Chudoff immediately sent another group of letters to Democratic Party officials advocating Alexander's appointment as ambassador to Haiti, a position that was then vacant. According to Chudoff, Dawson said that Alexander "should not be upset about the Ethiopia appointment." The *Pittsburgh Courier* reported that the State Department chose a career diplomat for Ethiopia "because of the strategic value of that county in an event of war with Russia." Chudoff reminded Boyle that Alexander was a friend of Haiti's president Paul Eugene Magloire and was qualified to serve as the U.S. ambassador there. Chudoff wanted Boyle to recommend Alexander to President Truman, but Boyle informed Chudoff that he was not sure he could obtain the position for Alexander.[40]

When Alexander discovered that he was not selected as U.S. ambassador to Ethiopia, he wrote Christine Ray Davis, the executive clerk to the Committee on Executive Expenditures. Alexander had previously attended a social event at Davis's home, but he did not want to discuss the ambassadorial position with Dawson and others persons in the room. Alexander reminded Davis of a meeting held a month earlier between Secretary of State Dean Acheson and "A Committee of Negroes" formed by twelve black leaders, including A. Philip Randolph and Mary McLeod Bethune. The group sought to advance American interests in the Cold War by improving race relations at home and countering Communist propaganda abroad. Alexander believed that after the meeting Acheson would appoint "one of our race as an Assistant Secretary of State with the same powers and opportunities" as his Harvard classmates. He mentioned to Davis that six of his white Harvard Law classmates "have been assistant secretaries of state" or worked in the Justice Department, reiterating the grievance he had preciously expressed to

Dawson. Alexander said he preferred to work in the State Department but was open to diplomatic posts in India, Asia Minor, or the Far East. In 1951, Truman appointed Edward Dudley as the first black ambassador to India, beyond the "Negro Circuit," giving African Americans the opportunity to serve in other countries. Alexander now stated that he did not want to work in Haiti because of the "bitter factions among the Haitians based on color and wealth" and because the Haitians "will fight for the appointment of a white man" to serve as an ambassador. The same issue of skin color and class status existed in the United States, but Alexander failed to see the comparison. He no longer viewed the ambassadorship to Haiti as a "Negro Job."[41]

During his unsuccessful campaigns for a federal judgeship and an ambassadorial post, Alexander remained active in Philadelphia politics. A month after the rumor that Truman favored Hastie rather than Alexander, Curtis C. Carson, a black attorney, told Alexander that Myers was still considering nominating a black lawyer from Philadelphia for the federal bench. Carson had written Myers a letter of recommendation on Alexander's behalf and believed that Myers's response had "implied that Mr. Hastie's recommendation had not received his official sanction." Alexander's pastor, Reverend Arthur Jones of Zion Baptist Church, sent a letter to Richardson Dilworth, a Democrat who was running for city treasurer in the upcoming election. Dilworth stated to Jones that he and Joseph S. Clark, who was running for city controller, supported Alexander and the two other black attorneys from Philadelphia for federal judge. However, after Clark and Dilworth spoke to Senator Myers and Finnegan, they discovered that "four of the six judges on the court" were from Pennsylvania, and the next judge had to be from another state in the third district. Alexander never mentioned that all of the judges were white men and that he firmly believed a black lawyer from Philadelphia must get the position. Dilworth stated that Governor Hastie would bring "luster to the Federal Appellate Court and break down bars to Negro appointments to Federal Courts." Furthermore, Dilworth indicated that Pennsylvania's next Governor would appoint a black judge on the state level, or as Reverend Jones told William Boyle, the Democratic Party might lose three hundred thousand black votes.[42]

Alexander was deeply frustrated with the Democratic Party on the national level and mobilized his local allies to push for change at the city and state levels. In October, Alexander planned a "political tea" at his home for all of the Democratic candidates. Alexander informed James Finnegan and Dilworth that he had invited more than "250 people representing the younger group of professional people" with "great influence over large numbers of people." When Dilworth received Alexander's invitation, he told Alexander that he could not attend, but Finnegan suggested to Dilworth "the campaign would be aided considerably by your attendance." Dilworth canceled his trip and attended Alexander's tea.[43] According to the *Philadelphia Tribune* "several hundred guests" attended the political tea, including Democratic incumbents and candidates Dilworth, Clark, Senator Myers, and Congressmen Earl Chudoff. The *Pittsburgh Courier* reported that during the affair, Dr. Harry Greene asked Myers why he had not nominated a black attorney from Philadelphia. Myers stated evasively that Hastie's "selection was made in Washington and he [Myers] merely gave his Senatorial approval." Not falling for political double-talk, Greene asked Myers point-blank if he had selected a district judge, and Myers answered that he had. While running for reelection, Myers sought to make it appear that he had played no role in Hastie's appointment. The *Philadelphia Inquirer* reported "political unrest" among Philadelphia's black Democrats and predicted that the Republicans might gain four wards in the 1949 election. The newspaper failed to realize that the political unrest came primarily from a few black lawyers in Philadelphia and not from the NAACP or the black community as a whole. In 1949, when Thurgood Marshall sought a federal judgeship in New York City, the NAACP supported him but the city's African American Democratic leaders did not. They wanted someone with political clout in Tammany Hall. Alexander had local political power, but Philadelphia was a Republican city and Philadelphia's thirty-six black lawyers did not have enough political power to get Alexander appointed to a federal bench.[44]

The Democratic Party Reform Movement in Philadelphia, 1951

Throughout the Trenton Six trial and his efforts to secure a federal appointment, Alexander was intimately involved in the Democratic Party reform movement in Philadelphia. After World War II, the Democratic Party was comprised of labor interests, ward politicians, African Americans, and progressive middle-class and elite whites. The Democratic Party wanted to reform Philadelphia politics by eradicating patronage. Alexander joined the Democratic Party in 1937, left in 1940, and rejoined in 1947. William J. McKenna noted that in 1947 Joseph S. Clark and Richardson Dilworth, two former Republicans, became Democrats. Dilworth ran for mayor in 1947 and lost. After 1948, Alexander became an integral part of the Democratic Party in Philadelphia. Alexander, Clark, and Dilworth were all Ivy League-educated graduates, upper-middle-class reformers who wanted to end bossism. These men formed the foundation of the Democratic Party in Philadelphia. White Democratic leaders were cognizant of Alexander's political power, and the party eventually rewarded Alexander with a judgeship.[45]

In May 1951, the Democratic Party accepted nominations for the fifth district city council position. *The Pittsburgh Courier* reported that the contest for the nomination for city council was between J. Thompson Pettigrew, an African American three-term state senator and "an inconspicuous figure" who did not pass any significant legislation, and Alexander, "the most distinguished Negro lawyer in America." The five ward leaders, however, formed a caucus and nominated Pettigrew, John K. Rice, and Granville Clark. Clark and Rice withdrew in June. The *Courier* reported that the ward leaders' "plot, however is not likely to succeed" because black and white Democratic Leaders opposed Pettigrew. Black leaders castigated the white Democrats who supported Pettigrew, a "mediocre Negro." The *Philadelphia Tribune* remarked that the Democratic Party supported Alexander for city council in order "to remove the noted lawyer from making the race for Congress" in the next year's election against the incumbent Earl Chudoff, who represented a majority-black district. Alexander had supported Chudoff in 1950 against a black candidate, and in return Chudoff supported Alexander's candidacy for city council. According to Carolyn Adams, the tension between the black ward leaders and the Democratic Party mirrored the class tensions among white Democrats in Philadelphia. The ward leaders supported political patronage, so they nominated Pettigrew and feared that Alexander, an upper-middle-class black, would eradicate patronage if he were elected.[46]

Alexander won the July primary for city council. In a letter to J. Austin Norris, a black Democrat, he revealed the expenses that gaining the nomination had entailed. In one week he had visited "forty democratic committeemen and committee women in the 47th ward" and "spent $1000.00" to pay election workers. Alexander did not disclose how much money he had spent on the primary but stated that "the amount was not just a token." As the November election approached, Alexander and Marshall Shepherd, a black Baptist minister, conducted "street corner rallies" in most of the black wards. In October, Alexander campaigned five nights a week but told Democratic leaders that he did not spend enough time in his own district. He wanted the North Philadelphia Democrats to schedule more meetings in his ward.

Alexander maintained that Joe Baker, a "conservative, reactionary, Republican of our race," emerged as a threat; therefore Alexander recommended to Finnegan that Clark and Dilworth attend an award ceremony where African Americans from the "upper bracket, conservative colored" met.[47]

According to the *Philadelphia Tribune*, Alexander's campaign addressed police brutality and their "indiscriminate raiding of Negro hotels and Negro homes without warrants and without an actual crime being committed." Increasing the number of black city employees was a major plank in his platform. Alexander told the *Philadelphia Tribune* that in 1950, Philadelphia's city budget was $3.6 million with 1058 employees, but the Fairmount Park Commission only employed "six Negroes and two as park guards." The Democratic campaign committee contended that the Republican Party had overlooked African Americans for city employment. The Democratic Party printed a twelve-page pullout in the *Philadelphia Tribune* that referred to City Hall as "A Citadel of Prejudice and Discrimination." The ad contained pictures of black victims of police brutality and accused the Philadelphia police conducted of racial profiling by "arresting inter-racial couples, in private and public spaces." The Democratic candidates wanted to end patronage, but to retain the black vote they needed to reward the black community with government positions.[48]

Alexander and the Democratic Party's reform leaders won by a large margin, ending sixty-seven years of Republican rule in Philadelphia. Charles A. Erkstom notes that between 1949 and 1959, the Democratic Party shifted from a "Democratic reform era" to the "consolidation of Democratic control." Joseph Clark was elected mayor, Richardson Dilworth district attorney, and Alexander city councilman. R. R. Wright Jr. congratulated Alexander and declared, "before you are sixty till time of retirement you should be a federal judge." In November, the John Mercer Langston Law Club and the Barristers Club, an organization of black lawyers in Philadelphia who passed the bar after 1943, held a testimonial dinner for Alexander to celebrate his campaign victory and his work in the Trenton Six case. Judge William Hastie and Thurgood Marshall were listed in the *Amsterdam News* among a group of African Americans from New York who attended the banquet. Alexander's wife told attorney Eustace Gay that the banquet "will always stand out as marking the contribution of the Negro lawyer and the status he has gained in the community." By 1951, the status of African American attorneys significantly improved in both the black and white communities of Philadelphia.[49]

The Cold War had a dual impact on Alexander and the civil rights struggle. The Cold War provided opportunities for black lawyers nationally and internationally. In order to improve the U.S.'s image abroad, the State Department sought to hire black professionals to extol the nation's democratic virtue. A plethora of black attorneys such as Alexander and others took advantage of these opportunities, while others such as William Patterson of the CRC remained committed to left-wing politics in spite of McCarthyism. Alexander campaigned for appointments to a federal judgeship and a U.S. ambassadorship. He was unsuccessful in both because he lacked national recognition, but his legal successes added to his prestige in Philadelphia.

The civil rights struggle in Philadelphia and other northern cities had gained momentum after World War II. In spite of the Cold War, the expanding black vote forced the Democratic Party to embrace civil rights, but black leaders had to denounce communists and avoid tactics associated with the left, such as mass demonstrations and propaganda. All organizations used publicity to obtain support; however, Cold War ideology differentiated between publicity and propaganda. The CRC and the left used propaganda while the NAACP and liberal organizations used publicity. In 1947, Alexander rejoined the Democratic Party and became a part of the Democratic Party reform movement in Philadelphia, where he practiced a politics of civil rights that consisted of litigation, voting, and interracial coalitions with white liberals. By the late 1940s and late 1950s, black attorneys including Alexander, Robert C. Nix Sr., J. Austin Norris, Sadie Tanner Mossell Alexander, and Harvey Schmidt were part of a black Democratic machine. White Democratic leaders identified them as power brokers in the black community. After playing an instrumental role in the Democratic takeover in 1951, Alexander used that victory as a springboard for his political career. As an upper-middle-class black Democrat, he became a party loyalist, but he had to balance patronage with meritocracy, a precarious proposition at best because black expectations had increased as political officials failed to provide the resources. While Alexander and other liberal Democrats advocated an end to patronage, his own campaign for city council was based on increasing the number of black city employees. Ironically, not only did attaining political power require compromises, but wielding it brought additional difficulties.

Not long after the black political machine was established, new black leaders challenged its authority. Nationally, working-class African Americans as well as college-aged students started to challenge local black leadership. In most cities throughout the nation, New Negro professionals were in power, but after the successful Montgomery Bus Boycott, black ministers took center stage and became the new leaders of the civil rights movement. By the late 1950s, Reverend Leon Sullivan and attorney Cecil B. Moore, along with working-class African Americans, emerged and added a new twist to the civil rights struggle in Philadelphia.

Part Three

A NEW NEGRO JUDGE DURING THE CIVIL
RIGHTS/BLACK POWER ERA, 1954–1974

Chapter Five

PARTICIPATING IN THE CIVIL RIGHTS
MOVEMENT FROM THE BENCH, 1954–1964

On May 17, 1954, the United States Supreme Court ruled in *Brown v. Board of Education* that "separate but equal" was unconstitutional. Some historians consider this landmark historic case as the genesis of the modern civil rights movement. In February 1954, while the nation was waiting for the *Brown* decision, Alexander filed a lawsuit to desegregate Girard College, a private school for "white male orphans" that was governed by the City Board of Trusts. For Alexander and many other black Philadelphians, Girard College symbolized white supremacy, resembling the de jure segregation of school systems in the South. On May 21, 1948, Alexander explained the significance of black youths' exclusion from Girard College in a letter to Earl Shelby, editor of the *Philadelphia Bulletin*, "I was born and raised in the shadows of the cold, grey and forbidding walls of Girard College. We, as the City's colored population, knew these walls meant discrimination—and I grew up to hate walls. I swore, were I ever able to become a lawyer, or legislator or both, I would try every legal means to break that evidence of segregation and discrimination that Girard College symbolized in the heart of the most populous [sic] Negro community in the City of Philadelphia."[1] Girard College was supported by taxes paid by black citizens, but black male orphans could not attend the school. The principle of racial discrimination that the school followed was inscribed in the donor's will—or so the Orphans Court reasoned.

Before the *Brown* decision, most liberal whites and blacks agreed that Philadelphia had made significant racial progress, despite persistent racial discrimination. In 1948, the city council passed the Home Rule Charter that prohibited racial discrimination when hiring for municipal jobs. In northern cities, racial progress consisted of improved housing, political, educational, and economic opportunities for African Americans. In southern cities, racial progress meant racial desegregation and suffrage. During the 1950s, a gradual trend toward racial integration occurred in some southern cities. According to historian Micheal Klarman, "black challenges to various aspects of Jim Crow were beginning to bear fruit in the early 1950s—there was desegregation of the Montgomery police force . . . and some department stores and public facilities in Greensboro."[2] In both southern and northern cities, a substantial black middle class had emerged and white business and political leaders who realized their economic impact; in this situation, white elites had good reasons to conciliate black leaders by yielding to some of their demands. Klarman argues that the Brown decision created "southern racial backlash" and white moderate politicians turned into racial extremists. However, in Philadelphia, the racial progress that was made up to the mid-1950s came without costing most whites much, but the claims that black residents made for equal citizenship in relation to public institutions from the mid-1950s on were more formidable.[3]

By 1953, Alexander believed that he had enough political support to desegregate Girard College. He was a prominent member of the Democratic Reform Movement and enjoyed support from liberal organizations such as the Commission on Human Relations (CHR). His wife, Sadie, had been a member of President Truman's civil rights task force, helped to design the CHF, and served on this policy advisory board for over a decade. The time seemed right to desegregate the college. In spite of the *Brown* decision, and the previous racial progress in Philadelphia, the judges in the Orphans Court were not swept up in civil rights liberalism. Indeed, their decision may have been influenced by the massive white backlash that swept the nation in the wake of *Brown.*

During the Girard College desegregation suit, a new movement emerged in Philadelphia to address white reaction and to create more opportunities for African Americans. From 1923 to 1953, Alexander's strategy for civil rights had worked because the number of black city employees had increased and race relations had improved. Middle-class professional blacks and whites dominated the civil rights coalition in Philadelphia, By the late 1950s, however, working-class blacks were not satisfied with the liberal policy of a "few black faces in high places," which they dismissed as "tokenism." Although African Americans had more opportunities, they still had a higher unemployment rates than whites. Reverend Leon Sullivan, pastor of Zion Baptist Church, emerged as a new civil rights leader in Philadelphia. Alexander's civil rights strategy relied upon the courts and on forming interracial coalitions with white liberals, but Sullivan mobilized the black church and working-class African Americans to take direct action. In 1960, Sullivan started the "400 ministers," an organization of black clergy in Philadelphia, and he began the "selective patronage" campaign in order to force companies to hire more African Americans. Sullivan's tactic was not new—during the 1930s, African Americans in northern cities had participated in the "Don't Buy Where You Can't Work" campaign, boycotting against white stores if the owners refused to hire African Americans—but it was effective in bringing black consumers' power to bear upon white employers who discriminated.[4]

In 1946, Alexander and other liberals sought to have Joseph Rainey, the progressive president of the local NAACP branch who wanted to mobilize working-class blacks, removed from office. After the 1930s Popular Front dissolved, white conservative and moderate leaders considered mass demonstrations and economic boycotts, communist-inspired tactics. By the late 1950s, these tactics returned to the civil rights struggle; Alexander believed that militant, confrontational tactics were unnecessary in Philadelphia. He viewed the all-black strategy as exclusionary, divisive, and not practical. One individual who represented this new style of leadership was Cecil B. Moore, an attorney originally from West Virginia. From January 1963 to 1968, Moore was instrumental in the civil rights movement in Philadelphia as he led demonstrations on construction sites, forcing them to hire more African Americans. Moore castigated black middle-class leadership, and on numerous occasions he referred to Alexander as an "Uncle Tom."[5]

In 1959, Governor George Leader appointed Alexander as the first black judge in the Court of Common Pleas in Philadelphia. Alexander was a judicial activist who addressed poverty, juvenile delinquency, and free legal aid for the poor. While Alexander did not participate in demonstrations, he fought the civil rights struggle from the bench. Through his long experience as a criminal lawyer, he understood that poverty and crime were major issues in the black community. Poor African Americans could not afford good lawyers, and as a result received unfair sentences. He created programs such as the Spiritual Rehabilitation Program (SRP), which provided job training for first-time offenders, and Community Legal Services (CLS), which provided free legal assistance to poor people. The SRP ended because of a lack of resources, but CLS is still in operation today.

During the 1960s, Alexander applauded the mass demonstrations in the South but vehemently opposed demonstrations in Philadelphia. Alexander feared that demonstrations in northern cites might force white working-class Democrats into voting for Barry Goldwater, the conservative Republican. In August 1964, a race riot occurred in Philadelphia, and Philadelphia mayor James Tate asked Alexander, Congressman Nix, and Moore to go to North Philadelphia to calm down the community. After Alexander left the riot area he was devastated, but, similar to King after the Watts riot, he realized that poverty and institutionalized racism were the major obstacles to justice. As a judge, Alexander could not participate in the civil rights movement, but in a decade, the civil rights movement in Philadelphia expanded and many African Americans questioned Alexander's civil rights strategy of relying on the law and the good will of white liberals.

Girard College Desegregation Case, 1954–1958

On the front cover of the October 1, 1957, issue of the *Philadelphia Tribune*, an African American newspaper, is an article on Arkansas governor Oral Faubus's attempt to prevent nine black children from desegregating the all-white Central High School. The white mob that gathered outside of the school angered African Americans. After the mob scene in Little Rock, jazz great Louis Armstrong stated in the *Philadelphia Tribune:* "The way they have been treating my people in the South the government can go to hell. . . . It's getting so a colored man hasn't got any country." Faubus's picture in the schoolhouse door is as famous as Bull Connor's dogs and hoses during the Birmingham movement. Underneath the Faubus story was an article titled "Orphans Court Joins South in Upholding School Segregation." Judge Charles Klein ruled in an unanimous decision that "the Board of Directors of City Trusts of the City of Philadelphia, as a state agency, could not bar Negro Orphans from Girard College, (but) a private trustee should be appointed, who would have the power to bar Negro boys." While the nation was engaged with Little Rock, for Alexander and other liberals in Philadelphia, Judge Klein had just ruled in favor of state-sanctioned segregation.[6]

Following the Orphans Court decision, a plethora of editorials in the *Philadelphia Tribune* discussed the Orphans Court decision that made the nexus between school desegregation in the North and South. An editorial titled "Court Follows South" states that the Orphans Courts decision was similar to "the Southern officials who seek to nullify the anti-segregation public decision of the United States Supreme Court."[7] During the Little Rock affair, racial violence had intensified in Philadelphia. According to the *Philadelphia Tribune* in 1957, a group of whites formed the Philadelphia Branch of the Seaboard White Citizens Council, an anti-African American hate group led by John Kasper, who had provoked race riots the previous fall in Clinton, Tennessee. In fact, during the summer of 1957, rumors of racial violence were so rampant in Philadelphia that Pennsylvania's Democratic senator Earl Chudoff was forced to write a letter to the Justice Department demanding to put the "subversive organization . . . out of business."[8]

White backlash associated with the modern civil rights movement did not occur only in the South; it was national. In the North, most whites resisted housing desegregation. Thomas Sugrue and Arnold Hirsch have studied white backlash and racial violence in housing in northern cities that occurred during the 1950s.[9] White backlash was also expressed in newspaper editorials and hate mail. These letters represent the sentiments of those who participated in violent resistance. During the 1950s in Philadelphia, white racial violence was evident in schools and neighborhoods as they became more African American. The post–World War II growth of the black population, similar to the first Great Migration, resulted in heightened racial tensions. However, during the fifties, television kept all citizens informed about the atrocities in the South, and many working-class whites and white ethnics in the North empathized with white southerners' support of states' rights. School and housing desegregation were two critical issues in the North, and as more African Americans moved to Philadelphia and as the Democratic Party distributed patronage to black voters, northern whites felt that their party was catering only to African Americans. For example, a letter from a white Philadelphian to the mayor:

Dear Mr. Mayor
The negroes are getting enough "free things" more so than the poor whites "They have been beating up our children in schools long before Little Rock." Nor, Mr. Mayor, if you aspire to the Governship or even for election—you may have the colored vote but will lose the white vote.[10]

Following the mob violence in Little Rock, some white teens started race riots in Philadelphia schools. In 1957, Philadelphia's district attorney Victor

A. Blanc blamed the race riots in South Philadelphia High School, a new integrated school that had black students, on "a report which points up conclusively that our juvenile problems have not been concerned with racial antagonism until the terrible Little Rock situation exploded." Prior to Little Rock, youth violence was intraracial; after Little Rock it shifted to intergroup disturbances. During the Little Rock Nine, the *Philadelphia Tribune* reported on the increase of racial violence in West Philadelphia. For example, in West Philadelphia, black parents organized a meeting in order "to stem the wave of terrorism" that derived from a white police officer who "slapped and choked" a young African American girl.[11] In addition, the black residents claimed that white youth met in a local bar and went outside and beat up black residents. White youth were watching television and, similar to southern whites, decided to defend their turf and attack black people. By the 1950s, South and West Philadelphia neighborhoods shared one thing in common: more African Americans were moving in and white backlash followed.

Stephen Girard was born in Bordeaux, France, and made his fortunes in shipping. During the last decade of the eighteenth century, Girard's ships made numerous trips to Haiti. Girard owned slaves in Louisiana, and, as with Thomas Jefferson and other men of the European Enlightenment era, for him slaveholding served as an avenue for status and wealth. Girard died in 1831, leaving the largest estate in the nation's history. According to Ken Carpenter, Girard's will stated that he did not want any "ecclesiastic, missionary, or minister . . . hold or exercise any station or duty whatever in the said college." His will further stated: "I am particularly desirous to provide for such number of *poor, white, male, orphan* children," those boys without fathers. However, Girard placed the college under control of Philadelphia's Board of Directors of City Trusts.[12]

From 1948 to 1954, most liberal whites and blacks agreed that the city experienced racial progress, in spite of the structural inequality. In fact, this same trend of racial progress existed in southern cities. One year before *Brown v. Board of Education*, Alexander believed that he had enough support to desegregate Girard College; therefore, in February 1954, three months before the historic Brown decision, he filed a lawsuit against Girard College. There was not massive resistance or white backlash of the magnitude seen in the South, but the Girard College alumni and whites in Philadelphia, whose children did not even qualify to attend the school, voiced their backlash in the newspapers and to mayor.

Alexander was not the first African American to protest Girard College, and on numerous occasions black parents in Philadelphia voiced their discontent about the school. In 1891, Nathan Mossell, Philadelphia's first black lawyer, sought to desegregate Girard College. During the 1950s, black parents asked Alexander when Girard College would admit black students. In May of 1953, attorney and *Philadelphia Tribune* columnist E. Washington Rhodes encouraged black boys between six and ten to apply to Girard, and he promised, "Free legal services will be given by the writer to battle for admission." In June, Alexander sent a letter to Robert Stern, the acting solicitor general of the United States, stating that he had told Thurgood Marshall about his "attack against the Stephen Girard Will," and he wanted Stern to provide him the briefs from the "Sweatt, McLaurin and Henderson cases." These were the civil rights cases that addressed educational segregation in the South. In July, Alexander sent a letter to the registrar at Girard with "the names of four or five young Negro boys . . . for entry into Girard College." While Alexander was conducting research on the case, he wanted to give the college an opportunity to desegregate before he went public.[13]

On July 23, 1953, Councilman Alexander introduced Resolution #433, stating that Girard College must desegregate or they would lose their tax-exempt status and that "the school is thus being subsidized by taxpayers, many of whom are Negroes." Moreover, in 1953, Girard's endowment was third behind Harvard and Yale Universities. Alexander had discovered that Girard College had difficulty recruiting students from Philadelphia, and he thought that it was "reprehensible that they should go begging for pupils" when there were qualified black youths in Philadelphia. Prior to Alexander's resolution, most whites in Philadelphia had benefited form the Democratic reforms, but when Alexander sought to desegregate Girard College, the white backlash began.[14]

The majority of Girard College alumni, students, and administrators opposed Alexander's quest to desegregate the college. After Alexander mentioned in city council that Girard College must integrate, discontented whites sent a barrage of letters to Alexander and local newspapers. One letter sent to John Gillen, secretary of the Girard College Alumni, stated, "During slavery Negro children were provided for by their parents or their masters." Girard created the college for the segment of society "for whom there was not adequate care—white orphans." For example, Alexander received a letter from Milon A. Manly from the CHR. Manly informed Alexander they had obtained a letter addressed to Alexander from John J. Fleck, "a well known racist, [who] is under surveillance by the Counter Espionage Division of the Army Intelligence Department, and is a known distributor of scurrilous literature." In September, Alexander stated to George Schermer, from the

Commission on Human Relations, that they "were the target for all kinds of anti-Negro letters, usually anonymous, and often very nasty phone calls." Alexander noticed that both local white papers had published "the photograph of the colored man who assaulted" a white man with the intent to "excite the rabid Negro hating and Negro baiting white man." Alexander wrote to Melville Ferguson, editor of the *Evening Bulletin*, that most whites thought Alexander wanted to "break the will of Stephen Girard" and that his "Resolution will cause racial discord." Alexander asked Ferguson if he would publish a shortened letter explaining his position. Alexander argued that his case had nothing to do with the will. If public officials operate a private institution, do taxpayers have a right to equal access? Alexander's main point was a civil rights issue that used litigation and moral suasion. As a result, he obtained support from Philadelphia's white liberal community.[15]

The case boiled down to Girard's intent and if the court had the power to break a will. A week after Alexander mentioned desegregating Girard College, John A. Diemond, the president of the Board of City Trusts and a Girard College graduate, stated in the *Philadelphia Inquirer* that his group was "bound by the will to do what Mr. Girard wanted done." According to college administrators, Girard established a standard of "preference" with "orphans born in old Philadelphia," with second preference given to those born in Pennsylvania counties and out of state based on a variety of characteristics. By 1953, the college was located in a black neighborhood—perhaps one reason that the school's enrollment had declined.

[Some of the strategies used in the civil rights movement in the South were duplicated in the North. One strategy was the "politics of respectability." In order for a test case to work, Alexander made sure that the boys he picked met all of the qualifications: they were orphans and, just as important, they did not have any character flaws.] For example, George J. Amonitti, principal of John F. Reynolds Elementary School, had to "not recommend" Ivan Felder because "with so much at stake, we should not jeopardize the boys' chances nor supply ammunition to those who might not be in accord with the idea." John Bright from the African Methodist Episcopal Church told Alexander that he "would try hard to get another boy of the type that I am sure you want." In other words, they had to be well-mannered boys and their mothers upstanding citizens.[16]

In December 1954, Alexander sent letters to black ministers and schoolteachers looking for boys between the ages of six and eight because they would be eligible to attend Girard College, if the case lasted more than a year. It took two months to get six boys and their mothers who met the quali-fications. In February 1954, six African American male orphans applied to Girard College, and on March 19, 1954, the Board of Directors of City Trusts reviewed the applications and denied the boys admission for two reasons: the board had "no power to admit other than white boys to Girard College" and the applicants were not "a poor white male orphan." In April Alexander described to Floyd Logan the negative responses he had received: "I have had, literally, scores of nasty letters, phone calls and threats, and ugly remarks, from our adversaries. It appears that the white man is vocal in his objections and denunciations of any effect on our part for freedom and equality as guar-anteed us by our city, state and federal constitution." After the college rejected the students based on race, Alexander filed a lawsuit and asked the mothers of the plaintiff to attend a city council meeting in order to make their case. Alexander requested them to "Please wear your very best clothes, conservative clothes, and have your son dressed in conservative clothes, preferably not too light in color." On May 27, 1954, the city council adopted Alexander's resolu-tion, and the city solicitor added his name to the lawsuit. One month before the Brown decision, there was resistance to desegregating Girard College.[17]

Local black attorneys such as Alexander were at a financial disadvantage. The costs of a case include mailing, filing briefs, copies, appeals, and transpor-tation for the plaintiffs. Fortunately, the national NAACP had the resources from membership and donations from liberal organizations to assist, but Alexander, his colleagues, and local organizations funded the majority of the Girard Case. For example, in 1955, Alexander wrote to Lawrence Smith, a white lawyer in Philadelphia, and mentioned the "rather burdensome and continuous expenses" in the Girard Case. Since Alexander was a city coun-cilman, he spent less time working in his law firm, and a significant portion of funds came out of his pocket. Alexander asked for funds from Rever-end Marshall Shepard and the rest of "The Baptist Churches of Philadel-phia" because, by 1956, Alexander had spent two thousand dollars of his own money. Looking for some financial assistance, Alexander wrote a letter to Maurice Fagan of the Philadelphia Fellowship Commission and stated that he "never charged or received a dollar for legal services rendered in thousands of civil rights cases," but the "bitter resistance" from whites forced him to ask for money from friends and organizations who were connected with the case. Alexander realized that the NAACP was spending money "for hundreds of school segregation cases . . . and the very legality of the NAACP in Alabama and Louisiana." In 1956, Alabama made it illegal to form a NAACP chapter.

In spite of the financial disadvantages, Alexander never lost a case owing to a lack of funds, but this local study demonstrates how the resources were collected from the community and allies.[18]

The Girard case started in Philadelphia's Orphans Court in 1955 and reached the Pennsylvania Supreme Court in 1956. Both courts ruled in favor of Girard College. Summarizing the case, the *Philadelphia Evening Bulletin* stated that Judge Robert Bulger of the Orphans Court had ruled "the will could not be changed and that the color ban must remain," and the Pennsylvania State Supreme Court Chief Justice stated "a man's prejudice are a part of his liberty." During the litigation process, white backlash was minimal because the local media did not provide a daily account of the trials. After both defeats, Alexander appealed the decisions and the case reached the United States Supreme Court. On April 29, 1957, the U.S. Supreme Court ruled that Girard College had violated the Fourteenth Amendment, but, according to Joseph P. Gaffney, the Court "didn't decide that these boys are to be admitted." It would be up to a state court to instruct the board on "how to act." Nevertheless, newspapers and journals across the country carried the story. A. W. Dent, president of Dillard University, a historically black college in New Orleans, told Alexander that the *New Orleans Times Picayune* mentioned the case but did not mention Alexander's name. The *Tallahassee Democrat* stated that it was "another crass violation of states' rights in the fact that it overrules a will . . . that the Pennsylvania Supreme Court upheld." An editorial in the *Saturday Evening Post* quoted Michael Perry, an African American from Philadelphia who grew up near the college and was upset that "a sane man's will, regardless of its right or wrong, has been set aside." Martin Luther King Jr. applauded the Supreme Court's decision and declared this "shuts the door in the face of southern states attempting to create private institutions for the education of white youths with the use of tax funds from the whole citizenry of the state." Unfortunately, King's assessment was incorrect, as large number of southern whites abandoned public schools in the South and attended all-white private schools."[19] The defendants appealed the Supreme Court's decision and waited for an answer from the lower courts in Pennsylvania.

During the fall of 1957, the nation's attention focused on Little Rock and Central High School. Three years after the Brown decision, southern states refused to desegregate their schools. After the Supreme Court ruled in April that Girard College had violated the Fourteenth Amendment, a number of whites voiced their concerns to Alexander, the newspapers, and Richardson Dilworth, the mayor. White backlash varied from Dilworth who supported

Alexander politically in order to attract the black vote to racist attacks about the character of black folks. Walter V. Sienkiewicz of Comegy's Food in Philadelphia told Dilworth that "integration will be solved more intelligently if it is not motivated by selfish interests." In September 1957, this person referred to Dilworth as a "Nigger Loving Skunk": "What Philadelphia needs and will have before long is a new White Supremacy party to keep these overbearing niggers in line. [Signed] Disgusted Democrat." Another letter stated, "If you like the Negroes so much why don't you have your Daughter or son marry one. Signed Was a Friend." These whites were upset with Dilworth, who supported Alexander, and many contemplated leaving the party. This backlash was a response to the expanding black political power in Philadelphia, though African Americans were still behind whites in every social category.[20]

Some letters criticized black behavior, a precursor to the underclass debates of the 1980s. For example, one letter to Alexander from a white person who "moved from Strawberry Mansion to Suburbia" declared that she respected Paul Robeson, Ralph Bunche, and Dr. Du Bois, so she and others like her were "not haters." However, she added, "It is said that hundreds of Negroes are fathered every night in Fairmount Park in the summer." In addition, African Americans "are able to get on relief more easily than white people are." In another letter to Alexander, the person commented on the "young negroes . . . disgusting . . . and frightening in their physical strength." Moreover, the letter mentioned her cousin who worked in a hospital where black women were "breeders" and a "white nurse resigned . . . in fear of threats she received from this human scum." A white girl who lived in a black neighborhood wrote a four-page letter describing her neighborhood's shift from "fine colored people" to a new type of black folk. She listed twenty-seven "tendencies" of black people exclusively, such as "Children stealing anything they can lay their hands on," "Fighting and arguing all though the night," and "People sitting on their front porches watching everyone else go to work." She did not sign the letter because she feared for her safety, but she advised Alexander to examine civil rights "from a white person's point of view."[21]

In spite of Alexander's efforts, a year and a half after the U.S. Supreme Court's decision, the local courts in Philadelphia allowed Girard College to be controlled by a private board. The four-year litigation struggled ended in a defeat; by the late fifties, a new cadre of black leaders emerged who castigated Alexander's "exclusive focus on legislative goals and the sole reliance on the leadership of middle-class professionals." In fact, in 1959, some African Americans started to picket outside of Girard College. A dozen years after Alexander wanted Rainey the progressive local president removed from office, mass demonstrations and economic boycotts—tactics that were used during the 1930s—had returned to the civil rights struggle, and Alexander did not believe those tactics were necessary in Philadelphia.[22]

Campaigning for a Judgeship in the Court of Common Pleas

In 1957, Congressman Earl Chudoff, who represented the Fourth District, where 75 percent of voters were black, and was a strong supporter of Alexander's bid to become an ambassador, resigned from Congress in order to become a Court of Common Pleas judge in Philadelphia. Chudoff asked William Green Jr., chair of the Philadelphia Democratic Organization, to support his bid for the judgeship. Green supported Chudoff, who had won the November election. Alexander intimated to the Democratic Party that he was interested in replacing Chudoff as congressman. Alexander did not want to become a congressman, but he used that as a threat to make the Democrats appoint him to the bench.

Chudoff's term on the Court of Common Pleas Court began in January 1958. Four prominent black candidates emerged for the vacant congressional seat: Alexander, a city councilman; J. Austin Norris, on the Board of Revision of Taxes; Reverend Marshall Shepard, a city councilman; Reverend E. Luther Cunningham, on the Civil Service Commission; and Robert Nix Sr., an attorney. Green and the Democratic machine supported Nix because he did not have a political appointment, but there was a power struggle within the Democratic Party. Green was the Democratic city chairman, but John Kelly Sr., a local businessman, was a key power broker in the party. Clark, Dilworth, Kelly, and Alexander were instrumental in the Democratic Reform movement, but they had fallen out of favor in the party. Some believed that Alexander's connection with Clark and Dilworth might hurt his chances of being nominated. Alexander stated in the *Philadelphia Tribune* that many African American and white Democrats did not support him but concluded that "when they cool down a bit and look at the record I have achieved during the last 30 years I will undoubtedly be endorsed by the organization." Alexander was confident that his civil rights activity in Philadelphia would speak for itself. But Eugene Haggerty, sergeant-at-arms for the city council, circulated a rumor that Alexander "was not a 'real organization man.'" Haggerty was running for congress and felt he deserved the nomination because he "gave up the City Councilman spot for Ray Alexander." Haggerty made these remarks about Alexander to get the Democrats to appoint him to magistrate. Two months after Alexander announced his candidacy for Congress, the *Philadelphia Tribune* reported that organized labor and other Democrats were so outraged at Green's decision to support Nix that they formed a "Citizens Committee" opposed to "the high-handed, undemocratic method used in choosing a Congressional candidate for the coming primary." Despite their concerns, the Democratic Party supported Nix.[24]

In 1940, 1952, 1954, and 1956, four black Republicans had run for Congress and lost. Two of the candidates were black attorneys, Edward Henry and Theodore Spaulding. In every election except 1940, Alexander had voted for the white Democratic candidate, Earl Chudoff. After Alexander announced that he was running for Congress, John Saunders, journalist of the *Philadelphia Tribune*, stated that a rumor had circulated that the party bosses had advised Alexander that if he withdrew from the special primary and publicly supported Nix, he would be in a "position to obtain the party's endorsement for the Common Pleas bench." Saunders does not mention the name of the individual who advised Alexander to withdraw from the race, but eleven days after Alexander announced that he was running for Congress, the *Philadelphia Tribune* reported that the "Democratic State Executive Committee" will inform Nix that he received the Party's support. In this same article, Alexander announced his support of Nix and that he could not "reveal my contacts at this time, but I am quite pleased since the law in all it's [sic] ramifications is where my deepest interests lie." Alexander was never interested in becoming a congressman, but he used his political leverage to force the Democratic machine to appoint him to the Court of Common Pleas.[25]

After Chudoff resigned to serve in the Court of Common Pleas, Governor George Leader called a special election for May 20 in order to fill the vacant position until the November election. Green was worried that Nix might not win the special election because of the splits in his party. The anti-Nix and anti-Green faction nominated Harvey Schmidt, a black attorney, who ran as an independent Democrat. Senator Joseph Clark Jr. organized labor and the Baptist Ministers Conference, who all supported Schmidt. The day before the primary, Congressman Green, Nix's greatest supporter, was concerned about the challenge from his own party. Yet in the special election held on May 20, Nix had a landslide victory, but he would have to run in the November general election. The *Philadelphia Tribune* reported that Nix won every black majority district, and during the swearing-in ceremony,

Green stated Nix's "victory means as much to me as my own victory in the Fifth congressional district." After the special election, many of the "independent Democrats" such as Reverend Marshall Shepard stated that they were "interested in electing the entire Democratic slate." Commenting on the historic occasion, Alexander referred to Nix as "a high type man," and he congratulated the voters for electing former Governor George Leader as the Democratic nominee for Senate and nominating his "good friend" David Lawrence to run for governor of Pennsylvania. According to Alexander, "The whole Democratic ticket indicates that this state is interested in progressive government—not the reactionary ruling leadership given our people by the Republicans."[26]

In the November election, Nix ran against the Republican candidate, Cecil B. Moore, a black attorney, originally from West Virginia and a former Marine. Moore served as on the "law enforcement committee" for the Citizens Committee Against Juvenile Delinquency and Its Causes (CCADJ), a grassroots organization that conducted "antitavern pickets" in black neighborhoods in Philadelphia.[27] Nix defeated Cecil B. Moore by thirty-eight thousand votes, and David Lawrence was elected governor. Reporting on the election, Jack Sanders wrote in the *Philadelphia Tribune* that since the black vote had such an impact, "Negro leaders are urging the appointment of Councilman Raymond Pace Alexander to one of the vacancies created on the Common Pleas Court bench."[28] The Democratic Party reform movement promised to remove patronage from city politics, but patronage is a major part of the American political system. Since black votes made the difference in the election, Saunders, the black community, and Alexander argued that Alexander must be appointed to the Common Pleas Court.

Alexander spent the entire year working to get appointed. However, judges were supposed to be recommended by the judiciary committee from the Philadelphia Bar Association. The *Philadelphia Tribune* noted that since 1922 the judiciary committee had supported only three African Americans for judgeships. Becoming a black judge in Philadelphia was extremely difficult. Relying on the Democratic Party was the best opportunity to circumvent the white bar's stranglehold. According to the *Philadelphia Inquirer*, during the fall election, the judiciary committee submitted five names to Governor Leader for judgeship, but Alexander's name was not on the list. However, it reported, "the Governor has adequate precedent for appointing Alexander": numerous Republican governors had appointed lawyers who were not recommended by the judiciary committee. The twenty-member judiciary committee voted the day before the November election; nineteen voted not to add Alexander's name to the list, and one was absent. Back in September, the judiciary committee had recommended eight lawyers and left Alexander off the list. The rejection came as a surprise because, the previous year, "Alexander was one of several lawyers approved for a Common Pleas Court judgeship."[29]

While the Bar Association's judiciary committee did not endorse Alexander, a number of attorneys from Philadelphia supported Alexander and encouraged Leader to appoint him. For example, Joseph Varbalow, a Jewish lawyer from Camden, New Jersey, who described himself as "a Democrat, whose vintage goes back to the days of Woodrow Wilson," had worked with Alexander for over thirty years. He called Alexander "an advocate and champion of the underprivileged." Varbalow and Alexander had worked on an extradition case in New Jersey that involved a "colored youth who had been maltreated and railroaded in the South." The two attorneys won the case with a total of "$3000.00 in court fees." Varbalow stated that Alexander was a well-respected attorney "irrespective of race, religion, or geographic origin." Varbalow believed that Alexander was an exceptional attorney and qualified for the position. Varbalow advised Leader that he could "safely ignore this action of the committee" because most of the members of the bar were not "sympathetic and understand the aggressive pioneering advocacy of the rights of the poor by Mr. Alexander." Varbalow reminded Leader about the courage that President Wilson had demonstrated when he supported Justice Louis Brandeis, whom the American Bar Association (ABA) had opposed because he was Jewish. This three-page letter summarized Alexander's long career and why the local bar association was wrong for not recommending him. James J. Regan, who was white, male, Catholic, and Republican, told Alexander that he was "shocked and dismayed" that the Philadelphia Bar did not endorse him and "deplored the crass ineptitude of so many of our brethren at the Bar." Although Regan did not always share Alexander's views on "law and policy," he recognized that Alexander would be an excellent judge. Regan invited Alexander to give him a call if he needed any assistance. Alexander's work appealed to a broad segment of Philadelphians. His civil rights work had an impact on the city and among his black and white colleagues, but those few white attorneys who failed to support Alexander still wielded considerable influence.[30]

Alexander's appointment was a last-minute decision. According to John Saunders, Leader refused to appoint Alexander because the judiciary committee did not endorse him. Before Leader relinquished his power to Governor-elect David Lawrence, he gave a speech in Philadelphia. Congressman Green attended Lawrence's speech at the Bellevue Stratford Hotel. The two men discussed Alexander's situation, and, according to Saunders, Green told Leader, "if you don't appoint Alexander, we will support Alexander against your appointee in the next Primary election—and beat him!" Green also told Leader that he would get Lawrence to appoint Alexander and Leader would not get the credit for appointing the first black Common Pleas Court judge. Green's political influenced worked. The front page of the *Philadelphia Tribune* presented two stories on Alexander's installation as judge. On January 5, 1958, two thousand people from "all walks of life as well as a cross section of white citizens" attended Alexander's swearing-in ceremony at City Hall. Alexander borrowed a robe from Judge Louis Levinthall, and a number of prominent judges and lawyers attended the historic event. Alexander stated: "This is the dawn of a new era. I consider this honor not as a personal one, but as a symbolic recognition of an ever struggling and rapidly advancing race." Most of the participants were African American; some were former clients, and others may have been city employees who were keenly aware of how much race relations had improved in Philadelphia. It took Alexander thirty-six years to become a judge. He had to fight to the end and use all the political leverage that he had acquired in Philadelphia. Now, Alexander could use his power as a judge to improve race relations in the city. Once Alexander became a judge, he had to stop practicing law, and he closed his practice. It was the end of an institution, but the beginning of new struggle.[31]

Addressing Juvenile Delinquency and Poverty

After World War II, an emerging youth culture emerged across the nation. These young Americans aged thirteen to nineteen were a new demographic boom for American businesses but a growing concern for adults. Adults were concerned about middle-class white youth as well as poor and working-class black youth and about girls as well as boys. More teenagers were spending time together in high schools and developing a popular culture of their own that took a rebellious stance toward the dominant adult society; rhythm and blues and rock and roll music were seen as dangerous, in part because they were sexually explicit with these youths who, regardless of race, had time to get into trouble. Adults feared an epidemic of teenage pregnancy. Whites' concern stemmed in part from the rapid movement of mothers into the paid labor force; white women were coming to resemble black women in their pursuit of employment after marriage and motherhood, an economic imperative that contradicted the prevailing cultural norm that mothers ought to stay at home. These fears were not so prevalent in the black community, where mothers had always been in the labor force, some households were disproportionately headed by women, and young people were more likely to drop out of school and have difficulty finding jobs. Black parents in Philadelphia were also seriously concerned about their children, but they tended to worry more about the poor quality of most public high schools, the lack of recreational facilities open to blacks and located in the black community, the high unemployment rate, and the bad influences to which children and youth were subjected by the numerous "taprooms" (taverns) and illegal enterprises (such as numbers running, other forms of gambling, and the drug trade) that were visible on the streets in black neighborhoods.

During the late 1950s, juvenile delinquency—strictly defined as a tendency among youths to commit criminal offenses but more loosely understood as the disorder that resulted from young people's disconnection from school and work and their lack of adult supervision—was perceived as a major problem in Philadelphia and the nation. As a Common Pleas Judge, Alexander was in a good position to understand the phenomenon of juvenile delinquency in the black community. Alexander dealt with many types of criminal offenses, seeing youths and others who had been charged with crimes running the gamut from petty offences (such as loitering or disorderly conduct) to very serious acts (such as murder), at all stages of the legal process from arraignment through trial and sentencing. He linked young people's legal offenses to racial inequality and poverty, and he vehemently opposed tough sentencing policies. Alexander attributed the increasing number of black youthful offenders to the major structural transformations in post-World War II Philadelphia.

After World War II, North, West, and South Philadelphia contained three large black neighborhoods that contained a larger percentage of unemployment, crime, poor housing, and poor schools than white neighborhoods. As a result, black young men in Philadelphia had a higher crime and incarceration rate than white males. The *Philadelphia Tribune* reported that "a crime wave" had hit the city and that juvenile delinquency was a major problem in the black community. The newspaper contained numerous headlines and stories about drug-related crime. In 1956, E. Washington Rhodes, editor of the *Philadelphia Tribune*, published a three-week series titled "The

Noose Is Crime," a study of black crime in Philadelphia. In 1956, African Americans comprised 10 percent of the population but committed 40 percent of the crime. Moreover, African Americans between the ages of seven and seventeen were 23 percent of the population but represented 55 percent of the juvenile delinquency cases. The city's black leadership was divided about the causes of crime in the black community. In April 1957, the *Philadelphia Tribune* reported that Reverend E. Luther Cunningham stated, "Negroes should be arrested for standing on street corners." "Militant attorney" Cecil B. Moore responded to Cunningham's statement: "Those handkerchief head Negroes would sell anybody down the river to satisfy their own craving for power." Some African Americans sided with Cunningham and others with Moore. Alexander stated in the *Philadelphia Tribune* that black juveniles needed a "social education" because a lack of education was responsible for crime, but he agreed with Cunningham that the police needed "to crack down on those smart alecks, those freshies, those jitter bugs and zoot suiters." Alexander was concerned with the growing crime among Philadelphia's black youth. There was a segment of black youth who committed crimes and needed to be arrested, but whites should not assume all young black men are criminals. Moreover, when the police arrest young African American males, he did not want the white press to put him "in a position to be making apologies for their conduct."[32]

After his first month in court, Alexander was appalled at the high number of black criminals and the system's failure to handle first-time offenders in a constructive manner. Alexander created an alternative probationary system called the Spiritual Rehabilitation Program. He stated that the defendants brought before him ranged from "many hardened criminals with long police records" to first-time offenders. The new program concentrated on first-time offenders, whom Alexander described as adults from all "races and social backgrounds who, had good souls, and good prospects of rehabilitation." Alexander was not going to try to rehabilitate long-time offenders or violent criminals, but he realized that the current system failed to prevent crime and rehabilitate offenders before they embarked on a criminal career. Labor, church, and civic organizations supported the SRP. Alexander created an executive committee composed of clergy and social workers that recruited volunteers to work with offenders. After offenders met their court-assigned probation officer, they met with a church-sponsored committee who worked with them individually. The SRP received national attention from the press because of its innovative character, which combined the ways in which crime was understood by social work experts with the tradition of mutual aid that flourished both within the black community and among predominantly white religious organizations. The *Baltimore Afro American* mistakenly referred to the SRP as a "probation plan for Negro defenders." The *Sunday Evening Bulletin* reported that Alexander stated that "poverty and crime we will have with us always, and this was not a Negro Problem, but a problem of the entire community of all its citizens." He maintained that crime did not have "a particular color, religion, or nationality" and that churches and synagogues must work together to decrease crime.[33]

After Alexander announced the SRP, he was a guest on a local television program called *The Bulletin Forum* to discuss crime and punishment in Philadelphia. Alexander declared that he was more concerned with "the weaknesses or disease in our society that produces juvenile delinquents and the criminal element" than with meting out harsh punishments. The rise in crime coincided with an increase in the black population in urban areas. Alexander linked the increase in crime rates to poor education, unemployment, racism, and poverty. He opposed the "get tough policy," which was based on the "fallacious assumption" that having a curfew law and building more jails deterred crime. Alexander attributed Philadelphia's get-tough policy to "police pressure, public hysteria," and the press. Judges, prosecutors, and politicians used urban crime as a political issue to advance their own careers and to appease the whites who feared black criminals. According to Alexander, Philadelphia spent forty-two million dollars on crime in 1959, a "shocking admission of our waste of money on the wrong end of this whole problem." As a black judge and criminal lawyer, who grew up poor in Philadelphia, Alexander was cognizant of the origins of crime and tried to create a program that prevented it. The majority of the judicial system had remained white, and, in addition to poverty, racism was responsible for the higher crime rate as white police offers and jurors gave tougher sentences to African Americans.[34]

The SRP program started in November 1959. Churches and synagogues were supposed to be the major financial contributors and to provide progress reports and evaluations. The majority of the offenders came from Alexander's court. After conviction, individuals volunteered for the program. Most of the participants had failed to complete high school and were not permanently employed when they committed their crimes. The 1960 SRP report concluded that "there was a greater emphasis than intended placed on the Negro clergy and congregations." The report cautiously criticized the minimal support received from the Roman Catholic Church and Jewish synagogues, stating tactfully that the Roman Catholic and Jewish communities could have provided "a stronger arm of support." Leaders feared, if they were too critical, those communities would not participate at all. But gentle persuasion did not work. The SRP became an African American affair, and Alexander could rightly have been highly critical of other communities' lack of support. According to the report, only four Roman Catholic defendants who appeared in Alexander's court that year participated in the program. Alexander informed Carl Murphy, editor of the *Baltimore Afro American*, that in 1960, 70 percent of his criminal cases were African Americans. Historically, whites have associated urban crime as a black problem; in Philadelphia, this became a self-fulfilling prophecy.[35]

In 1959, the Pennsylvania Association on Probation, Parole, and Correction, composed of probation officers and administrators, invited Alexander to discuss the problem of crime and punishment in American society. Alexander asked the audience; "What is being done at every level of our social structure to find the causes of this ever present and most disturbing problem?" According to Alexander, judges were overworked and defendants did not receive adequate individual attention for their cases. During sentencing, some judges acted like a "police commissioner . . . and became a mere echo of the crowd shouting for blood." Alexander suggested that private corporations contribute funds to get at the root of the problem, which he defined as "congested neighborhoods, over-crowding, poorly equipped and staffed schools . . . where the social problems of the community are dumped" on overworked teachers.[36]

In a commencement address he gave at William Penn High School in Philadelphia in 1958, Alexander discussed the nexus between education, deindustrialization, racism, unemployment, and crime. Alexander stated, "Never before in history have the distribution and manufacturing industries produced so much with so few people." African Americans who migrated North had been denied anything beyond a rudimentary education in the South, so they were "totally unprepared" for the skilled, technical, and professional jobs that were available in the city. Alexander asked the audience, "Do you blame them? If you do you are unjust." He gave the students an example from court. When a judge asked a black man why he did not support his wife, the man replied, "I can't get a job." The judge declared that if the man did not find a job in two weeks he was going to jail. The man replied that he was "a strong muscle man. And today there is no place in America for strong backs and weak minds." He told the judge what happened to him at a recent job search.

When he arrived at the job site there was a long line of African Americans. This story was a microcosm of the endemic underemployment in the black community.[37]

During the postwar period, Philadelphia lost a large number of manufacturing jobs as industries decentralized and then globalized. As the social history research project directed by Theodore Hershberg has documented, by 1970, Philadelphia lost a large number of manufacturing jobs, and African Americans experienced a higher level of residential and job segregation than white ethnic groups and were overrepresented in low-skilled employment. Alexander's speeches enumerated the structural disadvantages that plagued the black community in northern cities. In 1970, Alexander remarked pointedly: "White America is largely, if not totally, responsible for this terrible condition we are caught up with. Why didn't white Philadelphia see so clearly the handwriting on the wall of what we now see in the 70's way back in the 20's, 30's, 40's and 50's?" Alexander's analysis of poverty and crime identifies the causes, sown during the 1920s, of the 1960s race riots and urban poverty that gave rise to unrest. High unemployment, poor housing, inadequate education, and police brutality were long-term problems for African Americans in Philadelphia, as in other northern and western cities, but white politicians had failed to address the them.[38]

Debating Direct Action for Civil Rights

Just a month after Alexander was inaugurated as Common Pleas Court judge in February 1960, the direct action phase of the civil rights movement began in Greensboro, North Carolina. Five years earlier, the Montgomery Bus Boycott had served as a catalyst for the southern movement, but after the four black college students staged a lunch counter sit-in to protest the policy of not serving black customers, a new phase of mass mobilization began. A number of black middle-class leaders, including Thurgood Marshall and Roy Wilkins of the NAACP, vehemently opposed the student-led demonstrations. Both men were more comfortable with the litigation approach. However, as the ranks of student protestors swelled, so did their need for legal assistance. "Since March our lawyers have gone into court in behalf of more than 1600 students," wrote Thurgood Marshall to Alexander, requesting a contribution for the NAACP Legal Defense Fund. Marshall vowed that these young people "will not live lives crippled by second-class citizenship." Alexander contributed fifty dollars to the cause and praised the students' effort, declaring that the students "shame the faces of so called law abiding white people in the bigoted, bitter, hostile South." In November, Martin Luther King Jr. asked Alexander to join the Committee to Support the Southern Freedom Struggle, an interracial organization that included A. Philip Randolph, Harry Belafonte, Sidney Poitier, and Eleanor Roosevelt. Alexander and Randolph represented liberal civil rights leadership. Like King, Alexander advocated integration, civil rights, equal opportunity, and interracial cooperation.[39]

To mark the one hundredth anniversary of the Emancipation Proclamation, African American civil rights advocates adopted the slogan "Free in '63." In January, *Ebony*, a black magazine, selected Judge Alexander as one of the hundred most famous black leaders. According to Adam Green, the magazine had an "obsession with stories on 'the first, the only, the best' in black life." Instead of highlighting the negative impact of racial discrimination, *Ebony* magazine provided black readers with inspirational figures who made an impact on America. During the same month, the *Philadelphia Tribune* published a front-page feature on Alexander and black attorneys in Philadelphia. The article stated that black lawyers have earned "a level of prestige," but they had a "struggle on two fronts." The black lawyer (who was discussed in the male gender, despite the legal credentials of black women such as Sadie Alexander) had to win acceptance from African Americans and demonstrated his competency to "his white counterpart . . . before sometime hostile juries and unsympathetic courts." The article mentioned the discrimination that Alexander had encountered in Philadelphia and the civil rights cases that he had litigated. "It is said that he never accepted a fee for a civil rights cases," the *Philadelphia Tribune* reported. Alexander made this assertion on numerous occasions, but in truth it requires qualification. Alexander did not accept fees for any of his public accommodation cases, but he did accept money for criminal cases such as the Trenton Six case, in which civil rights was a key issue.[40]

The civil rights movement in the South had an impact in Philadelphia. The black press reported on the movement, and the young activists inspired black leaders in Philadelphia. In January 1963, Cecil B. Moore was sworn in as the president of the Philadelphia Branch of the NAACP. Moore had grown up in a middle-class family in West Virginia, graduated from Bluefield State College, which trained black teachers, and then worked as a salesman for Atlanta Life Insurance. During World War II, Moore joined the Marines. After leaving the service, he moved to Philadelphia, attended Temple Law

School at night, passed the bar in 1951, joined the Republican Party, and ran for Congress in 1958. Moore admired Adam Clayton Powell Jr., the controversial and flamboyant black congressman from Harlem. If an African American committed a crime, these men did not apologize to whites, and they were not afraid to make comments that made white people nervous. Their style was more confrontational than that of leaders who sought to persuade whites to support their civil rights agenda; they aimed to pressure whites to concede their demands. Many younger and working-class African Americans who experienced police brutality, unemployment, and racism came to believe that the strategy of litigation, legislation, and the formation of interracial coalitions espoused by black middle-class leaders and practiced by the NAACP black middle class had failed to improve their situation substantially. From 1963 to 1968, Moore's activism in Philadelphia epitomized the militant new style of leadership that was emerging in mass movements across the country. Many African Americans who had grown tired of the rhetoric of racial progress that was not followed by concrete gains believed that direct action produced results. As Countryman observed, Moore advocated "all-black protests that used confrontational language and tactics on trade-union-style picket lines." Mass demonstrations in Philadelphia resembled civil rights demonstrations in the South, but tended to focus on expanding employment opportunities and asserting control of black neighborhoods and local institutions. Moore's criticized established black leaders such as Alexander, occasionally condemning them as "Uncle Toms" who cared more about conciliating white people and advancing their own careers than about improving the lives of the majority of black people.[41]

Another major issue in urban America was urban renewal. Urban renewal had begun to earn the nickname "Negro removal" because it was carried out in ways that discriminated against poor black citizens. Blacks were displaced from their neighborhoods and were not provided with new affordable housing. Criticism of urban renewal policies and practices was developed enough that it seemed crucial to some black citizens to have substantial control over the entire process, starting with the research that could be used to justify destroying whole neighborhoods. The first major disagreement between Moore and Alexander was over a $1.7 million Ford Foundation-funded study in North Philadelphia. The Philadelphia Council for Community Advancement (PCCA) stated in the *Philadelphia Tribune* that the study was designed to investigate the conditions in North Philadelphia, which had the "worst substandard housing and was a neglected section of the city." In December

1962, the Philadelphia Council for Community Advancement (PCCA) hired Samuel Dash, a prominent white attorney, who grew up poor in Philadelphia. Dash was a Democrat and worked with former mayor Richardson Dilworth. Moore demanded that an African American be chosen instead; if he were not replaced by a black director, Moore threatened, the NAACP would boycott Ford Motors, but the Ford Foundation was governed by liberals and independent of Ford Motors.[42]

After Moore made this demand, Judge Alexander and other prominent African Americans in Philadelphia, including his wife Sadie, Congressman Robert N. C. Nix Sr., attorney J. Austin Norris, and E. Washington Rhodes, signed a petition supporting Dash and denouncing Moore. This group was composed of upper-middle-class professionals whose average age was sixty-five; they represented the New Negro generation who had been in the forefront of the civil rights struggle in Philadelphia for the previous forty years. Alexander stated in the *Philadelphia Tribune* that Moore's flamboyant and confrontational style "presented a false image of Negroes" to whites. Moore replied that it was "pathetic that allegedly prominent Negroes should direct their energies to attack the NAACP." He argued that the NAACP was trying to help the black community and that other black leaders should not attack the organization. Countryman notes that Moore received support from the *Philadelphia Independent,* whose readers were critical of the cautious black leadership. In March 1963, Moore led "twenty-five pickets" to increase the number of African Americans on the PCCA executive staff. In 1965, Reverend William H. Gray Jr. of Bright Hope Baptist Church, recalled in an interview published in the *Evening Bulletin* that he had refused to sign Alexander's letter because there were "strong feelings in my church on both sides." The controversy between Moore and Alexander illustrates tensions that emerged between the New Negro generation and the new black leadership of the 1960s. According to the *Philadelphia Tribune,* Alexander and the committee agreed with Moore that the PCCA should hire more African Americans, but Alexander did not "agree with his method to achieve his end." Both men wanted African Americans in decision-making power, but Alexander sought to persuade white people that it would be to everyone's advantage to hire an African American. Moore made demands on the power structure and mobilized people in the black community to support those demands; he rejected interracial coalitions, criticized black middle-class leadership as overly cautious, and advocated mass organization and direct action as means of making change.[43]

Moore's protest and demonstrations attracted more participants and received more press. The *Philadelphia Tribune* reported that all the "men on the streets" supported Moore. Paul Lemarck says that Moore "denounced whites," referred to established black leaders as "Uncle Toms," and developed a "populist leadership" of grassroots activists. This group of black leaders was not connected to the white power structure and relied primarily upon the black community. Alexander represented the mainstream civil rights group who formed pragmatic relationships with white liberals. By the 1960s, older mainstream black leaders such as Alexander were caught in a trap. The government used their success to illustrate racial progress but refused to make substantial changes in accord with their political agenda. As the civil rights movement progressed, support from white liberals decreased, working-class white resistance increased, and the black community demanded equality now.[44]

Alexander had certainly used mass mobilization in the past, but at this moment, when he thought black citizens could wield some political and economic power, he seems to have been concerned about retaining support from white liberal allies. In view of what happened in Philadelphia when fiscally conservative and racially reactionary white ethnic leaders won control of the city, it's reasonable to argue that Alexander's view was borne out by future events. Moore's confrontational mode was effective in mobilizing masses of black people and winning a few concessions, but not at making institutional or structural change. Unfortunately, Alexander's and Moore's shared awareness of the central importance of economics to racial inequality did not enable either of them to devise strategies and tactics that addressed this dimension of race. In that regard, though, they were no different from civil rights leaders across the country, militant and moderate alike, whose best efforts to promote economic justice were met with a positive response only when programs such as expanded access to education affected relatively few white people and produced a small black middle class, not when they would have threatened white working-class people's privileges of living in exclusive neighborhoods and holding reasonably well-paid, stable jobs with benefits. Whites (at least white men) seem to have thought they owned these public goods exclusively, and nobody—including white liberals who thought of themselves as the national leadership class—figured out how to persuade the majority of white Americans to redistribute these assets in a more just manner. So the state and the economy turned out to play crucial roles, just as Alexander himself understood by the late 1950s. The fact that the militant civil rights movement went around him in its militant tactics does not mean it went ahead of him in actual achievements.

The feud between Moore and Alexander was tactical. They agreed on goals; equal opportunity in education, employment and housing, and democratic representation in the major institutions that affected the quality of people's lives. The two leaders also exemplified a difference in style that was as much generational as political. New Negroes like Alexander had opened doors for their generation and laid the basis for the Black Power Movement, by increasing expectations for younger African Americans, but when they were not met, younger black leaders resorted to new tactics. Black Philadelphians born after World War II were frustrated with the slow pace of progress toward racial equality, and militant black leaders like Moore articulated their impatience.

1964, Year of Crisis

In January 1964, retired baseball star, Jackie Robinson, wrote guest editorials for the *Philadelphia Tribune*. According to Robinson, northern white liberals viewed the "Negro Revolution as a sectional revolution"; therefore, white liberals and even Alexander had supported mass demonstrations in the South. However, "when a Negro protests against conditions in the backyard of the liberals their shoes begins to pinch." Robinson's insights were correct. Robinson played for the Brooklyn Dodgers, lived in New York City, and witnessed the impact of northern-style racial discrimination.[45]

By 1964, the southern violence and white backlash had an impact on James Baldwin, whom many middle-class whites and blacks admired. His earlier works such as *Go Tell It on The Mountain*, an autobiographical novel, discussed his coming of age in America. However, *Blues for Mr. Charlie* represented Baldwin's disgust with southern violence. In May 1964, while in New York to attend a meeting, Alexander went to see the play. According to *Newsweek*, the play was loosely based on the 1955 horrific lynching of Emmett Till, a fifteen-year-old black boy from Chicago who was lynched in Mississippi for whistling at a white woman. The reviewer stated that the play was full of racial stereotypes, such as the "Uncle Tom, wise mammy, Southern white liberal, and the southerner who lusts after Negresses." The article concluded that James Baldwin "has become a Negro chauvinist" because he presented stereotypical characters, specifically southern whites who despised blacks and paternalistic white liberals. After Alexander saw the play, he sent the editor of the *New York Times* a four-page review titled "To Sir (James Baldwin) with Deep Regrets." Alexander stated he "made one mistake"; he should have returned to Philadelphia instead of seeing the play. Alexander castigated Baldwin for overemphasizing the "hate of the Negro for the white man" and for using white and black stereotypes. Alexander wanted Baldwin to portray segregation in relation to the "social, economic, political, and educational facts of American life." Alexander contended that Baldwin's play implied that "there is no true white friend of the Negro, only phony liberals." Alexander argued that *Blues for Mr. Charlie* was "more of a liability to us than demonstrations such as the stall-in fiasco, at the first day of the World's Fair."[46] During intermission, Alexander spoke to a white Presbyterian minister who remarked, "I would have a great difficulty in supporting my stand on Civil Rights for the Negro in my community" if his congregation saw the play. The white minister's reaction to Baldwin's play is what Alexander feared—losing support from whites or at the least making a moderate white anti–civil rights. Alexander disliked Baldwin's play so much that he wanted to participate in the Mississippi Freedom Summer, the massive voter registration campaign that drew student volunteers from the North to support grassroots organizing in the South's most oppressed rural black communities.[47]

Two weeks after his scathing critique of Baldwin's play, Alexander sent Martin Luther King Jr. a telegram asking him what role he could play in the movement. King suggested to Alexander that he could participate "in a direct action confrontation of segregation," give a speech in a city where they were demonstrating, or contribute funds to the movement. Alexander asked his longtime friend Sidney Redmond, an attorney from St. Louis, about his desire to march in Mississippi. Redmond reminded Alexander that he was "a judge and was expected to follow the law." If Alexander participated in a march, he would not be able to "preside at . . . a hearing" in Philadelphia where there "might be demonstrations;" he would have to recuse himself from similar cases in the future. Redmond believed that it was unusual and would be counterproductive for a judge to participate in a march. Three days later, Alexander received a letter from Charles A. Hall, a black attorney in Jackson, Mississippi, stating that he was "concerned" with Alexander's plan to march in Mississippi. Baker understood Alexander's desires "to be a more active participant in our nation's struggle"; however, he argued that Alexander's most important role in the movement was ensuring justice for demonstrators in Philadelphia. Hall asked, "Who *really* gave these youngsters the courage they are showing now?" Protests and demonstrations needed young people, and civil rights activists needed black judges when they were arrested and appeared in court. Hall cautioned Alexander about the heat of the Mississippi summer and reminded him that the conditions were not suitable for someone of Alexander's age. He emphasized that Alexander contributed in numerous ways to the civil rights struggle and assured him that "your contribution in Philadelphia is bigger than what you could contribute to Mississippi." Hall's letter demonstrates his understanding of the significance of local struggles in the North as well as the South to the civil rights movement. While Freedom Summer captured the nation's attention, civil rights activities in Philadelphia and the nation continued as well.[48]

Alexander responded to King's letter in mid-July, two weeks after President Lyndon B. Johnson signed the Civil Rights Act of 1964 that prohibited discrimination in hiring in government jobs. Alexander suggested to King that African Americans should start "rethinking a strategy and a new approach." According to Alexander, Goldwater's speech at the Republican National Convention in San Francisco denouncing "all moderates and liberals," even in his own party, demonstrated his right-wing extremism. Alexander feared that if Goldwater were elected he might allow "the army or permit vigilantes to 'cut down' individuals who were *striking*, or *picketing* or *peacefully marching* or *protesting*." Alexander took Redmond and Baker's advice and informed King he would not participate in Freedom Summer because "as a judge I am sworn to uphold the written law—which law may indeed be both unjust and unconstitutional." However, he supported King's civil disobedience campaigns in the South and suggested that he start a committee called the "Alliance for Better Racial Understanding," an interracial organization composed of middle-class professionals who would present speeches to all Americans on race relations to all Americans. Alexander believed this organization would "*cease* the *needless demonstrations,* stall-ins, uncalled lie downs especially in the North which bring discredit upon us. *Lets stop this for the duration of the campaign*"—that is, until the presidential election. Alexander made a thousand-dollar donation to King and SCLC. The organization he projected was in line with his generation's liberal approach to civil rights; middle-class black and white professionals talking about race relations would persuade whites to relinquish power in order to realize American ideals of equality. At the same time, his caution about arousing opposition during a crucial national election made him especially anxious about the conservative backlash that disruptive tactics might provoke.[49]

King thanked Alexander for his financial contribution, but he stated that the SCLC could not start another committee. King suggested that the civil rights movement needed a campaign that included all liberals, instead of running a campaign "encouraging the fear of Fascism." King told Alexander that "we will be extremely cautious when it comes to dealing with demonstrations" and did not suggest that demonstrations should cease in the North. Alexander's letter did not mention any names, but his critique of northern demonstrations was a shot at Cecil B. Moore. Alexander feared that northern demonstrations only intensified white backlash among white northern Democrats. Most northern whites supported the civil rights movement in the South, but they preferred to ignore the existence of racism and poverty in their own cities.[50]

In the summer of 1964, Alexander's fears about the Democrats losing the election came to fruition. In July, President Lyndon B. Johnson signed the historic Civil Rights Act of 1964, but the celebration was cut short as racial tensions in the North worsened. A race riot broke out in Harlem that lasted for five days, and weeks later another riot broke out in Rochester, New York. According to *Time*, after the Harlem Riot, King met with Robert Wagner, mayor of New York City. King, Roy Wilkins of the NAACP, John Lewis of SNCC, and A. Philip Randolph decided to "voluntarily observe a broad curtailment, if not total moratorium, of all mass marches, mass picketing and mass demonstrations until after Election Day, next Nov. 3." An editorial in the *Philadelphia Inquirer* titled "Rights and Rioting" referred to Alexander's July 20 letter to King. The article agreed with Alexander's suggestion that King should continue with nonviolence but must cease "needless demonstrations." However, the author misquoted Alexander, who wanted demonstrations to end in northern cities but not in the South. Alexander had viewed the civil rights movement as a southern movement, but, similarly to northern white liberals, he vehemently opposed mass demonstrations in the North. Many whites failed to see that the northern race riots were in response to civil rights violations in the black community, but Alexander believed that Moore's protests in Philadelphia were undesirable because they might push working-class white ethnics to vote for Goldwater.[51]

A week before King and the civil rights leaders publicly requested a moratorium on mass demonstrations, the *Philadelphia Evening Bulletin* published Alexander's letter to King. The editorial titled "Alexander Asks For Freeze on Rights Protests" agreed with the other civil rights leaders that mass demonstrations only improved Goldwater's chances of becoming president.

Ester Eyre from North Philadelphia was surprised by Alexander's stance. She reminded Alexander how he had obtained his judgeship—"because and only because you fought for it." Eyre thought that Alexander's recommendations were "based on the emotion of fear" that Goldwater and the extremists would win if demonstrations continued. To her, Alexander's position seemed self-contradictory; Alexander's letter implied that "we must not protest and yet we must not remain silent!!!!!! and he can't have it both ways." However, Alexander had relied on his political clout, which was based on the black vote and his service to the black community in elected office, to attain his position on the bench. Unlike black leaders far from the halls of power, he had considerable political savvy. Lois Mark Stalvey, a "white mother of three" stated that "the average white citizen should not criticize the tactics of the Negro drive for equality until we, as whites" improve schools, housing and employment opportunities. Stalvey agreed with Alexander that, if Goldwater were elected, it would "increase the hopelessness in the Negro community, and lead to an overwhelming wave of rioting." She suggested that the civil rights movement should concentrate on a less controversial issue such as voter registration. Most moderates and liberals agreed that the November election was very important and that demonstrations should cease. This was a major problem with the liberal component of the civil rights movement. Even though President Johnson supported and signed two major civil rights laws, liberals conceded too much to the right wing. The cautious stance by Alexander and other leaders who recommended a cessation in demonstrations during the election campaign only intensified the growing ideological gap in the black community. Protest leaders such as Moore wanted to maintain the pressure, while Alexander and others wanted to cease demonstrations and on good faith hope the Democrats would continue to support civil rights.[52]

One month after the passage of the Civil Rights Act of 1964, and almost a year after the historic March on Washington, a race riot occurred in Philadelphia. On August 28, 1964, a team with one black and one white police officer received a call to check on a stalled car in North Philadelphia. A black woman, Odessa Bradford, and her friend had appeared to be in an argument. The white police officer tried to force Bradford from the car, but a black spectator saw him abuse Bradford and threw a rock at the white officer. Another black resident saw the event and yelled that the white cop had killed a pregnant black woman. Police brutality was such a serious grievance in black neighborhoods that a mere rumor could trigger a riot. For the next three nights, rioting and looting took place in North Philadelphia. Philadelphia mayor James Tate imposed a curfew and closed all liquor stores and tap-rooms in the area. He also ordered the police not to abuse the rioters. Tate understood that it was politically expedient to appear empathetic rather than antagonistic to the rioters. On August 29, Tate called black leaders to visit the riot-torn area. The *Philadelphia Inquirer* reported that Alexander, Moore, and Congressman Nix went about on "sound trucks" broadcasting messages in a vain effort to regain control. In fact, Moore was attending the Democratic National Convention in Atlantic City, New Jersey. Alexander admitted later to Maurice Litman, editor of the *Philadelphia Inquirer*, that he "implored the people to cease, desist and go home, without success, I regret to say I left heart broken and in tears." Marcus Foster of the YMCA stated, "Bad as the rioting was wrong," it was "insignificant when measured against centuries of injustice." Black leaders understood the problems that existed in northern cities, but most agreed rioting was not the answer. Even the "militant" Moore denounced the riots; however, he asked in the *Philadelphia Inquirer*, why does black leadership have to "accept responsibility for Negro criminals?" In other words, whites should be intelligent enough not to indict the entire black community. But getting black leaders to warn African Americans to return home was the strategy that local authorities used to end riots. Alexander and Moore knew that all of the rioters were not criminals. The majority of looters were law-abiding citizens who viewed this tumultuous moment as an oppor-tunity to strike back at the system. The *Philadelphia Inquirer* reported that the 1964 race riot was caused by "alleged police brutality and lack of jobs" and that most of the rioters were young African American men.[53]

A week later, the *Philadelphia Inquirer* printed a front-page picture of what Alexander referred to as "five kind-hearted, Christian Negro women" who served coffee and hot dogs to the black and white police officers who worked during the riot in North Philadelphia. Alexander stated to Maurice Litman that London and Paris newspapers reprinted this picture, and fortu-nately African Americans in Philadelphia did not face "growling police dogs and high pressure hoses," as demonstrators did in Birmingham, Alabama. He was differentiating the southern movement from the northern move-ment. The Philadelphia police department did not use dogs, but there were instances of abuse when they arrested some of the rioters. Alexander compli-mented the editor of the *Philadelphia Inquirer* for their September 9 feature, "We Salute Them Proudly," applauding the newspaper's effort to illustrate the "respectable and upright lives" that the five African Americans women represented. Alexander was concerned that the entire white community viewed all African Americans as rioters, and this image of respectable black women would signal to whites that most African Americans were exceptional citizens. After saying that he did not want to explain the cause of the riot, Alexander did so anyway. Most whites never visited a "Negro ghetto with overcrowding, stopped-up plumbing and single parent families, these were not exaggerations." Economic deprivation and poor social conditions generated resentment and anger that were stirred up into destructive forms by irresponsible leaders. Alexander stated that "The Negro's greatest handicap is the loud, profane, and boastful type of leadership that leads the masses of Negroes." Alexander was referring to Moore, who after the riot declared in *Time* magazine that he was "the goddam boss." Alexander believed that Moore's controversial statement prohibited whites from supporting civil rights, and the civil rights movement needed responsible leaders like King, Wilkins, and himself, who worked with white liberals and touched "the more, ethical, and Christian conscience" of white America. They, he believed, were more effective in advancing the interests of African Americans than those whose militancy aroused the masses to act destructively.[54]

When the modern civil rights movement gathered momentum in the postwar period, the New Negro generation of black leaders such as Alexander, had attained public office as judges or local politicians or leaders of social organizations. Although Alexander could not participate in marches and demonstrations, he continued his civil rights struggle in Philadelphia from the bench by addressing civil rights issues, crime, poverty, and employment. As a criminal lawyer, he saw how poor black defendants were mistreated and sought to prevent juvenile delinquency from leading to a criminal career. This type of approach would not be on the front page of the newspaper or on the daily news broadcast; it was not dramatic but involved people-to-people, long-term, social interaction. What made Alexander most upset was that most younger activists had no idea how racist Philadelphia had been and how much had been achieved by previous generations of activists and advocates.

In 1964, a decade after the Supreme Court declared racial segregation unconstitutional, whites were still responding with massive resistance. The summer after President Johnson signed the Civil Rights Act of 1964, northern cities were convulsed by race riots. Despite the costs to the black community in deaths, injuries, and damages, they did call public attention to the problems that existed in inner-city black communities. For example, white journalist Drew Pearson of the *Philadelphia Inquirer* traveled to Washington, D.C., to interview Adam Clayton Powell Jr., the congressman from Harlem.

Pearson explained that "with riots devastating Philadelphia," he asked Powell for suggestions on how to improve race relations. Powell stated: "The Civil Rights Act is of no value to the Negro in the North."[55] In northern cities, the most powerful forms of racial discrimination were economic, and black political power was not sufficient to overturn many of its most malignant forms in the labor and housing markets, as well as the public school system. After the Philadelphia race riot, Alexander wrote numerous letters to several newspapers to convince white liberals that militant black leaders such as Moore were not the real leaders of the black community. Moreover, his writings and speeches increasingly addressed poverty and the economic inequality, two issues that King and Black Power leaders focused on during the second half of the sixties.

Chapter Six

A NEW NEGRO JUDGE IN
BLACK POWER AMERICA, 1965–1974

The June 1968 celebration of the United States Supreme Court's ruling that Girard College had to desegregate was full of ironies for Raymond Pace Alexander. The victory rally was a joyous occasion for the black community. Cecil B. Moore had led mass demonstrations protesting segregation, called "Operation Girard," since 1965. Alexander, who had begun putting political and legal pressure on Girard a decade earlier, did not support Moore's demonstrations. Moore, a self-styled militant, castigated him as a do-nothing, middle-class black leader. In spite of their differences, Moore invited Alexander to the ceremony to provide a historical account of the Girard case. The crowd booed when Moore called Alexander to the podium, but Moore told the crowd to stop. According to Gerald Early, a Philadelphia native and English professor at Washington University, "Moore was a large enough man to realize that Alexander had deserved something infinitely more for his extraordinary effort than just another form of heartbreak." Between 1963 and 1968, Moore and Alexander castigated each other over the direction of the civil rights struggle in Philadelphia. However, a decade earlier, two thousand Philadelphians, a majority of them African American, had attended Judge Alexander's swearing-in ceremony at City Hall. In 1958, Alexander was a race hero, but in 1968, he had been transformed into an upper middle-class "token"

who was out of touch with the masses. The booing crowd was not cognizant of Alexander's contributions to the long civil rights struggle in Philadelphia. A new generation of leaders like Moore and Stokely Carmichael
(now Kwame Toure) of the Student Non-violent Coordinating Committee
(SNCC) had emerged to replace Alexander and moderate civil rights leaders
such as Bayard Rustin and Roy Wilkins.[1]

As the civil rights movement gained momentum, the leaders of national
civil rights organizations, referred to as the "Big Six," included Martin
Luther King Jr. of the Southern Christian Leadership Council (SCLC); Roy
Wilkins of the National Association for the Advancement of Colored People
(NAACP); Whitney Young of the National Urban League (NUL); James
Farmer of the Congress of Racial Equality (CORE); John Lewis (SNCC);
and A. Philip Randolph, longtime leader of the Brotherhood of Sleeping
Car Porters (now heading the A. Philip Randolph Institute). These lead-
ers formed strategic alliances with labor and, most important, with Lyndon
Johnson. In June 1965, Alexander published an article in *Negro Digest*, "The
Five Civil Rights Groups Should Combine Forces Now," suggesting that the
major organizations pool their resources, create a common ground, write "in
a joint statement a series of resolutions of demands in every area of human
rights," and take the resolutions to the federal government.[2]

Roy Wilkins recalled that at the height of the civil rights movement's
power, when its agenda had come to define national politics, the movement
seemed to be collapsing from within: "Between the beginning of August 1965
and the end of the following year, it sometimes seemed as if the roof had
caved in and the floor was about to give way, too. A new generation short
on history and long on spleen chased after me and the N.A.A.C.P. day and
night. Some said we were just too old, others that we were playing Uncle Tom
for white America. If the attacks hadn't been so unfair, so divorced from the
actual record, so patently one-sided, they would have hurt more; as it was,
they still hurt plenty."[3] Many in the black community viewed the Big Six
and local leaders such as Alexander as more concerned with not offending
whites than with obtaining justice for African Americans. As Wilkins stated,
the new generation was "short on history" and not aware of the central role
Alexander and the NAACP had played during the civil rights movement.
From the 1920s to the 1960s, black leaders had fought to improve the quality
of life for African Americans in northern cities. Using the legal system, boycotts, voting, and demonstrations, and forming coalitions with white radicals
during the 1930s and 1940s and with white liberals after World War II, black

activists had measurably improved race relations in cities such as Philadelphia and the nation.

Yet, African Americans continued to experience higher rates of unemployment, poverty, incarceration, and crime than whites. This paradox of black progress and stagnation existing simultaneously continues to be the major conundrum in post-civil rights America. In 1964, the federal government passed the Civil Rights Act and President Johnson's War on Poverty program began. In August 1965, Johnson signed the historic Voting Rights Act. Ironically, in both 1964 and 1965, race riots occurred in northern cities not too long after the ink dried on those two historic policies. The riots shocked many Americans who thought that this legislation marked the end of the civil rights movement. In reality, those two acts ended only de jure segregation, and 1965 represented the beginning of the next phase in the fight for equality, eradicating institutionalized racism and poverty.

Black Power was a response to the white liberal retreat from racial and economic justice. Regarding Black Power as a mere slogan, Alexander and most moderate black civil rights leaders despised the term. But they had more sympathy with Black Power as an ideology that addressed the limits of American liberalism. As longtime civil rights leader Julian Bond notes, "We did not abandon liberalism; liberals abandoned us."[4] For him and others, the crucial betrayal took place during the 1964 Democratic National Convention in Atlantic City, when the Democrats forced King and the Mississippi Freedom Democratic Party to accept a token "compromise" rather than unseating the all-white Mississippi delegation. Many grassroots activists realized that the real issue in America was power. So did black Philadelphians: at the very same time, the "City of Brotherly Love" was convulsed by a race riot. Historians Timothy Tyson and Matthew Countryman argue that Black Power and the Civil Rights Movement existed simultaneously rather than sequentially. Recent scholarship on the Black Power movement interprets it not as a dark moment in American history but as deeply rooted in the past and leaving a lasting legacy. We must examine the New Negro understanding of the intertwined issues that confronted black America in the post–civil rights era: racism and poverty. Moderate leaders disagreed with the style tactics and rhetoric adopted by Black Power activists, but Alexander had advocated some of the same themes that were associated with Black Power.[5]

The media played a major role in generating tension between civil rights leaders and Black Power spokespersons. According to Judson Jeffries, "by 1966, for many Americans," television had become "the primary source for news and entertainment."[6] That summer, Stokely Carmichael introduced the term "Black Power." Wilkins recalled Carmichael shouting out the phrase "Black Power" and "the unreflecting eye of the TV cameras caught it all and those of us who did not endorse or embrace the new concept were rhetorically lynched."[7] The ideas articulated by Wilkins, Alexander, and other moderate leaders about liberalism, patience, and building coalitions did not resonate with the growing number of dissatisfied African Americans. The black working class and poor regarded civil rights rhetoric as obsolete. During the civil rights movement, the print media such as *Time, Newsweek,* and the *New York Times* empathized with activists and demonized white racist extremists, such as Eugene "Bull" Connor of Birmingham. Journalists interviewed leaders and activists who described the horrific conditions in the South. Edward P. Morgan argues that by the "late sixties media discourse increasingly focused on the most flamboyant actions, sights, sounds, and rhetoric of the 'outsider'": "Drama made political activity newsworthy; it helped to sell news programming to wider audiences as the 'society of spectacle' was coming of age."[8] While the Panthers used media to get attention, their radical message got lost in their regalia, guns, and black berets.

What also got lost in translation was the fact that Alexander's New Negro generation had articulated concepts that are associated with Black Power. Civil rights leaders and Black Power activists were unable to find common ground, and the media intentionally focused on the differences. Alexander and other mainstream civil rights leaders rejected the term "Black Power" because they believed that the slogan marginalized white liberals and called into question the United States' inclusive, egalitarian promises. These leaders believed that the only way for African Americans to obtain equality was to work with white liberals to extend rights and liberties to all. The white media portrayed Alexander and King (until he spoke out against the Vietnam War) as "responsible leaders," while Black Power advocates translated that stance as "selling out" to white liberals. In so polarized an atmosphere, even Alexander himself failed to recognize that some aspects of Black Power ideology were an extension of ideas that he expressed during his civil rights struggle in Philadelphia.

A New Negro Lawyer and Black Power

In the summer of 1966, during the March Against Fear in Greenwood, Mississippi, as marchers camped out during the evening, the leaders of the march, King of SCLC and Carmichael, the new leader of SNCC, gave talks to the marchers. When it was Carmichael's turn to speak, Willie Ricks, a SNCC colleague, gave Carmichael a prearranged signal. Carmichael shouted to the crowd, "What Do We Want?" and the crowd responded, "Black Power." Black Power was not an entirely new term. In 1954, novelist Richard Wright wrote a book titled *Black Power*, though at the time very few knew about it. Historian Peniel Joseph argues that other black leaders and activists such as Adam Clayton Powell Jr., the black congressman from Harlem, and Gloria Richardson, leader of the Cambridge Non-Violent Action Committee (CNAC), a civil rights organization in Cambridge, Maryland, who advocated civil rights, economic justice, and self-defense, "had embodied the phrase, even before its widespread use."⁹ According to Ruth Feldstein, Nina Simone's 1963 song "Mississippi Goddamn" represented the shift toward Black Power, but Simone was a black woman and Black Power represented "assertions of black *male* pride."¹⁰ In spite of the term's earlier use and gendered meaning, for most whites and moderate black leaders, the slogan sent shock waves across America. Media grabbed the term and interviewed anyone to get a definition. All the mainstream civil rights activists, including King, Wilkins, Randolph, Rustin, Lewis, and Alexander, denounced the term because it excluded white liberals and encouraged violence. Three months later in Oakland, California, Huey Newton and Bobby Seale founded the Black Panther Party for Self Defense. The organization created a Ten Point Program that addressed improving housing, education, and ending police brutality in black communities, but they were armed with rifles and wore black berets. The Panthers rapidly became the government's number one enemy.

While the nation was engrossed with the Black Panthers, Black Power, and the new militancy, moderate civil rights leaders such as Bayard Rustin organized a group of black and white liberals to design a "Freedom Budget." Rustin, who vehemently did not support Black Power, wanted to continue to build interracial coalitions and concentrate on eradicating poverty. In October 1966, Rustin presented his Freedom Budget in Harlem. Expanding upon Johnson's War on Poverty, the Freedom Budget sought to end poverty not by increasing taxes but through federal programs to expand employment, with funding based on "estimates of economic growth projections."¹¹ In layman's terms, Rustin's pamphlet told its readers that the new budget would provide jobs. This revolutionary proposal was not televised, and it was not as militant or scary as Black Power. The War in Vietnam destroyed the Freedom Budget and the War on Poverty. The Vietnam War split the Democratic Party, and during the 1966 midterm elections the Republicans elected nine governors, including Ronald Reagan, and along with conservative Democrats shifted the nation's resources from fighting poverty to the Vietnam War. Rustin's Freedom Budget, like Alexander's commitment to providing legal aid to the poor, ultimately lost ground to the war.

By the end of 1966, the civil rights movement was over, Black Power emerged as the new movement, and many local and national organizations focused on eradicating institutionalized racism and poverty. The media continued to focus on the Panthers and King's protests in Chicago, while Rustin and others continued trying to get the federal government to maintain its commitment to addressing poverty. Three years after King's historic "I Have a Dream Speech" in Washington, D.C., Alexander gave a speech at the African Methodist Episcopal (AME) Church in Bermuda. The title of his address was "We Still Have A Dream." This speech exhorted Christians and Jews to "declare that segregation, discrimination, hatred and bigotry defy and degrade the teachings of God." Churches and synagogues must tell their members that "fleeing to the suburbs, threatened the very life of the cities that made America great." White religious leaders had a moral obligation to educate whites about racism and inequality.[12]

The second half of the address disparaged Black Power. Alexander stated that civil rights leaders must unify in order to defeat "the bitter, frustrated, young vociferous advocates of 'Black Power', a hazardous and meaningless 'catch phrase.'" Black Power amounted to "black racism," which "is as dangerous and divisive a course for the Negro as 'white racism.'" According to Alexander, "Black Power has caused the loss of many thousands of our friends and serious damage to the heightened Negro image" that he had striven to develop. He feared that Black Power was a roadblock for African Americans, in part because it served as a scapegoat for white backlash.[13]

In February 1968, the ASNLH invited Alexander to New York to accept the organizations Carter G. Woodson award. The *Philadelphia Inquirer* reported that Alexander's speech referred to Black Power as "a cry without a format or a program" and suggested that Black Power advocates should use the term "Negro Renaissance or a Negro Cultural Revolution" in order to avoid long hot summers and riots that fueled white backlash. During the New Negro movement, studying African American history was a component of vindicating the race. Alexander mentioned that as a high school student he had met the "Father of Black History," Carter G. Woodson; in law school, he attended a lecture by Marcus Garvey; he was a founding member of the Philadelphia Chapter of the ASNLH. Ralph McGill, editor of the *Atlanta*

Journal Constitution, commented, "Black Power has no relevancy to the laudable ideal of improving the Negro's image in America." Like Alexander, McGill preferred the term "Renaissance" because the term "is more and more a cutting edge against the status quo, apathy, and the fortifications of white prejudice." Black Power was a distraction from the pressing issue of poverty in America.[14]

The Harlem Renaissance, like the Black Power movement, emphasized studying African American history. Alexander stated that universities "should hire black scholars to lecture on black history, in order to inform whites that they created a Negro Problem." Most Black Power advocates agreed that universities needed to hire black faculty. During the late sixties, working-class citizens, blacks, Latinos, Asians, and progressive whites viewed American universities as intellectual bastions of American imperialism and racism. Universities hired black faculty, and in 1968 San Francisco State University created the nation's first Black Studies Department. Alexander may not have agreed with the tactics that students used to force universities to hire black faculty and offer Black Studies courses, but he agreed that studying history was a viable method of improving race relations and understanding racial oppression. The Black Power movement led not only to the creation of African American and Africana studies programs but indirectly to the genesis of Chicano, women's, Asian, and gay and lesbian studies.[15]

Black Professionals and Black Power

Black attorneys were in the forefront of the civil rights movement from the 1920s to the 1954 *Brown v. Board of Education* decision. Black lawyers had organized the National Bar Association, an organization of black attorneys, where they discussed civil rights issues. However, after King's successful Montgomery Bus Boycott, ministers emerged as the leaders of the black community, and lawyers were relegated to the courtroom rather than television. During the Black Power era, younger militant black activists replaced ministers, and lawyers continued their work on a local level. On April 4, 1968, James Early Ray murdered King on the balcony of the Lorraine Hotel in Memphis, Tennessee. King was in Memphis supporting the municipal garbage workers' strike. After King's death, urban riots erupted across America, and, for some young black activists, King's death signaled the beginning of the revolution. What would or should be the role of black lawyers in this highly charged political moment?

In August 1968, the NBA invited Alexander to speak at the forty-third annual convention in Washington, D.C. The first half of his address was a history of the NBA, "the American Negro lawyer and his contribution to the on-going and difficult struggle for better race relations in America." Alexander stated that "the National Bar Association was the lone voice, organized law association" crying in the wilderness "for justice and equality for the American Negro." In northern cities, white hotel managers excluded the NBA, so they had to meet in local Young Men's Christian Associations. During the 1920s, there were only five hundred black lawyers nationally and only fifty in the South. Southern African Americans often lacked legal representation. He mentioned the work of the "Father of Civil Rights," Charles Hamilton Houston, the attorney who trained Thurgood Marshall at Howard University. Alexander stated that "The NBA is needed more today than ever before in its history."[16]

In the second portion of the address, Alexander stated that "the Negro lawyer can fill the void" left by King's untimely death. Alexander maintained that black lawyers "must always demand *equal opportunity, equal treatment* and *full justice* and have *good, quality education.*" According to Alexander, the three most important priorities for African Americans were "education, employment and non-segregated housing." Black lawyers needed to eradicate the "hard-core ugly ghetto areas, and unlock its store of treasures." He charged black attorneys to challenge "northern segregations dedicated to Negro inferiority." Alexander's agenda detailed the problems that confronted black Americans in the post–civil rights era.[17]

During King's last few years, he advocated a restructuring of American society, a democratic socialism. Alexander made a similar plea: "It is *not* too much to ask America to unlock its store of treasures and give to the poor and disadvantaged in the richest country of the world." America is the only industrialized nation without a "family or children's allowance." Canada and Scandinavian nations "have model family allowance laws," and if the United States had such a law it would restore hope in black America. Alexander encouraged his colleagues to support a "guaranteed income plan" in order to make poor families a "productive part of the American community." Today, Alexander is not remembered for his radical positions. He might not have considered his proposal of a guaranteed income radical because Canadian and European democracies had such a policy, but in an American context many politicians, including Democrats, considered it a form of socialism. The Democratic Party never embraced the radical social and economic reforms that Alexander advocated.

The *New York Law Journal* published Alexander's address, and a number of his colleagues responded in print. Timothy L. Jenkins, an African American attorney, planned a conference for black lawyers to address the issues that Alexander had put forth.[18] In November, Alexander recommended to Jenkins that "a black lawyers conference" be convened to address the ills of the ghettos. Alexander suggested to Jenkins a number of issues to consider, such as increasing the number of black law students. He recommended avoiding "sloganism," the repetition of such catch-phrases as "Don't call me Negro," "Wear your hair Afro," "Call me Afro American," and "Ending apartheid in America" as advocates of Black Power used. Alexander suggested that black attorneys provide weekly race relations updates to the media and aid with the reform of American prisons. According to Alexander, the black community must "avoid further polarization and what appears to be a struggle between upper and lower class American Negroes." Finally, black attorneys must eradicate the racist myth that the "Negro is lazy, worthless and biologically inferior and try to bring back to the Negro cause the willing whites who want to help (as their children did from 1954–1965)." Alexander voiced both a critique of Black Power and a growing concern about the widening class gap in black America.[19]

In December 1969, Timothy Jenkins and a group of seventeen lawyers, including Derrick Bell, currently a law professor at New York University, and Floyd McKissick, then president of CORE, created a new professional organization for black attorneys, the National Council of Black Lawyers (NCBL). According to Jeffrey Ogbar, from 1968 to 1970, a number of black professionals created their own organizations, such as the National Conference of Black Political Scientists and Association of Black Sociologists, to address issues in the black community independently of white organizations. The NCBL was part of this movement because its members were "unapologetic in their quest for independence and self-determination."[20] The NCBL's "Declaration of Concern and Commitment" stated that "white racism is at the core of the nation's domestic problems" and "white America does not intend to deal with Black people" fairly. According to the Declaration, "The Black revolution demands Black attorneys must organize in order to achieve dignity and a fair share of power of Black people." The NCBL was intended to be "an ongoing body of all Black lawyers determined to join the Black revolution." Robert Carter, an attorney for the *Brown* decision, was a founding member, so younger militant black attorneys were not the only members of this new organization.[21]

Alexander wrote to Robert Carter, co-chair of the National Conference of Black Lawyers, stating his concerns about the organization's objectives. Jenkins's letter "greatly disturbed" him. Alexander wrote a six-page response to Jenkins that discussed potential themes at the black lawyers' conference. In spite of Alexander's concerns, he joined the NCBL and paid his fifty-dollar membership fee. However, Alexander stated that he fought "to destroy RACISM, both black and white racism, urge the end of race bigots, both black and white." The NCBL stated that white racism was the problem, but Alexander suggested "that we not put all the blame on white America, bad as, admittedly, they are."[22] The NCBL's claim that racism was the primary problem reiterates the conclusion of the 1968 Kerner Report, which stated "racism was the underlying cause" of the riots, and warned that America was "moving towards two societies, one white and one black, separate and unequal."[23] Alexander admitted that racism was the problem, but he worried that the NCBL's approach might not win political support from white allies. This dilemma constantly confronted Alexander: he understood that white racism was the problem, but in order to get white liberal support, he must use terms that did not offend whites. From Alexander's perspective, focusing solely on racism would only create white backlash and decease support from white liberals.

During the late sixties, Black Power had taken root on college campuses as black students organized to secure black faculty, black studies courses, and black dorms. Referring to this issue as the "last battle of my own with a new form of black power," Wilkins contended that demanding separate space was a form of "black apartheid." Separating from whites was a sign "of weakness, not strength."[24] Alexander expressed similar disappointment with the growing militancy of college students, who are "taking over the offices of college officials, burning records, looting files, and shutting out the lawfully designated college officials." Viewed by millions of people across America, the black student protest "creates a perverse, destructive image of the black man throughout the world" and maintains the gap between the races.[25] In 1970, Alexander criticized African American college students who demanded "separated eating halls, separate dormitories, separate libraries, separate study halls." According to Alexander, these students disrespected the work of African American leaders "who literally gave part of their lives" so they could be "free from the restrictions of a segregated life." The New Negro despised segregation because segregation connoted inferiority and second-class citizenship. Alexander assumed that black separation justified racist myths and excluded African Americans from becoming part of America. To the younger generation, however, black separatism connoted self-determination, the same drive that motivated Alexander's New Negro generation. Most if not all New Negro activists participated in all-black organizations where they decided what was best for African Americans. But Alexander and his generation failed to make this connection later on.[26]

Alexander also commented on the Black Power protest at the 1968 and 1972 Olympics. Historically, black athletes used the Olympics to demonstrate their hard work and loyalty. In 1936, Jesse Owens won four Gold Medals in Berlin in front of Adolph Hitler. Alexander's generation also extolled the accomplishments of other black Olympic athletes, such as Alice Coachman, the first black woman to win a gold medal in the Olympics.[27] African Americans used these victories to debunk racist myths about African Americans. According to Mark Dyreson, Owens provided an "interracial education" to white America.[28] Most white Americans were familiar with the accomplishments of Joe Louis, the black heavyweight champion, and they were comfortable with Louis and Owens. During the late sixties, some black athletes stopped asking for respect or trying to prove they were qualified for citizenship; they demanded justice. At the 1968 Olympics in Mexico City, Tommie Lee and John Carlos, two medal-winning black runners, wore black socks and raised a clenched fist with a black glove during the singing of the U.S. national anthem. Both runners were banned from the Olympic Village for embarrassing the United States. In the 1972 Olympics in Munich, Germany, which are widely known for the murder of Israeli athletes,[29] a black coach and three black athletes "elected to live apart from their white teammates." Two of the runners missed the 100-meter event because "they were not present when the continental time was explained." The *Philadelphia Inquirer* asked Alexander to comment on "voluntary segregation" at the 1972 Olympics. Referring to this stance as "reverse racism,"[30] Alexander said he could not understand why these African Americans wanted to separate from their teammates. Two African Americans had finished first and second in an event, but "with the world looking on," Wayne Collett, one of the winners, "gave the Black Power Salute" and was "barred from further competition." Alexander encouraged younger African Americans to "rethink your obedience to catchword phrases" and avoid "the use of so much unnecessary regalia," which, he reminded them, "is not accepted in the new republics of Africa." Alexander advised African Americans to "avoid those so-called new opportunities in new fields for black actors and actresses, such as Black Movies, which are now, unhappily the vogue in Hollywood."[31] This short interview epitomizes Alexander's disgust with Black Power and "black consciousness." In reality, however, what plagued the black community were not dashikis, Afros, and black film, it was the malignant combination of racism and poverty.

Another major issue during the Black Power Era was affirmative action. In September 1965, President Johnson signed Executive Order 11246 that formed the Office of Federal Contract Compliance of the Department of Labor. This office was designed to ensure that construction companies that received federal contracts "practice affirmative action." In 1969, President Richard Nixon instituted the "Philadelphia Plan" to increase the number of black city construction workers on city projects. According to Thomas Sugrue, "the plan attempted to meet civil rights protesters' demands for quantitative evidence of minority employment while skirting the hot-button issue of quotas."[32] A number of black activists protested in front of construction sites demanding jobs, and some of "the protests turned violent as hardhats and picketers clashed." While Alexander did not join protesters, he agreed with the protestors that the city must hire a higher percentage of African Americans.

In 1972, Alexander wrote an article in the *Philadelphia Inquirer* about the Philadelphia Police Department's efforts to hire more African American police officers. Alexander stated that black representation on the police force should be equal to their representation in the city's population. In 1972, African Americans comprised 35 percent of the population. The city had 7,500 police officers, but only 1,337 were black. "On a strict ratio basis, there should be slightly more than 2,500 Negroes on our police force," Alexander contended. Controversially, he stated that there "is nothing fundamentally wrong with a quota system" since historically "the black worker was denied any semblance of right to this and similar public or private employment." Alexander's support of a quota system was in line with the Philadelphia Plan, but Sugrue argues that many white working-class Philadelphians viewed quotas "as a part of a large cultural attack on the white working class world." Alexander reasoned that African Americans paid city taxes, so they should have their fair share of employment. Affirmative action emerged as the major white backlash issue during the 1970s, but it origins are evident in post–World War II America. Alexander's reasoning was one he made throughout his life: as long as African Americans are taxpayers they are entitled to their fair portion of city resources.[33]

Poverty in Post–Civil Rights America

Another major component of the civil rights movement was poverty. According to Martha Davis, between 1960 and 1973, "a new breed of lawyer-activist-
poverty lawyer" had emerged.[34] These lawyers were committed to assisting the
poor, and Alexander was part of this movement. Michael Harrington's *The
Other America: Poverty in the United States*, published in 1962, laid the foundation for Johnson's War on Poverty Program, which, similar to the New Deal,
provided a social safety net for Americans. In the same year, an influential
but not so widely known book appeared; in *The War on Poverty: A Civilian
Perspective*, coauthors Jean and Edgar Cahn discussed providing free legal
services to the poor. The civil rights movement had focused on voting and
ending Jim Crow in the South and de facto segregation in the North; poli-
cymakers were talking about the devastating impact of poverty. As a criminal
lawyer and judge, Alexander was cognizant of the relationship between crime
and poverty. As a judge, he could not participate in demonstrations or act
as a leader of the masses, but he was active behind the scenes, talking about
poverty and providing a sociological analysis of urban poverty. By the late
sixties, lawyers sought to fight poverty by providing legal assistance to poor
people, and Alexander supported these progressive social programs. However,
the media did not focus on the fight against poverty; they were busy chasing
black militants.

In March 1965, Central State College, a historically black college in Ohio,
invited Alexander to address the students. A week before Alexander arrived
on campus, he read an article in a new campus publication, *Grape-Vine*, cri-
tiquing an "apathetic attitude that is generally found on this campus." These
students wanted more "controversial speakers" who were not "pre-occupied
with the so-called 'negro problem.'" Alexander told the students that he hoped
his comments would energize them to address "the struggle of the American
Negro for basic human rights." He proposed that the leaders of the five major
civil rights organizations—SCLC, the NAACP, Urban League, CORE, and
SNCC—combine their resources in order to address human rights.[35]

The recent issue of *Grape-Vine* concerned Malcolm X as well. Although
Malcolm sought to bring U.S. human rights violations before the United
Nations, Alexander remained skeptical of Malcolm's transformation and
interpreted his death as a result of black extremism. In the second part of his
address, Alexander castigated the Nation of Islam (NOI) and other extremist organizations. He described Malcolm as "a peculiar, complicated and

egocentric man who, from all reports was changing" when he was assassinated. Malcolm's pilgrimage to Mecca had transformed his categorically negative views about whites, but his death illustrated the problem with extremism. Alexander called the Nation of Islam a "Negro Far Right extremist group," the Communists "Far Left," and the KKK and White Citizens Council "Far Right." Alexander's interpretation of the NOI is similar to Mike Wallace's 1959 documentary, *The Hate That Hate Produced*, which viewed the Nation of Islam as a black KKK. Alexander believed that those who joined extremist organizations were "easy prey to the simplistic slogans and absolutist solutions of even the most difficult problems." Alexander was also concerned that media in Europe, Asia, and Africa portrayed Malcolm's death as a "conspiracy of 'white anti-Negro groups'" and referred to him as an "American Lumumba" who "fought for the emancipation of the Negro."[36] Many African Americans viewed Malcolm's assassination as a government plot and saw Malcolm as a revolutionary figure. Alexander was concerned with how Communists and developing nations understood race relations in the United States. According to Kevin Gaines, "criticism of U.S. foreign policy was decidedly off limits for prominent African Americans." Unlike King, Alexander did not make any antiwar statements, nor did he criticize American race relations while representing the United States in foreign nations. Alexander, similar to Pauli Murray and Edith Sampson, two prominent black attorneys, followed the State Department's "unspoken but widely understood restriction of black leadership to the purview of domestic civil rights."[37]

While refraining from taking any stand with regard to foreign relations, Alexander issued a biting indictment of the domestic situation. Toward the end of his address, Alexander told these aspiring members of the black middle class "to sacrifice much of his time to help his brother at the lower level" and said they must demand "integrated education" and "high-quality education by the best and most qualified teachers." Insisting that education is essential to improve race relations, he maintained that African Americans would "support an increase in the tax rate" to improve education. Alexander's recommendations are similar to those programs supported by Johnson's Great Society. In order to close the racial gap in occupational achievement, the government must fund early education and improve schools. In addition, these schools must include the historical accomplishments of African Americans.[38]

During the 1930s and 1940s, the black freedom struggle had emphasized economic as well as political equality. The modern civil rights movement is associated with dismantling Jim Crow, while the Democratic Party sought to address poverty and economic inequality. In June 1965, two months before the passage of the Voting Rights Act and three months before Johnson signed Executive Order 11246 that introduced the term "affirmative action," he gave his famous commencement address at Howard University, "To Fulfill These Rights." Johnson's speech addressed the major issue in America, the yawning economic gap between blacks and whites. Johnson could not understand why there was "a widening gulf" between the races. Johnson noted that in 1948 the black male teenage unemployment rate was 8 percent, but in 1964 it increased to 23 percent. In 1930, the black and white unemployment rates were similar; in 1965, the black rate was twice the national average. According to Johnson, there was a difference between black and white poverty. Black poverty was linked to "slavery; and a century of oppression, hatred and injustice." The ideas that Johnson mentions in his speech are echoed in a number of Alexander's speeches in the following years.[39]

Another section of Johnson's address examines the role of the black family. The first part of Johnson's address declared that racial injustice was the major cause of black poverty, but Johnson argued that "the breakdown of the Negro family structure" was a major problem: "A majority of all Negro children receive federally-aided public assistance sometime during their lifetime." Johnson shifted the blame from racism and poverty to single black mothers. Three months later, Daniel Patrick Moynihan, Undersecretary of Labor, and Richard Goodwin, a presidential speech writer who coauthored Johnson's "To Fulfill These Rights," published a report titled "The Negro Family: The Case for National Action." According to Stephen Steinberg, Moynihan cited federal welfare programs, especially Aid to Families with Dependent Children (AFDC), as a cause of black poverty, while failing to mention that the unemployment rate for African Americans had risen. Moynihan suggested that there should be a period of "benign neglect" when the federal government ceased funding social programs to aid the poor. Steinberg remarks, "Moynihan had brought the nation to the threshold of truth—racial equality as a moral and political imperative—and then, with rhetorical guile, deflected the focus onto the tribulations within black families." In spite of Moynihan's rhetorical slight of hand, Alexander continued to address poverty from a structural perspective. Alexander and other civil rights leaders were shifting their attention to poverty and getting the federal government to create policies to decrease poverty, but this agenda was overshadowed by the demonstrations in Selma and the riot in Watts.[40]

In May 1965, a month before Johnson's Howard University address, Alexander gave the commencement address at Savannah State College, a historically black college. The title of his address was "In Our Other America." Using Harrington's title, Alexander's address examined the black poor. According to Alexander, "Poverty to the Negro embraces much more and is more complex than the poverty of the white man." If race were not a factor in economics, "the Negro would not be twelve percent of the nation's unemployed while the total unemployed is at 4.7 percent level; nor would the incidence of Negro crime, proportionally, be approximately three times that of white persons charged with crime." Alexander differentiates between black and white poverty and presents the data to prove his point. Alexander stated that the black poverty rate was twice the national average and African Americans faced not only the legacy of slavery, segregation, poor schools, and discrimination but also *"inherited poverty."*[41] Alexander's structural analysis of racism and poverty predates the recent studies that examine the gaps in wealth and income between blacks and whites.[42]

Another portion of the address suggested solutions to black poverty. According to Alexander, "American Negroes deserve special and preferential treatment. It is a debt long overdue and too long postponed." Alexander's recommendation for "affirmative action" came three months before President Johnson signed Executive Order 11246 officially introducing the term "affirmative action," which was designed to correct and compensate for decades of discrimination.[43] Alexander proposed a "Marshall Plan" for black America similar to that instituted by George Marshall, former Secretary of Defense, to aid war-torn Europe in economic reconstruction. Alexander stated that the Marshall Plan gave billions of dollars to *"allies* and *enemy alike* to maintain their free democratic government and to rebuild their economy...." However, for "this unprecedented charity we are rewarded by scores of our Embassies being broken into, windows smashed, and chants such as 'Yankee go home.'" Alexander criticized the French for not supporting the United States' efforts "to resolve present international unrest in the Caribbean, in South America and in Asia." With this rhetorical strategy, he sought to convince the federal government that African Americans are loyal citizens who deserve a "federally operated Marshall Plan for Negroes." Booker T. Washington had used a similar strategy in his famous 1895 Atlanta Exposition Address, when he told white industrialists not to rely upon European immigrant labor but to employ loyal black citizens. Alexander was never out of touch with the problems that confronted the masses of black America.[44]

In October 1966, Alexander delivered an address at the annual conference of the National Legal Aid and Defender Association (NLADA), founded in 1911 to provide legal aid for the poor. Alexander's speech addressed poverty and what role lawyers could play in assisting poor Americans. "America's poor have been 'blowing in the wind,'" Alexander declared. African Americans residing in the overcrowded cities constituted the main body of poor people in the country. Poor people needed free legal aid to address such symptoms of poverty as juvenile delinquency and nonpayment of rent. According to Alexander, these problems "perpetually plague all the poor but especially and particularly the Negro poor." Black workers suffered from discrimination: for example, "the hard-working father who lost his job because a biased union unlawfully withdrew his membership privileges; the able-bodied Negro men who are refused union apprentice training." The "Negro poor . . . know no lawyers," he noted. The first part of the speech addressed urban poverty, but, Alexander points out, "to those of you who think these problems of the ghetto are peculiar to the Negro, let me remind you that these very same problems" existed with white ethnic immigrants. In this room full of lawyers, Alexander made sure that they did not see poverty solely as a black problem. Using a comparative historical approach, Alexander proceeded to inform his audience about American poverty.[45]

Alexander told the audience that poverty existed in rural white America and among Irish and Italian immigrants when they first came to America. He deracialized poverty by comparing the status of Irish and Jewish immigrants in turn-of-the-century America. According to Alexander, the objectionable term "family pathology" was first applied to the Irish in an 1872 report titled "The Dangerous Classes of New York." He stated that President Theodore Roosevelt wrote in his diary that "The average Irishman is a low, venal, corrupt and unintelligent brute." Women often headed Irish families and "immigrant slums were far worse than today." Alexander demonstrated that the problems African Americans faced in the slums were not unique; they had existed when the white immigrants came to America. The major difference between European ethnics and African Americans was owing to racial segregation.[46]

Referring to Moynihan's 1966 report on the Negro family, Alexander agreed that "the breakdown of the Negro family is at the very root of the Negro problem in America." After analyzing structural barriers to equality, why focus on families? Alexander traced the connections. Having a strong family is beneficial, but if both parents are unemployed or working low-wage jobs, it is difficult to keep that family together. Alexander admitted that the "ghetto family is overwhelmingly matriarchal," and when the husband left, the woman became "intertwined with the law." He argued that "the pathology of the Negro family is not endemic with or to the Negro, neither is it indigenous to the Negro." Alexander emphasized that crime was color-blind and the problems that African Americans encountered were not a black problem but an American problem. Using history and sociology, he demonstrated that poverty is not racial or cultural in origin but rather economic. Alexander insisted that lawyers must improve the lives of the poor in America because so many problems the poor faced derived from a lack of legal representation.[47]

The final portion of his address was a warning to the lawyers if they failed to address these important issues. In 1966, the segregationist Lester Maddox was elected governor of Georgia, and George Mahoney, a conservative Democrat, whom Alexander characterized as "another racist," defeated the liberal Democrat Carlton Sickel. Two months before his address, Stokely Carmichael (later Kwame Toure) of SNCC shouted the term "Black Power," and within weeks it became a new rallying cry for the movement. Alexander placed the blame for the Maddox and Sickel victories as well as Black Power on the lawyers who are fearful of "white backlash." "Black power distorts our reasoned and intelligent aims as American citizens," he said. Alexander believed that Black Power advocates and Lester Maddox were cut from the same cloth.[48] Alexander's addresses and speeches articulate an analysis of the interconnections between racism and poverty, but the media focused on Black Power militants and white backlash. Unfortunately, he blamed Black Power for white backlash instead of blaming racism and white politicians who warned whites that African Americans were threatening to take over America.

An American Representative in Southeast Asia and the Middle East

Earlier in his career, Alexander had wanted to work for the U.S. State Department. During the Cold War, the State Department started to hire more African Americans to inform the world about the progress of race relations in America. This pattern continued during the Vietnam War, despite the fact that some civil rights organizations opposed U.S. military intervention in Southeast Asia. SNCC was one of the first civil rights organizations to criticize the nation's participation in the Vietnam War. By 1967, King announced his dissent regarding the war, and in response Johnson and many white liberals marginalized King. In 1967, Whitney Young supported Johnson, whom he believed was more supportive of civil rights than Kennedy, and in return, Johnson appointed Young to serve as an "observer of the South Vietnamese elections."⁴⁹ A year earlier, the National Urban League paid for Young to study the condition of black soldiers in Vietnam. Young's strategy was to ensure that black soldiers were treated well in Vietnam, and he felt free to castigate the president. Alexander used the opportunity movement to address youth in Southeast Asia about the struggle against communism and to disprove negative propaganda about American race relations.

In July 1965, Alexander was accepted as an American Specialist to Southeast Asia and India. As the Vietnam War escalated, Southeast Asia was an increasingly vital part of the world. According to Alexander, "America does not deserve the ugly picture that has been drawn by those in far off sections of the world who do not provide democratic elections." He was committed to "correcting the image of America." During the Cold War, Alexander was among the anticommunist African American liberals, such as Ralph Bunche, who criticized American racism at home but not abroad.⁵⁰ As an "American Specialist," Alexander traveled to ten Southeast Asian countries in ten weeks. In each country his audience was composed of college-age students. In Saigon, Alexander spoke at the National Institute of Administration of Saigon. He encouraged the students to choose "freedom" over communism, and he compared the Vietnamese students' struggle against communism to American students' struggle for equality. According to Alexander, the Vietnam War was maintained by a "cruel and relentless foe who is intent on destroying their freedom." Using the civil rights movement as the model for democratic reform and student activism, Alexander extolled the democratic virtues of the civil rights movement to the Vietnamese students.⁵¹

Alexander reported to the State Department that "the image of the American Negro in the far off corner of the world is not a very happy one." Most Southeast Asians and Indians "know nothing of the true relationship between the white and Negro Americans and the progress of the American Negro." The reason his audiences were not cognizant of black progress was that "only the bad news gets through of race riots, bombing by the KKK of Negro churches, murders of Negro and white civil rights workers." From 1960 to 1965, the media assisted the civil rights movement by displaying these images to the world, forcing the federal government to address the nation's image abroad. However, this was the only image of African Americans that these students had seen. Many were not aware of the number of black lawyers and other professionals in America. Alexander stated, "I sincerely believe that our country and our government would profit immeasurably by the appointment of highly qualified and talented Negro men and women to high positions in the embassies." This would eliminate the nonwhite world's impression of the United States as an "imperialistic, industrialist power hungry nation" out "to superimpose white domination of the entire world." Alexander believed that African American foreign affairs officers would be the most effective examples to counter the propaganda that Asian students were fed.[52]

Throughout Alexander's professional career, he believed that racism prohibited him from obtaining positions that he deserved. He ran for judge during the 1930s and lost, because both parties would not support a black judge. When he applied for an appointment in World War II, he was denied. At every opportunity, he would point out a white Harvard Law classmate of his with less experience who got the position. At the end of his report, Alexander made some observations about his trip. He should have received "first class transportation for an overseas flight, especially when your specialist is of senior citizen status." When he arrived at the airport, officials with a "Diplomatic Passport" had received "VIP, and very high priority privileges." He intentionally did not mention their race, but in 1965, the majority of foreign diplomats were white. The regular diplomats did not have to wait at customs, but, "in my own U.S.A.," he was "subject to endless delays and minute inspection of baggage." After his observations, he ended his letter by stating that it was a great service for his "great government" but that on his next trip he would like "passport privileges." In spite of his status, Alexander's recognized that his race prohibited him receiving from all of the privileges that white diplomats received.[53]

In 1968, the State Department hired Alexander as an American Specialist to the Middle East. Over five and a half weeks, Alexander presented twenty-five lectures on civil rights, black protest, and poverty in three countries—Turkey, Lebanon, and Cyprus. Alexander defined civil rights as "the achievement of equal justice" and defined its major historical stages. He placed the origins of the equal justice crusade after the Civil War with the passage of the Thirtieth, Fourteenth, and Fifteenth amendments. The next phase of the civil rights movement started during the 1920s and continued to the Civil Rights Act of 1964. But "the law has not yet dealt adequately with the problem of *de facto* discrimination—that discrimination which is inherent in Ghetto living."

Now the nation needed to shift its energy to eradicating poverty. Alexander reiterated to his audience the structural inequalities that remained in wages, housing, and education. Next he addressed a "broader concern, the plight of Americans who suffer from the evils of poverty." Alexander summarized some aspects of the War on Poverty, such as the role of the Office of Economic Opportunity (OEO) and the Community Action Programs (CAP), and complimented the role lawyers played in the fight against poverty.[54]

Following his trip to the Middle East, Alexander wanted to continue with his work in foreign affairs. However, the newly elected president, Richard Nixon, was a Republican. Alexander sent a letter to three high-ranking African Americans: Senator Edward W. Brooke of Massachusetts, the first black senator since Reconstruction; Ralph Bunche, the first African American recipient of the Nobel Peace Prize; and Andrew F. Brimmer, the first African American appointed to the Federal Reserve Bank and the highest-ranking black official in the administration. Alexander noted that Nixon was going to appoint an African American to serve as "Deputy Ambassador to the United Nations." President Johnson had appointed James A. Nabrit, an attorney and Alexander's colleague, to the position. Alexander wrote that he heard that Nixon would appoint any African American regardless of party affiliation and that, although he was "a registered Democrat," it would not "affect my loyalty to our President." In 1969, Alexander was seventy years old, but in true Alexander fashion, he mentioned to Brooke that Ambassador Averill Harriman, who was white, was seventy-eight. Alexander was open to serving as an ambassador "to the newly-emerging Black Nations of African; or the new Independent Nations of the Caribbean, or to the problem areas of the white world." Alexander did not get this or any other position. At the age of seventy, after years of discouraging experiences, he used the same strategy that he used during the 1940s: he relied on persuasion and the racial contradictions that existed within the United States to prove his point that he was entitled to the same opportunity as any white American.[55] This strategy did not work, and Alexander did not get the appointment.

Old Leadership and New Leadership

By the mid-sixties, two types of black leaders had emerged in Philadelphia and other northern cities. Alexander represented the older, moderate leadership, while Cecil B. Moore represented the new, militant leadership. In January

1965, the *Philadelphia Evening Bulletin* published a fourteen-page study titled "The Negro in Philadelphia," with one section focused on black leadership. Moore's comments after the Philadelphia race riot attracted national attention. In the September 11, 1964, issue of *Time* magazine, Moore declared that he was "the goddam boss," given his rapport with the man and woman on the street. Taking aim at the sixteen-member committee that criticized his decision to demand a black director of the Ford Foundation study in Philadelphia, he declared that "16 Uncle Toms and an Aunt Dinah Don't Speak for the NAACP." According to the *Evening Bulletin*, Alexander said that Moore had "brought to the front in a blazing fashion the inequities, but he was irresponsible." Alexander acknowledged Moore's impact in Philadelphia, but he did not agree with his methods. From 1963 to 1968, pickets and protests had increased the number of black workers on local construction projects. As a result, Moore was regarded as the "unofficial" leader of the common man. Moore's charisma and flamboyant personality made great news. By the late 1960s, the media defined the movement by concentrating "on aspects of protest that will arouse the curiosity and hold the attention of potential audiences; they focus on behaviors, appearances, and personal stories of the protestors and on any dramatic conflicts." Moore emerged as a major leader in large part because he was valuable to the media. Alexander believed that Moore's personality and style had a negative impact on whites, but black people admired Moore's brash and uncompromising stands.[56]

James O. Williams of CORE made an interesting observation about the black community's response to black leadership during the riot. When Moore and Alexander visited North Philadelphia during the riot, Williams said, "Rocks, that's what they got." According to Williams, the rioters only knew Alexander "when they appeared before him in court," and when Moore arrived people "threw rocks at the truck." Moore's rhetoric did not end poverty or prevent the riot, and black residents were not going to allow Moore to pacify their anger.[57] Local people had a different perspective on black leadership than the media.

In 1967, Claude Lewis, a black journalist for the *Evening Bulletin*, wrote an editorial on black leadership in Philadelphia summarizing the differences between the "old leadership" and the "new leaders." According to Lewis, Judge Alexander, Congressman Robert N. C. Nix Sr., and J. Austin Norris represented the old leadership. The old leadership "gained its strength from the white power structure," was educated in the Ivy League, and had grown up in poverty. Lewis maintained that "today's leaders got their power from the people themselves" and the majority of them were born in the ghetto. New black leaders included Alice Lipscomb, chairperson on the Hawthorne Community Council, and Charles Bowser, deputy to the mayor. Lewis neglected to add that the new black leadership benefited from the massive amount of federal money that the government funneled into the black community to end rioting. All of the new leaders Lewis cited agreed that they were "providing a hand-up instead of the usual hand-out." Most thought that the black community needed to help itself, but in Lewis's essay, not one leader contributed a structural critique of the problem. Finally, Lewis failed to analyze black leadership in historical context.[58]

After Alexander read Lewis's essay, he wrote to the *Evening Bulletin*'s editor protesting that Lewis, "a native New Yorker," demonstrated a "recurrent naiveté." Alexander wanted to correct Lewis's interpretation of the "old leadership." Alexander stated that the "old leadership" came from the "ghetto league" in the Seventh Ward of Philadelphia or migrated from the South. Many were poor, although some, such as Sadie Tanner Mossell Alexander and Dr. R. R. Wright Jr., came from the middle class. In black Philadelphia, the middle class was defined not by wealth but by education and occupation; Alexander made the distinction that Lewis had failed to make. Alexander vehemently disagreed with Lewis's statement that the old leadership derived its power from the white power structure. He reminded readers that when he fought to desegregate downtown restaurants and theaters, even as late as the 1940s, "the white power structure—unlike today—fought us at every turn." The civil rights struggle had expanded political and economic opportunities for African Americans, and, as a result, by 1967 the white power structure was more receptive to African Americans in order to retain the black vote and prevent riots. Alexander referred to himself as a "peaceful activist." He lamented that he used to believe in the "myth of inevitability," but by 1967 he believed that the "future is no longer inevitable." He did not say why he worried that continued progress in race relations was not assured, but white resistance and black rioting seemed an ominous combination.[59]

This debate about black leadership is best understood in historical context. The New Negro generation of the twenties viewed the turn-of-the-century "old guard" as out of touch and too dependent on the white elite. At that time, the leadership was composed of caterers and barbers who served wealthy whites, were Republicans, and advocated integration. After the Great Migration, a black business and professional elite replaced the old guard. Most served black, rather than white, customers and clients. Some

black businessmen discouraged integration because they benefited financially from a captive market. In the 1920s, the New Negro generation of
attorneys emerged in Philadelphia and the nation. The New Negro attorney
advocated equality and was able to call on the political power of the growing black urban population. During the thirties, Alexander castigated old
guard leaders such as Amos Scott, a black attorney, for accepting only minor
rewards in return for the black vote. From the 1920s to the 1964 Philadelphia
race riot, Alexander's generation dominated black leadership. Alexander and
his colleagues were the first to obtain important political positions in the
city government. As racial progress occurred, black expectations rose; by
1960, African Americans demanded more than just tokenism, a few black
faces in high places. However, as racism, poverty, police brutality, and deindustrialization devastated the black community, the old leadership's mantra
of patience failed to meet the rising demands of the black community. Para-
doxically, the civil rights movement improved the quality of life for a large
segment of the black community; black poverty had decreased but remained
twice as high as white poverty. The riots gave the black poor a voice and, as
a result, the federal government put money into the black community. Consequently, a younger group of black leaders conducted most of their work in
the black community.

Historicizing the Struggle

Civil rights leaders and Black Power advocates shared some central ideas. For
example, Alexander supported black political power; while Black Power leaders advocated independent rather than party politics, both believed in political participation. Alexander and Black Power advocates supported studying
African American history to build self-esteem and race pride and to eradicate
racist myths about African Americans. Alexander was a lifelong member of
Carter G. Woodson's Association for the Study of African American Life and
History (ASALH) and emphasized black contributions to American history.
Black Power leaders emphasized African history and wanted African Ameri-
cans to embrace an African value system that promoted unity and rejected
Western culture. While Alexander supported studying African history, he did
not agree with African Americans who adopted African names and clothing.
He insisted that African Americans were Americans. Segregation had forced
Alexander and the New Negro generation to create all-black social and

professional organizations to combat racism. Alexander was a member of the National Bar Association and many other black social clubs, but during the late 1960s, when black college students in predominantly white universities protested for black dorms and Black Studies courses, Alexander vehemently denounced the students' effort. He could not understand why black students at his alma mater, the University of Pennsylvania, wanted all-black dorms. When he attended Penn he could not eat in the cafeteria. Ending involuntary segregation was not consistent, in his mind, with voluntary separation in the name of racial solidarity.

What disappointed Alexander most during the Black Power Era was how little anyone knew about the history of the civil rights struggle in Philadelphia. By the 1960s, the New Negro generation was older, and many had opportunities that they could only have dreamed of during the 1920s and 1930s. Some worked in white law firms and taught at white universities. From Alexander and the New Negro generation's perspective, racism in the 1960s was not as formidable as it was during the 1920s. Alexander realized in 1968, when he was booed at Girard College, that most Americans, black and white, were not aware of his or his generation's contributions to the civil rights struggle. Similarly, Rayford Logan, born the same year as Alexander, had graduated from Williams College and received his Ph.D. in history from Harvard, the accoutrements of a New Negro. During the 1960s, Logan was concerned with the younger generation's lack of historical knowledge about his generation's contributions. According to his biographer, Kenneth Janken, "The Black Power activists and the civil rights movement in general were, according to Logan, ignorant of their past and therefore had forgotten the pioneering role of Logan and his generation."[60] Alexander and Logan sought to make sure that their contributions to the civil rights movement and profession were known.

In March 1970, Robert Levine, editor of the *Cornell Law Journal*, asked Alexander to write an article titled "Blacks and the Law" for the spring issue. Levine stated that he was "not seeking only an establishment view"; he wanted "many different political and social views." The editor requested Alexander to "write from personal experience" about how he fought discrimination and to respond to the question, "can one be an activist within the law?" Alexander assured Levine that he was "in touch with the situation as it 'really is' today and I expect to tell it 'as it is' but more significant in my case, tell it like it was (awful) in those days." Alexander described numerous episodes of racism. For example, in the 1940s, a "Philadelphia Negro of good repute" on his way to South Carolina accidentally struck and killed a white girl. After the incident, the convicted man called Alexander. Alexander consulted his Harvard Directory and called a white Harvard-educated attorney, a "deep down southerner." Alexander intentionally did not tell him that he was African American and did not have the white attorney meet him at the airport. When Alexander arrived, the white attorney said, "Oh yes, so you're Alexander." The white lawyer did not say "Mr.," but Alexander did not say anything. According to Alexander, when he entered the court, he "was compelled to sit in the segregated section." His "lawyer friend" did not ask Alexander to sit in the lawyers' section. During the three-day trial, the prosecution reiterated to the jury that the man drove a "brand new cream colored Cadillac car." According to Alexander, that was his "worst guilt"—being a black man driving an expensive car. Alexander won the case, but his client remained in jail until his insurance agent paid the settlement fee.[61]

Next, Alexander discussed the status of black attorneys in Philadelphia. He complimented Bernard G. Segal, president of the American Bar Association, for providing ample opportunities for black attorneys in the city. In 1970, eight African American attorneys were employed in white law firms, including the "lily-white totally WASP" firm that had rejected Alexander in 1923. William T. Coleman Jr. was the first black attorney to work at a white law firm in Philadelphia. Coleman graduated from Harvard Law and served as a clerk for U.S. Supreme Court Justice Felix Frankfurter. Alexander praised the civil rights work performed not only by lawyers and clergy but also by "the poor and untrained, the denied and oppressed." Nonetheless, discrimination continued in Philadelphia because "knowledgeable whites" were ignorant to the plight of African Americans. "We must pay and pay and pay for the sins of malign neglect," he concluded.[62]

A number of publications reprinted Alexander's "Blacks and the Law." This essay represented the ideals of New Negro attorneys and judges across the nation. Civil rights attorneys and judges such as Alexander used the law to change society. The process was difficult, with more victories than defeats. Professionally, black attorneys had to grind their teeth and keep their mouths shut when they encountered racism in the judiciary. Alexander could ill afford to upset a judge if he wanted to be successful in court. Southern courts were even worse for black attorneys. Alexander did not spend a great deal of time in the South; when he was there, his law degree did not shield him from racism.[63]

In 1974, Alexander served on the ASNLH Bicentennial Advisor Council. The ASNLH planned to have a special session on black lawyers and judges.

U.S. District Court Judge Constance Baker Motley recommended to Derrick Bell, a black Harvard Law professor, that the ASNLH should make a film or a scholarly book on the contributions of black attorneys. She stated that some students at Amherst were "working on a biography on Houston, Hastie and, perhaps Marshall." Alexander received copies of the Advisory Council correspondence, and three days before he died, he wrote Motley and applauded her for dedicating a program on the history of black attorneys and civil rights. He informed Motley that he was working on his autobiography and mentioned to her about his long fight against segregation in Philadelphia.

One of Alexander's last public appearances occurred in Philadelphia at the 1974 ASNLH conference. The ASNLH invited U.S. District Court Judge A. Leon Higginbotham Jr. to provide the keynote address. Alexander introduced Higginbotham to the crowd. A major controversy ensued after Judge Higginbotham's address on civil rights and the federal courts. During the conference, Higginbotham was serving as the judge for a racial discrimination suit against a labor union. After the labor union read Acel Moore's *Philadelphia Inquirer* article about Higginbotham's speech, they requested that Higginbotham be removed from the case. Moore quoted Higginbotham, who stated, "As I see it, we must make major efforts in other forums without exclusive reliance on the federal legal process." The union lawyers claimed that Higginbotham was biased because he spoke to an all-"black audience." Higginbotham discussed the entire controversy in a *Journal of Negro History* article titled "To the Scale and Standing of Men." Higginbotham acknowledged that he was black but observed that no one had asked a Jewish judge to be removed for a case because of bias. He also stated that the ASNLH was comprised of black and white scholars. Higginbotham mentioned that Judge Alexander's speeches at the ASNLH had established a precedent for black lawyers speaking about racism and the law at scholarly conferences. On numerous occasions, Alexander spoke on legal issues at the ASNLH, and Higginbotham asked, "should Judge Alexander have been disqualified from even hearing a case involving racial claims?" Some whites believed that black judges could not be objective in cases involving African Americans. Higginbotham agued that Alexander used the ASNLH to advance the cause of black lawyers, civil rights, scholarship, and black history. Segregation forced African American professionals to work closer together to dismantle racism and segregation. Alexander consistently advocated black professionals working together for economic and social justice.[64]

On Saturday, November 25, 1974, Alexander returned to his office from a meeting in New York. When he did not come home that night, his wife called the police. The police went to his office and found him dead at his desk. Alexander died of a heart attack. Many remembered Alexander's contributions to the legal profession, civil rights, race relations, and the black community. The obituary in the *Philadelphia Inquirer* stated that Alexander was "an activist for civil rights long before it was a popular cause" who spoke out against "philosophical mistakes by a younger generation of black leaders." "His death at 76," the obituary stated, "deprives Philadelphia and the nation of an outstanding fighter against racial discrimination who was equally active promoting good race relations."

The obituary neglected to include Alexander's support of affirmative action and a guaranteed income for poor Americans. It correctly stated that Alexander was involved in the civil rights struggle long before it became popular, but what made it unpopular was white resistance in Philadelphia. Instead of writing about Alexander's radical ideas, the author used Alexander's type of leadership as a model to discredit younger leaders who sought to eradicate racism and poverty, the same issues Alexander had talked about. Claude Lewis of the *Philadelphia Inquirer* wrote: "He never threw a bomb, he never tossed a brick. He simply learned the law and fought to have it enforced." As a lawyer and judge, Alexander believed in and remained committed to the legal approach to obtaining civil rights for African Americans and improving race relations. However, this method by itself failed to desegregate unions in Philadelphia or make the black unemployment rate equal to the white rate. While rioting was a tragedy, it forced the federal government to address the issues in the black community.[65] John Saunders of the *Philadelphia Tribune* reported that Alexander was a "great man of our time," and he recalled the numerous legal cases Alexander had won. Longtime colleague J. Austin Norris stated in the *Evening Bulletin* that Alexander "was the first of the very able trial lawyers that Negroes had at the Philadelphia Bar."

Alexander's funeral was held at the First Baptist Church in order to accommodate the large number of people. Numerous dignitaries attended the funeral, including Frank Rizzo, the city's mayor, who maintained that Alexander was a "pioneer of equal rights." Congressman Nix Sr. stated in the *Philadelphia Tribune* that Alexander's "efforts on behalf of the Blacks, the underprivileged and deprived" improved the quality of life for those groups. Pennsylvania Supreme Court Judge Robert N. C. Nix Jr. stressed that Alexander inspired disadvantaged youths.[66]

While he was serving as a judge, Alexander continued his civil rights struggle in Philadelphia. Focusing on what he knew best, the law, he produced results through litigation and interracial coalitions, not mere slogans.

In the last phase of his long life, Alexander focused on poverty and inequality. As a result of the media's obsession with Black Power, moderate civil rights leaders such as Alexander were marginalized. Moreover, his relationship with the federal government prevented him from criticizing the Vietnam War. The funding that had been devoted to social programs was diverted to the military. Rather than blame the war, Alexander focused on criticizing the term "Black Power." In spite of his criticism of Black Power, the federal government continued to support the Vietnam War. In addition, the government blamed Black Power as the major stumbling block to obtaining funds for social programs and creating white backlash. White backlash existed before Carmichael stated Black Power in 1966 or the Black Panthers were formed. As long as racial oppression exists and African American demand equality, white backlash will follow. In reality, however, if Black Power had not existed, the federal government would still have been committed to financing the war.

Alexander's ideas changed over time in response to the major issues of the period. He shared some of the radical views King expressed in his last book, *Chaos or Community: Where Do We Go From Here*: "the solution to poverty is to abolish it directly by a now widely discussed measure: the guaranteed income."[67] In 1965, when Alexander gave a commencement address at Savannah State University, a historically black university, he talked about poverty and the need for a guaranteed income. Alexander's leadership was not as exciting as the Black Panthers, and white liberals constructed an Alexander that fit well with mainstream white America. For example, a congressman read Alexander's obituary in the House of Representatives, but he never mentioned Alexander's comment on a guaranteed income, or his suggestion of a Marshall Plan for black America. Instead, he praised Alexander as a responsible leader who "had condemned the call for black power."[68] Alexander's radicalism fits right in with King, Rustin, and others who understood that the problem in post–civil rights America was poverty and that the federal government must create policies to address it.

Alexander advocated progressive social policies, but he did not join the antiwar movement and remained allied with the Democratic Party. Alexander, Wilkins, Young, and Rustin all followed this strategy, a carryover from the Cold War, which defined civil rights as a domestic issue. Black radicals such as W. E. B. DuBois and Shirley Graham DuBois, Julian Mayfield, and Alphaeus Hunton continued to critique American foreign policy and promote building political relations with African nations.[69] Remaining loyal to the Democratic Party allowed Alexander and Young to represent the United States abroad. But it did not enable them to stem the resurgent tide of racism in white America. By the early 1970s, many white Democrats had decided that black culture, rather than economic and environmental conditions, lay at the root of black poverty.

CONCLUSION

In 1971, Senior Judge Raymond Pace Alexander spoke at the NAACP's testimonial dinner held in his honor. Alexander explained how he had used a "nonviolent, yet vigorous action rather than by explosive methods" to obtain civil rights. He insisted that his "approach to these problems was right and I still have faith in God and my country."[1] Historians have recently identified a "long history of the civil rights struggle,"[2] but Alexander participated in the "longer history of the civil rights struggle" that began during the New Negro era, as black lawyers in northern cities spurred the fight for equality. This struggle originated a decade before the New Deal and before civil rights became a national issue. This distinction is crucial. During the economic boom of the 1920s, most working-class whites were not concerned about black equality or working-class inequality, but African Americans still confronted racism and segregation. The Great Depression expanded the need for equality, and black and white worked together and found their common interests.

Alexander lived through three generations of activism and leadership: the New Negro era, World War II, and the era of civil rights and Black Power. What was radical during the 1920s was moderate by the 1960s. In order to appreciate Alexander's radicalism during the 1920s, we must be cognizant of the impact of racism and segregation in Philadelphia. Eating in a white-owned restaurant, sitting wherever one wanted in a white-owned theater, and staying at a white-owned hotel were off limits to African Americans. By the Black Power Era, African Americas expected to be able to do all these things without encountering discourtesy. Alexander's generation planted seeds for the next generation, who rightfully expected more than what their parents received. Martin Delaney, a nineteenth-century black leader, Union officer, and "The father of Black Nationalism," stated it best about generational expectations. In 1852, Delaney wrote: "The colored people of to-day are not the colored people of a quarter of a century ago, and require very different means and measures to satisfy their wants and demands, and to effect their advancement. No wise statesman presumes the same measures for the satisfaction of the American people now, that may have been with propriety adopted twenty-five years ago; neither is it wisdom to presume that the privileges which satisfied colored people twenty years ago, they will be reconciled with now." Every generation of African Americans desire more than the last, and there will be new leaders with higher expectations. The New Negro generation increased expectations for the Civil Rights/Black Power generation. During the late sixties a generational shift had occurred in black America, and it took Alexander and white America by surprise.[3]

Alexander's life was a microcosm of a generation of New Negro lawyers. Born at the turn of the century, Alexander grew up in a working poor household and faced overt racial discrimination, but hard work, education, and mentoring by African American intellectuals and professionals provided him with wider opportunities. The New Negro generation fought to obtain the rights and privileges of American citizens, but in order to combat racism, they formed separate social organizations, including college fraternities such as Omega Psi Phi Fraternity and Alpha Phi Alpha Incorporated, sororities such as Delta Sigma Theta and Alpha Kappa Alpha, and professional organizations such as the National Bar Association and the National Medical Association. Alexander advocated race pride and encouraged all Americans to study African American history. As a high school student, he was fortunate to hear Carter Woodson, the "father of black history," give a talk at his church on black people's contributions to world history. Much later, black history became an important subject in the Freedom Schools established by SNCC. Studying black history has been an important component of the civil rights struggle that is often overlooked. Both New Negro and Black Power advocates stressed the importance of studying the past in order to understand the rich cultural heritage of African civilizations and the struggles and achievements of African Americans. However, Alexander did not support adopting African names as black cultural nationalists did.

During the 1920s and 1930s, the NAACP led a long, systematic litigation campaign against segregation in the South. During the same period, Alexander led a campaign against de facto segregation in Philadelphia. The majority of his public accommodation desegregation cases involved middle-class African Americans. Kevin Gaines refers to the black middle class's

determination to eradicate segregation in public spaces as "social integration."
Historian Evelyn Brooks Higginbotham argues that the black middle class
incorporated a "politics of respectability." For example, in Montgomery, Alabama, black leaders decided not to make a test case when Claudette Clovin,
an unmarried pregnant teenager, did not give up her seat for a white man.
Rosa Parks, who was eminently respectable, dignified, professional, and married, was the ideal person for the case. African Americans knew that they had
to send the best and brightest to prove to white America that they deserved
equality. Recognizing this fact, Alexander and others based their civil rights
strategy around this formula.[4]

At the same time, in criminal cases Alexander often employed a black
pathology argument to convince the jury that racism, poor education, and
structural disadvantages may have caused those accused to commit the
crimes. Alexander occasionally tried to prove that his clients were not intelligent enough to write or speak like the confessions the prosecutors used
against them. This strategy was effective, but it illustrates the impact of race
and class. The cases of Willie Brown, Walter Rounds, and the Trenton Six all
involved uneducated black men; therefore, he employed a strategy that reaffirmed racial and class assumptions that whites and some middle-class blacks
held about poor African Americans. In civil court, Alexander brought out
the best in the black community, but in criminal court he used the worst to
explain the connections between racism and crime.

As some scholars examined the growing class divide in the black community, a study of black lawyers reveals that in spite of the growing number
of black attorneys in corporate America, racism continues to plague the profession. According to Andrew Hacker, in 1990, black male attorneys aged
thirty-five to thirty-nine made $744 for every $1,000 white attorneys made
and black female attorneys made $926 for every $1,000 that white female
attorneys made. A wage gap still exists between black and white attorneys
of similar background. Self-employed black attorneys are still supported by a
black clientele. Furthermore, most black judges are still elected by a majority
of black voters. Obviously, a black attorney's income is much higher than that
of working-class African Americans, but when they are compared with their
white counterparts, a gap remains in status and in salary. There are also com-
paratively few black judges on the federal bench. The battle that Alexander
fought has not yet been won.

A growing number of African American attorneys are members of historically all-white bar associations, but their participation in black bar associations is still necessary. Since the 1960s, a large number of African American

professionals are more active in white organizations than in African American organizations. Alexander advocated African American lawyers participating in predominantly white bar organizations, but he also wanted black attorneys to participate in the NBA. He realized that mainstream bar organizations were not as committed to addressing the issues that black attorneys and the black community encounter. Alexander insisted that African Americans participate in both predominantly white and all-black organizations.[5]

During the Black Power era, younger leaders criticized the New Negro generation. Many were unaware of the long civil rights struggle Alexander had fought in Philadelphia. The 1964 Philadelphia race riot not only left damaging reminders in North Philadelphia but took with it the interracial understanding that Alexander, his wife, Sadie, and others had achieved. In 1964, most of the youth in the black community were entirely ignorant of the depth and pervasiveness of racism in Philadelphia during the 1920s. Cecil B. Moore's referring to Alexander as an "Uncle Tom" did not help, either. The oblivion into which Alexander fell in Philadelphia may be a microcosm for other attorneys in northern cities. When the race riots of the sixties began, it erased from memory the civil rights gains made in the North by Alexander and the New Negro generation of attorneys. Moreover, in post–civil rights America, black elected officials emerged as the new leaders in urban areas. Alexander played a central role in making Philadelphia a Democratic city, and he helped to create a black political leadership class that emerged after World War II and continues today.

Alexander never supported Black Power, but he suggested a more radical solution to racism by highlighting its base in structural poverty. He advocated a guaranteed income and a Marshall Plan for black America. King advocated these radical ideas during the late sixties. According to historian Thomas Jackson, King understood "poverty as a structural pillar of a capitalist society,"[6] and by the late sixties, King sought not merely reform but a fundamental restructuring of American society. Matthew Countryman argues, "Black Power advocates were never able to convince other elements of the New Deal coalition to bear the cost of its agenda for racial justice."[7] Coalition building was a major part of Alexander's strategy, but many whites in Philadelphia failed to see how improving conditions for African Americans would improve the lives of all Americans. Unfortunately, most white Philadelphians viewed racial progress as a zero-sum game; therefore, when there was an increase in the number of blacks in "white positions," whites felt that they were losing ground, even though inequalities persisted between blacks and whites.

Alexander's generation and the Black Power generation failed to find common ground. But as Alexander got older, he became more critical of the slow progress in race relations. The majority of civil rights and Black Power leaders concluded that the federal government must take steps to make amends for years of neglect, but the leaders disagreed about tactics. For example, Alexander warned young black activists not to take over buildings or use violent tactics. Most African Americans knew that armed tactics were not effective in the United States because they allowed the police to use force to control black militants. Ironically, it took race riots and campus takeovers to get the federal government and universities to become democratic and create social policies to address race, class, and gender inequality. Alexander's generation eliminated the de jure racism that plagued America and persuaded the power structure to increase black representation in middle-class society.

During the late sixties, younger activists criticized black tokenism and Alexander's civil rights strategy, but they undervalued the progress. For example, according to Algernon Austin, in 1940, 90 percent of blacks were in poverty; in 1966, the poverty rate for blacks decreased to 42 percent; and in 2000, the black poverty rate was 23 percent, an all-time low. In addition, Austin declares, "Blacks are more educated now than they have ever been."[8] In terms of poverty and education, there has been progress, but the insidious combination of structural racism and poverty continues to maintain higher black unemployment and poverty rates. By the late 1960s, younger leaders whose expectations had been raised and then disappointed adopted a militant discourse that demanded an end to racism. Younger militants may not have been aware of the declining poverty rates, but their impatience with the system was a product of institutionalized racism and poverty. Alexander's generation had recognized the problem of racism and poverty but clung to the conviction that only litigation and legislation, supported by popular mobilization and interracial coalitions, were capable of achieving the comprehensive solutions that ending racial inequality required.

NOTES

Introduction

1. UPT 50 A 74 Sadie Tanner Mossell Alexander Box 1 Folder 6, *The Philadelphia Bulletin*, January 24, 1965, in the Sadie Tanner Mossell Alexander Papers at the University of Pennsylvania Archives. I will refer to her papers as STMA Box # and Folder #.

2. W. E. B. DuBois, "Close Ranks," in Lewis, *W. E. B. DuBois*, 697.

3. Woodward, *Origins of the New South*; Hahn, *Nation Under Our Feet*.

4. Woodward, *Strange Career of Jim Crow*, 17.

5. For historiography of the civil rights movement see Eagles, "Toward New Histories of the Civil Rights Era"; Gaines, "Historiography of the Struggle"; Kluger, *Simple Justice*; Garrow, *Bearing the Cross*; Meier and Rudwick, *CORE*.

6. Carson, In Struggle; Dyson, *I May Not Get There With You*; Chafe, *Civilities and Civil Rights*; Dittmer, *Local People*; Payne, *I've Got the Light of Freedom*; Tuck, *Beyond Atlanta*; Fairclough, *Race and Democracy*; Ransby, *Ella Baker and the Black Freedom Movement*; Dudziak, *Cold War Civil Rights*; Morris, *Origins of the Civil Rights Movement*; Theoharis and Woodward, *Groundwork*.

7. Theoharis and Woodard, *Freedom North*; Hirsch, "Massive Resistance in the Urban North"; Wolcott, "Recreation and Race in the Postwar City"; Sugrue, "Affirmative Action from Below"; Biondi, *To Stand and Fight*; Self, *American Babylon*; Countryman, *Up South*; Sugrue, *Sweet Land of Liberty*.

8. Woodward, *Strange Career of Jim Crow*, 114.

9. Schneider, *We Return Fighting*; Boyle, *Arc of Justice*; Brisbane, *Black Vanguard*, 42; Tuttle, *Race Riot*; Haynes, *Night of Violence*; Jackson, *Ku Klux Klan in the City*; Weems, *Desegregating the Dollar*, 10.

10. Lewis, *When Harlem was in Vogue*, 24; Meier, *Negro Thought in America*, 258.

11. 2007; Work, "Negro In Business and the Professions," 140; Locke, *New Negro*, 11; James, *Holding Aloft the Banner of Ethiopia*.

12. Smith, *Emancipation*; Hine, "Black Lawyers and the Twentieth-Century Struggle for Constitutional Change," 34. Blakely, *Earl B. Dickerson*, is a biography about an influential New Negro lawyer in Chicago and Alexander's colleague.

13. McNeil, *Groundwork; Ware, William Hastie;* Williams, *Thurgood Marshall.*

14. Hardy, "Race and Opportunity," 283–84; Woodson, *Negro Professional Man,* 199; RPA, "The Struggle Against Racism in Philadelphia From 1923–1948" 2, RPA Box 97 Folder 19.

15. The sixteen states were Connecticut (1884), Iowa (1884), New Jersey (1884), Ohio (1884), Colorado (1885), Illinois (1885), Indiana (1885), Massachusetts (1885), Michigan (1885), Minnesota (1885), Nebraska (1885), Rhode Island, (1885), Pennsylvania (1887), New York (1893), Washington (1890), Wisconsin (1895), California (1897), and Kansas, (1905). Stephenson, *Race and Distinction in American Law.* Alexander quoted in the *Philadelphia Tribune,* April 11, 1935.

16. Pfeffer, *A. Philip Randolph;* Korstad, *Civil Rights Unionism.*

17. *Philadelphia Inquirer,* August 24, 1964.

18. Tompkins, *Pullman Porters;* Tushnet, *NAACP's Legal Strategy;* Mack, "Law and Mass Politics," 38–39; Gaines, *Uplifting the Race,* 238.

19. Williams, *Thurgood Marshall,* 247–48; RPA, "John M. Langston Law Club," *The Shingle* (December 1951), 233–34, in RPA Box 97 Folder 23; *Philadelphia Tribune,* May 9, 1925; *Pittsburgh Courier,* May 23, 1925.

20. Krenn, *Black Diplomacy;* Countryman, *Up South,* 1.

21. RPA Box 99, Folder 44; Ralph Ellison, quoted in Singh, *Black is A Country,* 55.

Chapter One

1. For biographical information on Raymond Pace Alexander's parents, see RPA to Dr. Clifton H. Johnson, September 15, 1969, 1, RPA Box 14 Folder 1; RPA, UPT 50 U74, Oversize Scrapbook, "A Brief Sketch of the Life of Raymond Pace Alexander," n.d.; "Obituary for Samuel Alexander," ca. 1952; RPA's Birth Certificate; Hillard B. Alexander's Birth Certificate, RPA Box 1 Folder 47; Hillard Alexander's Marriage Certificate, March 24, 1922, City Hall Archives, Philadelphia. On Philadelphia, see Roger Lane, *William Dorsey's Philadelphia and Ours,* 64–66; Gregg, *Sparks From the Anvil of Oppression,* 150–51.

2. On black migration, see Painter, *Exodusters;* Rabinowitz, *Race Relations in the Urban South;* Cohen, *At Freedom's Edge;* Taylor and Hill, *Historical Roots of the Urban Crisis.*

3. Lane, *William Dorsey's Philadelphia and Ours,* 63; Osofsky, *Harlem;* Kusmer, *Ghetto Takes Shape;* Trotter, *Black Milwaukee;* Lewis, *In Their Own Interests;* Thomas, *Life For Us Is What We Make It.*

4. Lane, *Roots of Violence in Black Philadelphia,* 62–67.

5. Du Bois, *Philadelphia Negro,* 47, 107; Hershberg et al., "Tale of Three Cities."

6. DuBois, *Philadelphia Negro,* 311–16. Only a minority was lower class and engaged in such morally dubious activities as drinking, gambling, prostitution, and crime. Like most sociologists, DuBois attributed these problems to environmental and economic factors rather than to racial factors or family pathology. *Philadelphia Tribune,* June 27, 1925; RPA Box 7 Folder 20; RPA Box 1 Folder 47; RPA's Birth Certificate, RPA Box 1 Folder Penn.

7. Lane, *William Dorsey's Philadelphia,* 128.

8. *Philadelphia Tribune,* June 27, 1925; RPA Box 7 Folder 20; RPA Box 1 Folder 47; RPA's Birth Certificate. For black Philadelphia's occupational structure, see DuBois, *Philadelphia Negro,* 107; Hardy, "Race and Opportunity," 15–17. On the Alexanders' riding business, see RPA Box 1 Folder Penn. On the changing structural position of the black community, see Kusmer, "Black Urban Experience in American History," 106–7.

9. For Virginia Pace Alexander, see Death Certificate 28288, City Archives, Philadelphia, Pennsylvania; DuBois, *Philadelphia Negro*, 152, 214; "Facts Concerning the Life History of Mrs. Georgia C. Pace," RPA Box III Folder 3.

10. *Philadelphia Tribune*, June 27, 1925; RPA to Carl Murphy, May 2, 1949, RPA Box 1 Folder 7; Franklin, *Education of Black Philadelphia*, 39–45.

11. Odum, "Negro Children in the Public Schools of Philadelphia."

12. RPA to Leon Sullivan, RPA Box 7 Folder 20.

13. *Philadelphia Tribune*, June 25, 1927; RPA to Carl Murphy, May 2, 1949, RPA Box 1 Folder 7; Labaree, *Making of an American High School*, 159–70.

14. Alexander, "Days of Glory," *Central High School: Alumni Journal* (May 1953), 3, 15–16; RPA Box 1 Folder 17; Alexander to Sullivan, RPA Box 7, Folder 20; Assorted Newspaper and Magazine articles, RPA Box 1 Folder 6.

15. Alexander, "Legal Education and Formative Influences in the Law," RPA Box 1 Folder 15; Alexander, "A Short Summary of the Life and Activities of Raymond Pace Alexander," May 1966, RPA Box 1 Folder 8; E. W. Moore, n.d., to RPA in RPA Box 1 Folder Penn; DuBois, *Philadelphia Negro*, 320.

16. Alexander, "Stranger in the House," RPA Box 99 Folder 28; Goggin, *Carter G. Woodson*, 42.

17. Alexander, "Legal Education," RPA Box 1 Folder 15; "Alexander, "Stranger in the House," RPA Box 99 Folder 28; Meier, *Negro Thought in America*, 260–63.

18. Alexander, "Legal Education," RPA Box 1 Folder 15. For biographical information on William H. Lewis, see Smith, *Emancipation*, 105–8.

19. RPA to Carl Murphy, May 2, 1949; RPA Box 1 Folder Central High. On Houston and Hastie's education, see McNeil, *Groundwork*, 24–31; Ware, *William Hastie*, 7–11.

20. Misc. Biographical writings in RPA Box 1, Folder 1; *Central High School Class Record* (February 1917), 11; Box III Folder 31; *Philadelphia Tribune*, February 24, 1917.

21. Johnson, *Negro College Graduate*, 9; STMA Box 1 Folder 6; RPA Box 1 Folder Penn.

22. "Short Biographical Sketches," RPA Box 1 Folder 5; RPA to Carl Murphy, May 2, 1949, RPA Box 1 Folder 7. On Millen, see RPA Box 98 Folder 56; Williams, *Thurgood Marshall*, 44–45.

23. Rudwick, *Race Riot in East St. Louis*,; Franklin, "Philadelphia Race Riot 1918," *Pennsylvania History Magazine and Biography* 99 (1975): 336–50; Tuttle, *Race Riot.*

24. On Penn's SATC, see *Pennsylvania Gazette*, October 4, 11, 25, 1918, and December 13, 1918; for black SATC students, see RPA Box 1 Folder Penn, SATC, U of Penn. Informal Dance sponsored by black undergraduate students. Discharge papers RPA Box 1 Folder Penn. DuBois, "Close Ranks."

25. Senior Grades, RPA Box 1 Folder Penn; RPA to Eustace Gay, May 12, 1970, RPA Box 14 Folder 27. Taylor and Ha, "A Unity of Opposites," 36–37.

26. Alexander, "Legal Education," RPA Box 1 Folder 15; Henry L. Abraham to RPA, March 30, April 3, 30, 1970; RPA Box 14 Folder 27; John C. Wheeler to RPA Box 14 Folder 27, March 31, April 6, 30, 1970; RPA to Eustace Gay, May 12, 1970, RPA Box 14, Folder 27; *Philadelphia Tribune* June 19, 1920.

27. Janken, *Rayford W. Logan*, 28.

28. University of Pennsylvania, *The Record*, 1920, 18, University of Pennsylvania Archives.

29. Schneider, *Boston Confronts Jim Crow*, 4.

30. Fox, *Guardian of Boston*; Sollors, Titcomb, and Underwood, *Blacks at Harvard.*

31. Alexander, "Blacks and the Law."

32. Alexander, "Blacks and the Law,"; RPA Box 99 Folder 66; RPA Box 7 Folder 20; Houston quoted in McNeil, *Groundwork*, 50; McNeil, *Groundwork*, 50–53; Dunbar Law Club, RPA Box 87 Folder 32.

33. Daniel C. McCarthy to RPA, July 25, 1935, RPA Box 9 Folder 4; RPA to McCarthy, July 31, 1935, RPA Box 9 Folder 4; "Biographical Sketch," STMA Box 1 Folder 6, STMA to RPA, May 16, 1921, STMA Box 3, Folder 1; *The Crisis* 24 (July 21).

34. Alexander, "Legal Education" (n.d.), RPA Papers, Box 1 Folder 15; James D. McLendon to Municipal Court of the City of New York, RPA Box 6 Folder 1; Murray, *State's Laws on Race and Color,* 305–06; *The Crisis* 24 (July 1921), 128. There is no record of the court's decision on Alexander's case; the docket file was destroyed.

35. A. Lawrence Lowell to Roscoe Conkling Bruce, in *New York Age*, 20 January 1923, quoted in Sollors, Titcomb, and Underwood, *Blacks at Harvard*, 196.

36. Alexander, "Voices from Harvard's Own Negroes"; Sollors, Titcomb, and Underwood, *Blacks at Harvard*, 189–94. Graham, *Senator and the Socialite*, 309–16.

37. McNeil, *Groundwork*, 53; Goggin, *Woodson*, 141, 151–52; Kornweibel, *Seeing Red*, 120–21.

38. Ware, *Grace Under Pressure*, 32.

39. Johnson, *Negro College Graduate*, 8; Leonard, *Black Lawyers,* 142; Banks, *Black Intellectuals*, 92; *The Crisis* 28 (July 1923), 108.

40. Segal, *Blacks in the Law*, 29; Liacourus, "Report," 150–60.

41. Biographical Sketch, RPA Box 1 Folder 7; RPA Box 1 Folder 1 "1900 Chestnut Street"; *Philadelphia Tribune*, June 25, 1927. The same incident is in Smith's *Emancipation*, 36–37. On Scott and Alexander's father, see *Pittsburgh Courier*, March 5, 1955, in Sadie and Raymond Alexander Joint Papers, UPT 40 STMA-RPA Box 1 Folder 4.

42. *Philadelphia Tribune*, January 26, 1924.

43. *Philadelphia Tribune*, October 24, 1925.

44. *Pittsburgh Courier*, October 24, 1925.

45. *Pittsburgh Courier*, October 24, 1925; *Philadelphia Tribune*, October 31, 1925.

46. *Philadelphia Tribune*, December 11, 1926; Woodson, *Negro Professional Man*, 203–4, 207.

47. *Philadelphia Tribune*, March 29, 1924; April, 19, 1924; *Pittsburgh Courier*, March 28, 1925.

48. Woodson, *Negro Professional Man*, 198; Meier and Rudwick, "Attorneys Black and White." For firm finances, see RPA Box 26 Folder 1.

49. *Philadelphia Tribune*, May 17, 1924.

50. "My Struggle Against Racism in Philadelphia 1923–1948," RPA Box 100 Folder 56.

Chapter Two

1. "The New Negro Fights For Justice," RPA Box 95 Folder 54.

2. Mack, "Rethinking Civil Rights Lawyering and Politics," 256, 280.

3. Mollison, "Negro Lawyers in Mississippi"; Smith, *Emancipation;* and Smith, "Black Bar Association and Civil Rights."

4. Smith, *Emancipation*, census data, 630–33, founding of NBA, 574, local black bar associations, 581–83; Hine, "Black Professionals and Race Consciousness"; for a copy of the NBA's Constitution, see RPA Box 85 Folder 1.

5. On local black bar organizations, see Smith, *Emancipation*, 581–83; Alexander, "John M. Langston Law Club," *The Shingle* (December 1951), 233–34, in RPA Box 97 Folder 23; *Philadelphia Tribune*, May 9, 1925; *Pittsburgh Courier*, May 23, 1925.

6. *Philadelphia Tribune*, March 7, 1925, *Philadelphia Inquirer*, March 5, 1925; *Washington Daily American*, March 6, 1925.

7. Joseph B. Bowser to Robert Bagnall, February 2, 1925; White to Martin, February 24, 1925; all in the NAACP Local Branches Correspondence, Box G 186, Manuscript Division, Library of Congress; Schneider, *We Return Fighting.*, 358–60.

8. RPA to Walter White, March 20, 1925, in NAACP Local Branch Correspondence, Box G 186.

9. Rounds testimony in *Court of Oyer and Marsh Session Testimonies Nos. 15, 16, 17 1925*, 453; RPA to White, March 20, 1925, in NAACP Local Branch Correspondence, Box G 187; *Philadelphia Tribune*, March 7, 1925; *Philadelphia Inquirer*, March 5, April 25, 1925.

10. White to RPA, March 10, 1925; Martin to White, March 14, 1925; Julian St. George White to Walter White, March 16, 1925; all in NAACP Philadelphia Branch Correspondence, Box G 186.

11. White to RPA, March 10, 1925; Martin to White, March 14, 1925; Julian St. George White to White, March 16, 1925; all in NAACP Philadelphia Branch Correspondence, Box G 186.

12. RPA to White, March 20, 1925; White to RPA, March 21, 1925; all in NAACP Local Branch Correspondence, Box G 187.

13. Martin to White, March 24, 1925; RPA to White, April 2, 1925; Martin to White, April 6, 1925; White to Martin, April 8, 1925; all in NAACP Local Branch Correspondence, Box G 186.

14. White to RPA, April 13, 1925; White to RPA, April 15, 1925; White to Martin, April 28, 1925; all in NAACP Local Branch Correspondence, Box G 186.

15. White to Martin, April 28, 1925, in NAACP Local Branch Correspondence, Box G 186.

16. *Philadelphia Tribune*, September 19, 1925; Smith, *Emancipation*, 39.

17. *Philadelphia Tribune*, October 9, 1926; Hale, "Career Development," 68.

18. *Philadelphia Tribune*, March 19, 1927; STMA Box 1 Folder 20; *Hartford Observer*, June 25 1927; *Pittsburgh Courier*, July 18, 1927; STMA Box 2 Folder 15; Graham, *Our Kind of People*; Woodson, *Negro Professional Man*, 195; *Philadelphia Tribune*, March 19, 1927, March 17, 1928, and January 12, 1933.

19. "Specialization of Practice and Law Partnership or Association Needed to Enhance Position of Bar," RPA Box 95 Folder 29; Woodson, *Negro Professional Man*, 235–36; Smith, *Emancipation*, 558–59.

20. Louise J. Pridgeon to RPA, June 12, 1930, RPA Box 85 Folder 5; RPA to Moorfield Storey, July 26, 1930, RPA Box 85 Folder 5.

21. "The Negro Lawyer: His Duty in a Rapidly Changing Social, Economic and Political World," RPA Box 95 Folder 36.

22. *Philadelphia Tribune*, January 30, 1930; RPA to Elmer Carter, July 27, 1931, RPA Box 87 Folder 7; Alexander, "Negro Lawyer."

23. RPA to Louise Pridgeon, June 25, 1931, RPA Box 87 Folder 7; RPA to Perry Howard, July 27, 1931, RPA Box 85 Folder 12; RPA to Patterson, July 31, 1931, RPA Box 85 Folder 15; RPA

to Pound, June 22, 1931, RPA Box 85 Folder 12; Darrow to RPA, August 2, 1931, RPA Box 85 Folder 13; Walter White to RPA, July 17, 1931, RPA Box 87 Folder 7; RPA to White, July 21, 1931, RPA Box 85 Folder 15; RPA to Eugene Gordon, RPA Box 85 Folder 5.

24. Mack, "Law and Mass Politics," 39.

25. "Our Profession and Our Bar," RPA Box 95 Folder 38; Smith, *Emancipation*, 561–62; RPA to Claude Barnett, June 5, 1931, RPA Box 85 Folder 10; RPA to Mary Church Terrell, February 16, 1931; Terrell to RPA, February 19, 1931, RPA Box 85 Folder 11; Carter, *Scottsboro*, 143.

26. Carter, *Scottsboro*, 68; Tushnet, *NAACP's Legal Strategy*, 31; Meier and Rudwick, "Attorneys Black and White," 135.

27. "Address at the NBA Convention," RPA 95, Folder 45. Smith, *Emancipation*, 562–63.

28. "Address at the NBA Convention," RPA 95, Folder 45

29. RPA Box 87 Folder 7; for police brutality, see *Philadelphia Tribune*, October 2, 1930. The "third degree treatment" was a code for forced confessions; white police officers brutalized black men in order to get them to admit to crimes. If the crime involved a white female, the police used the "third degree" without any fear of punishment.

30. *Philadelphia Tribune*, March 24, 1932.

31. RPA to Walter White, March 25, 1932, NAACP Philadelphia Branch Correspondence, Box G 188; Nelson, "Race and Class Consciousness," 340–43.

32. RPA to Walter White, March 25, 1932, NAACP Philadelphia Branch Correspondence, Box G 188.

33. RPA to White, March 25, 1932, NAACP Branch Correspondence, Box G 188; Nelson, "Philadelphia NAACP," 255.

34. Millen to White, March 18, 1932; White to Millen, March 21, 1932; White to Arthur Spingarn, March 25, 1932; White to Spingarn, March 29, 1932; Spingarn to White, March 30, 1932; White to Spingarn, April 1, 1932; RPA to White, April 5, 1932; White to RPA, April 6, 1932; all in NAACP Local Branch Correspondence G 188.

35. Judge George W. Maxey opinion, *Commonwealth* vs. *William Brown* 307 PA 134, November 29, 1932; *Philadelphia Tribune*, December 1, 1932, January 1, 1933; *Philadelphia Record*, January 18, 1933; RPA to White, January 18, 1933; RPA to White, January 24, 1933; all in NAACP Branch Correspondence, Box G 188; *Philadelphia Tribune*, January 26, February 2, 1933.

36. Robert C. Nix Jr. to Walter White, April 22, 1933, in NAACP Local Branch Correspondence, Box G 188.

37. White to RPA, March 27, 1933; White to Millen, March 28, 1933; White to RPA, March 28, 1933; Houston to White, March 27, 1933; William Patterson to Houston, March 29, 1933; Houston to White, March 28, 1933; White to Millen, March 31, 1933; RPA to White, April 25, 1933; all in NAACP Local Branch Correspondence, G 188.

38. Meier and Rudwick, "Origins of Nonviolent Direct Action," 312–13. See also Pierce, *Polite Protest*.

39. RPA to White, July 13, 1933, NAACP Legal File, Box 48 Folder 6; Wiese, *Places of Their Own*, 51. For Chester County and Philadelphia data, see fisher.lib.virginia.edu/collections/stats/histcensus/php/county

40. Berwyn is not an incorporated place; its territory fell in both Eastown and Tredyffrin townships. Alexander, "Outline of the School Situation in Eastown and Tredyffrin Townships," October 18, 1933. NAACP Legal File Box 48 Folder 8; *Philadelphia Tribune*, August 28, October 13, 1932; *NAACP Annual Report 1932* (New York, 1933), 27.

41. *Philadelphia Inquirer*, May 16, 2004, A 22.

42. RPA to Walter White, July 13, 1933, NAACP Legal File, Box 48 Folder 7; RPA to Robert M. Bagnall, August 24, 1932, NAACP Legal File, Box 48, Folder 5; Roy Wilkins to RPA, September 8, 1932, NAACP Legal File, Box 48, Folder 5. The NAACP had filed or was about to file lawsuits in Vincennes and Gary, Indiana; Toms River, New Jersey; Hillburn, New York; Dayton and Mansfield, Ohio; Douglass, Arizona; Coffeyville, Kansas; and Vallejo, California. Meier and Rudwick, "Origins of Non Violent Direct Action," 307.

43. *Philadelphia Inquirer*, May 16, 2004, A 22.

44. *Main Line Daily Times*, October 12, 1932, NAACP Legal File, Box 48, Folder 5; *Philadelphia Record*, January 1, 1933, NAACP, Legal File, Box 48, Folder 6; *Philadelphia Tribune*, November 24, 1932, December 29, 1932, January 5, 1933.

45. Alexander, "Outline of the School Situation" (October 18, 1933), 2, NAACP, Legal File, Box 48 Folder 8.

46. Philadelphia Yearly Meetings of the Religious Society of Friends Committee on Race Relations Series I Box 1, December 20, 27, 1932, February, 21, 1933, Swarthmore College.

47. Alexander, "Outline of the School Situation" (October 18, 1933), 2, NAACP Legal File, Box 48 Folder 8; White to RPA, February 17, 1933; White, "Memorandum to the Pennsylvania Branches of the N.A.A.C.P.," February 21, 1933; Roy Wilkins to W. W. Hines, March 10, 1933; all in NAACP Legal Files, Box 48 Folder 7.

48. White to RPA, June 2, 1933; RPA to White, June 5, 1933; both in NAACP Legal File, Box 48, Folder 7; Wilkins to RPA, November 15, 1933, NAACP Legal File Box 48 Folder 8.

49. The Communist Party organized the LSNR in 1930 as a successor to the American Negro Labor Congress and was active in the Scottsboro defense. The LSNR opposed police brutality and supported the creation of an independent black nation in the South. It was dissolved with the Communist Party's shift to the Popular Front policy in 1935 and was succeeded by the National Negro Labor Congress.

50. *Harlem Liberator*, August 11, 1934.

51. W. L. Johnson to Walter White, October 12, 1933; Wilkins to Cobb, September 28, 1933; Cobb to Wilkins, October 4, 1933; all in NAACP Legal Files, Box 48, Folder 8.

52. RPA to Wilkins, October 20, 1933; O. B. Cobb to Wilkins, October 19, 1933; White to Herbert Millen, October 21, 1933; all in NAACP Legal File Box 48 Folder 8; *Philadelphia Tribune*, October 14, 1933; *NAACP Annual Report 1933*, 19–20.

53. Wilkins, "Memorandum on the Berwyn School Case," October 2, 1933; Wilkins to Bryan, October 25, 1933; Wilkins to Lucille Milner, November 3, 1933; all in NAACP Legal Files, Box 48 Folder 8.

54. *Harlem Liberator*, March 24, 1934.

55. Alexander, "Minutes of the First Seminar on Segregation," January 26, 1934, 10, CORR, Series 2 Box 2.

56. Helen Bryan, January 6, 1934, Committee on Race Relations, Series 2 Box 2; Ralph J. Bunche and Charles Hamilton Houston, "Seminar on Segregation," CORR, Series 2 Box 2; DuBois, "Segregation" *The Crisis*, January 1934, in Lewis, *DuBois*, 557.

57. Bates, *Pullman Porters and the Rise of Protest Politics*. For the Philadelphia protest meeting and the march on Washington for the Scottsboro case, see *Philadelphia Tribune*, January 26, February 2 and 16, March 20, April 13, 20, and 27, June 1 and 22, 1933. W. A. Richards

to Patrick H. Jeffries, May 6 and 11, 1933, in Floyd Logan Papers, Temple University Urban Archives, Folder 1 Box 2.

58. *Philadelphia Tribune*, February 10, 1934; Davis to Dear Friend, February 17, 1934, Logan Papers, Folder 1 Box 1; Logan to LeStrange, February 23, 1934, Logan Papers, Folder 1 Box 2; LeStrange to Theodore White, February 26, 1934, Logan Papers, Folder 1 Box 2; *Philadelphia Tribune*, March 1 and 8, 1934; Wilkins to Millen, April 27, 1934, NAACP Legal File Box 48, Folder 9; *Philadelphia Tribune*, November 23, 1933; Goings, *NAACP Come of Age*.

59. *Philadelphia Tribune*, April 19 and 26, 1934; Franklin, *Education of Black Philadelphia*, 141.

60. RPA to Wilkins, May 10, 1934; NAACP Legal File, Box 48 Folder 9.

61. *Philadelphia Tribune*, May 3, 1934; *Philadelphia Record*, May 1, 1934; Wilkins to RPA, May 7, 1934; Wilkins to Cobb, May 5, 1934 in NAACP Legal File, Box 48 Folder 9. Douglas, *Jim Crow Moves North*, 210–11.

62. *Philadelphia Record*, May 1, 1934; *Philadelphia Tribune*, May 10, 1934; *Philadelphia Independent*, May 6, 1934; NAACP Legal File, Box 48, Folder 9.

63. Smith, *Emancipation*, 156–57.

64. "The Negro Lawyer: His Part in a Reconstructed Race Program," RPA Box 95 Folder 21.

65. *Philadelphia Tribune*, April 11, May 2 and 9, June 6 and 13, 1935; McBride, "Mid-Atlantic State Courts," 580–82.

66. *Philadelphia Tribune,* August 22, 1935.

67. *Philadelphia Tribune* August 22, 1935. On racial discrimination, see *Philadelphia Tribune*, April 2 and 18, 1935. Thomas Gates to RPA, April 5, 1935, Box 9 Folder 3. Gates apologized to Alexander because the University of Pennsylvania prohibited Howard University Law students from staying on campus during a conference. Nelson, "Race and Class Consciousness," 335–37; *NAACP Annual Report 1935* (New York, 1936), 32.

68. RPA to J. V. Horn, August 9, 1935, RPA Box 8 Folder 2; ARK, V. P of Horn and Hardart, to RPA, August 19, 1935, RPA Box 8 Folder 2. Dr. Channing Tobias, secretary of the National Urban League, filed a discrimination suit against a Horn and Hardart restaurant in New York City. *Philadelphia Tribune*, July 6, 1933.

69. RPA to Houston, September 7, 1935; RPA Box 9 Folder 2; RPA to Wilkins, October 23, 1935; RPA Box 9 Folder 2. On the Stouffer's incident, see *Philadelphia Tribune*, October 14, 1935; Helen Bryan, CORR, November 26, 1935, 2; Series 2 Box 2, CORR Papers, Swarthmore College; *Philadelphia Afro American*, December 21, 1935.

70. On discrimination, see *Philadelphia Tribune*, November 21, 1935. For the Doris Theater case, see *Philadelphia Tribune*, December 19, 1935; *Philadelphia Independent*, December 22, 1935; *Washington Afro-American*, December 21, 1935; *Philadelphia Tribune*, January 23, 1936.

Chapter Three

1. Katznelson, *When Affirmative Action Was White*; Sitkoff, *New Deal for Blacks*.

2. Singh, *Black Is a Country;* Hall, "Long Civil Rights Movement." Singh argues that "the long civil rights era" originated during "the Keynesian transformation of the liberal capitalist state during the 1930s and the emergence of black social movements that were urban, nation, and transnational in scope and conception," 6.

3. *Philadelphia Tribune*, June 29, 1933; *Philadelphia Tribune*, July 13, 1933; *Philadelphia Tribune*, July 20, 1937; Robert S. Abbott to RPA, July 22, 1937 in RPA Oversized Scrapbook UPT 50 A 374; *Philadelphia Tribune*, July 1, 1937.

4. *Philadelphia Tribune*, October 12, 1933; *Philadelphia Tribune*, October 1, 1936; Perry W. Howard to Jay Cooke, July 20, 1937; Francis E. Rivers to Jay Cooke, July 19, 1937; Thurgood Marshall to Cooke, July 26, 1937; William L. Houston to Cooke, July 20, 1937; Nannie H. Burroughs to Cooke, July 31, 1937.

5. *Philadelphia Tribune*, July 1, 1937; *Philadelphia Tribune*, July 15, 1937; *Philadelphia Tribune*, July 19, 1937.

6. Excerpts of Cooke's speech in *Philadelphia Tribune* ca. August 1937; Ed Henry to Jay Cooke, August 20, 1937; Alexander Martin to RPA, August 15, 1937 all in RPA Oversized Scrapbook, UPT 50 A 374,

7. *Philadelphia Tribune*, August 26, 1937; *Philadelphia Tribune*, September 2, 1937; Ed Henry to Francis Shunk Brown, September 1, 1937; Ed Henry to Brown, September 4, 1937; in RPA Box 17 Folder 2; *Philadelphia Tribune*, August 7, 1937; RPA to Fellow Republican Worker, September 10, 1937, RPA Box 17 Folder 2.

8. Miller, "Negro in Pennsylvania Politics," 346–47; *Philadelphia Inquirer*, September 15, 1937, *Philadelphia Evening Bulletin*, September 15, 1937; *Philadelphia Tribune*, September 21, 1937; *Philadelphia Tribune*, October 7, 1937; *Philadelphia Independent*, n.d. 1937; in RPA Oversized Scrapbook UPT 50; Dr. N. F. Mossell to John B. Kelly, October 14, 1937; Harr to RPA October 6, 1937; RPA to Judge Curtis Bok, September 30, 1937; all located in RPA Oversized Scrapbook.

9. RPA to Arthur Huff Fauset, September 15, 1937; Fauset to RPA, September 16, 1937; Fauset to RPA, September 22, 1937 all located in RPA Oversized Scrapbook; Alexander "Why Philadelphia Needs the National Negro Congress," September 24, 1937, RPA Box 95 Folder 71.

10. RPA "Radio Address Over WIP," October 22, 1937, RPA Box 95 Folder 72; Editorial n.t. "Under the Microscope" October 28, 1937, in RPA Oversized Scrapbook.

11. Alexander, "In Support of the Democratic Candidate," November 1, 1937, RPA Box 95 Folder 73.

12. *Philadelphia Tribune*, ca. November 1937 in RPA Oversized Scrapbook; Hardin, "Negroes of Philadelphia," 15; Miller, "Negro In Pennsylvania Politics," 377.

13. *Legal Intelligencer*, July 4, 1937; *Philadelphia Afro American*, July 7, 1937, in RPA Oversized Scrapbook UPT 50 A 374; Time, 16 August 1937, 26; Smith, *Emancipation*, 565–66; *Philadelphia Tribune*, August 12, 1937.

14. *Philadelphia Tribune*, August 12, 1937.

15. Alexander, "Opportunities and Problems Confronting the Negro Lawyer in the North," RPA Box 95 Folder 20; *Philadelphia Tribune*, August 21, 1937.

16. Styles, *Negroes and the Law*, 156; Stradford to Alexander, August 20, 1937, in RPA Oversized Scrapbook.

17. Stradford to Alexander, August 20, 1937, in RPA Oversized Scrapbook UPT 50 A 374; *Time*, 14 August 1937; Roger Butterfield to RPA, August 19, 1937; RPA to Butterfield, August 19, 1937, in RPA Oversized Scrapbook UPT 50 A 374.

18. *Philadelphia Tribune*, September 2 1939; *Philadelphia Tribune*, October 27, 1939; Alexander, "Summary of the Two Arsenic Trials in Which Raymond Pace Alexander Esquire, Represented Alfonsi and Carina," RPA Box 47 Folder 13; Cooper, *Poison Widow*; *Philadelphia*

Tribune, October 4, 1941; Marshall, "Equal Justice Under the Law"; Fleming, "Philadelphia Lawyer"; *Philadelphia Inquirer*, December 31, 1939; *Opportunity* 29 (January 1940); Kaplan, "Legal Front."

19. Martin to Alexander, March 29, 1941; Martin to Alexander May 15, 1941; Martin to Alexander, May 31, 1941; all located in RPA Oversized Scrapbook.

20. Alexander, "Forward--Editorial The National Bar Association-Its Aims and Purposes" *National Bar Journal* 1 (July 1941), 2–3; Frankfurter to RPA September 12, 1941; Frankfurter to RPA, September 19, 1941, in RPA Oversized Scrapbook.

21. Smith, *Emancipation*, 569–70; Martin to RPA July 7, 1941; Rayford Logan to RPA July 14, 1941; Frankfurter to RPA, September 12, 1941; George W. Maxey to RPA, July 15, 1941; Alice Peppers to Martin, July 18, 1941; *New York Sun*, July 19, 1941; *St. Louis American* July 17, 1941, *Washington Afro-American*, July 19, 1941; *American Bar Association Journal*, 27 (October 1941), 617; Martin Popper to RPA, October 2, 1941; *America: A Catholic Review of the Week* "Racial Barriers are Raised Against the Negro Lawyer" 65 (September 1941), 595–97. All papers located in RPA Oversized Scrapbook; Alexander, "Comments From Bench, Bar and Press."

22. Alexander, "Let My People Live" (May 7, 1939), 1, Box 95 Folder 76.

23. Alexander, "What About National Preparedness for the Negro," 9, RPA Box 96 Folder 7; *Philadelphia Tribune*, February 21, 1942; RPA to General J. A. Ulio, August 10, 1942, in RPA Box 9 Folder 20; Ulio to RPA, August 21, 1942 Box 9 Folder 20; R. C. Butts to RPA, March 6, 1942 in RPA Oversized Scrapbook.

24. Alexander to Roosevelt, July 9, 1942, RPA Box 9 Folder 20; Alexander to Felix Frankfurter, July 13, 1942, Box 9 Folder 20; Alexander to Frankfurter, September 3, 1942, Box 9 Folder 20; *Philadelphia Tribune*, September 15, 1942.

25. RPA to Frederick Baldi, July 18, 1942, RPA Box 47 Folder 16; The Commonwealth of Pennsylvania ex rel Thomas Mattox vs. Superintendent of County Prison, Superior Court of Pennsylvania October Term 1942 No. 318, "History of the Case." RPA Box 47 Folder 17; *Philadelphia Tribune*, September 19, 1942.

26. Petition for a Re-Hearing on the Request of the State of Georgia For the Extradition of One Thomas Mattox, 6–8. RPA Box 47 Folder 17.

27. William Henry Huff to Alexander, August 1, 1942, RPA Box 47 Folder 16; Brief for the Philadelphia Chapter of the National Lawyers Guild, Amicus Curiae, October Term, 1942, No. 318, 8. RPA Box 47 Folder 16; Petition for Re-Hearing on the Request of the State of Georgia For the Extradition of one Thomas Mattox, 10 RPA Box 47 Folder 16; Johnson and Seligmann, "Legal Aspects of the Negro Problem," 97. Brundage, *Lynching in the New South*.

28. Answer of John H. Maurer, District Attorney of Philadelphia County, Made of Behalf of the State of Georgia in Re Extradition of Thomas William Mattox, 1–3,7. RPA Box 47 Folder 16.

29. Judge Clare Fenerty, Opinion in Commonwealth ex rel. *Thomas Mattox v. Superintendent of County Prison* 4–8 RPZ Box 42 Folder 10; Fair Clay to RPA, RPA Box 47 Folder 16; *Philadelphia Tribune*, October 24, 1942.

30. RPA to Wilkins, October 21, 1942, RPA Box 47 Folder 15; RPA to Houston, October 21, 1942, RPA Box 47 Folder 15; RPA to Arthur James, December 3, 1942, RPA Box 47 Folder 15; RPA to Keller, December 4, 1942, RPA Box 47 Folder 15; *Philadelphia Tribune*, December 12, 1942.

31. Alexander to Edward Martin, March 6, 1943, Alexander to John C. Bell, Alexander to White, March 11, 1943, all located in RPA Box 47 Folder 16; *Philadelphia Tribune*, March 6,

1943; *Philadelphia Inquirer*, April 17, 1943; *Philadelphia Tribune*, April 24, 1943; *Pittsburgh Courier*, April 24, 1943; *Legal Intelligencer*, April 19, 1943; all newspaper clippings in RPA Oversized Scrapbook; RPA to Mattox, May 12, 1943.

32. Leon Ransom to RPA, April 24, 1943; Rayford Logan to RPA, May 10, 1943; *Philadelphia Inquirer*, April 17, 1943; *Pittsburgh Courier*, July 24, 1943; all in RPA Oversized Scrapbook; RPA to Keller, May 25, 1943, RPA Box 47 Folder 16; Joseph Good to RPA, October 16, 1943, RPA Box 47 Folder 16; RPA to Good, October 19, 1943, RPA Box 47 Folder 16; Signed Democrat to RPA ca. 1944, RPA Oversized Scrapbook; "Scope of Habeas Corpus: Hearing on Interstate Extradition of Criminals," *Yale Law Journal*, 53 (March 1944), 359–64; "Extradition: Scope of the Writ of Habeas Corpus," *Temple Law Quarterly*, 17 (Spring 1944), 469–72; Alexander, "Thomas Mattox Extradition Case."

33. Capeci, *Lynching of Cleo Wright*, 187–93; NLG Brief, October Term 1942, 8; RPA Box 47 Folder 16; Alexander, "Summary of the Thomas Mattox Extradition Case," ca. 1943, RPA Box 47 Folder 19.

34. *Philadelphia Inquirer*, December 11, 1946.

35. *Philadelphia Inquirer*, December 11, 1944; *Philadelphia Evening Bulletin*, December 14, 1944; *Philadelphia Tribune*, December 16, 1944. *Baltimore Afro American*, December 23, 1944; RPA to Michael Saxe, December 11, 1944, RPA Box Folder.

36. RPA to Sykes, January 2, 1945; Ephraim Lipschutz to RPA, January 5, 1945; *Philadelphia Tribune*, January 6, 1945: *Baltimore Afro-American*, January 13, 1945; *Philadelphia Evening Bulletin*, January 29, 1945; *Evening Bulletin*, February 27, 1945; *Philadelphia Inquirer*, February 26, 1945.

37. *Philadelphia Evening Bulletin*, March 7, 1945.

38. *Philadelphia Inquirer*, March 13, 1945; *Philadelphia Tribune*, February 3, 1945; *Philadelphia Inquirer*, March 6, 1945.

39. RPA Box Folder

40. *Philadelphia Inquirer*, March 12, 1945

41. *Philadelphia Evening Bulletin*, March 15, 1945; *Philadelphia Inquirer*, March 16, 1945; *Philadelphia Tribune*, March 17, 1945.

42. *Philadelphia Inquirer*, March 13, 1945; *Philadelphia Evening Bulletin*, March 16, 1945.

43. *Philadelphia Inquirer*, March 18, 1945; *Philadelphia Inquirer*, March 23, 1945; *Baltimore Afro American*, March 24, 1945.

44. *Philadelphia Tribune*, May 12, 1945; *Philadelphia Inquirer*, May 13, 1945

45. *Philadelphia Inquirer*, June 7, 1945; *Philadelphia Tribune*, June 16, 1945; *Philadelphia Evening Bulletin*, November 11, 1945; *Philadelphia Tribune*, January 12, 1946.

46. *Philadelphia Tribune*, May 18, 1946; *Philadelphia Inquirer*, September 12, 1946.

47. *Philadelphia Inquirer*, September, 12, 1946; *Philadelphia Tribune*, September 14, 1946; *Philadelphia Inquirer*, September, 27, 1946; *Philadelphia Tribune*, September 28, 1946.

48. *Philadelphia Inquirer*, October 14, 1946; *Baltimore Afro American*, October 14, 1946,

49. *Philadelphia Tribune*, October 19, 1946; *Baltimore Afro American*, October 26, 1946; *Philadelphia Inquirer*, October 17, 1946.

50. Arthur Huff Fauset, "Sykes Case Echoes Heard," *People's Voice*, December 23, 1944; RPA Scrapbook.

51. RPA to Wendell Willkie, July 10, 1940, RPA Box 95 Folder 60.

52. Francis C. Rivers to American Citizen (RPA), October 15, 1940; Box 95 Folder 81; Alexander "New Deal Has Give Only Lip Service to Negro Aspirations," October 24, 1940, Box 9 Folder 15.

53. Hamilton, *Political Biography of an American Dilemma*, 167–73; *Philadelphia Tribune*, January 29, 1948; O'Brien, *Color of the Law.*

54. Alexander to William L. Dawson, December 15, 1948, RPA Box 17 Folder 6.

55. Alexander, "Democracy's Breach of Trust," RPA Box 96 Folder 39.

Chapter Four

1. Dudziak, *Cold War Civil Rights*, 12.

2. Mack, "Law and Mass Politics," 58; Gaines, *American Africans in Ghana*, 117; Horne, *Communist Front?* 24.

3. Countryman, *Up South*, 39.

4. Goldman, *Picking Federal Judges*, 98.

5. *Daily Compass*, April 27, 1951, in RPA Box 35 Folder 20.

6. "The Facts About The Trenton Six" by the Joint Committee to Secure a Fair Trial for the Trenton Six, ca. (March 1951), RPA Box 36 Folder 19, 1–2.

7. Horne, *Communist Front?* 132–34; Plummer, *Rising Wind*, 202.

8. Thurgood Marshall to RPA, March 28, 1951, RPA Box 36 Folder 25; RPA to Marshall, April 2, 1951, RPA Box 36, Folder 25; "The Fantastic Case of the Trenton Six" NAACP Legal Defense and Educational Fund, Inc. (January 1951), RPA Box 36 Folder 21.

9. Dr. Edward S. Corwin to Dear Friend, April 6, 1951, RPA Box 36 Folder 19; "The Princeton Committee," ca. 1951, RPA Box 36 Folder 20.

10. *New York World-Telegram and Sun*, April 2, 1951; *The Philadelphia Evening Bulletin*, April 2, 1951; *Philadelphia Tribune*, April 3, 1951; *Philadelphia Inquirer*, April 3, 1951; *Trenton Evening Times*, April 2, 1951; *Philadelphia Inquirer*, April 4, 1951; *Trentonian*, April 4, 1941, all located in RPA Box 36 Folder 20.

11. *Philadelphia Inquirer*, April 5, 1951; *Philadelphia Evening Bulletin*, April 6, 1951; *Trenton Evening Times*, April 4, 1951; *Trenton Evening Times*, April 6, 1951; *Philadelphia Inquirer,* April 7, 1951; *Philadelphia Inquirer*, April 6, 1951, all located in RPA Box 36 Folder 20; *Pittsburgh Courier*, April 28, 1951.

12. *Philadelphia Inquirer*, April 10, 1951; *Philadelphia Inquirer*, April 12, 1951; *Philadelphia Evening Bulletin*, April 10, 11, 12, 1951.

13. *New York Post*, April 12, 1951; *Pittsburgh Courier, Philadelphia Edition*, April 14, 1951; all located in RPA Box 36 Folder 20.

14. *New York Herald Tribune*, April 14, 1951; *New York Times*, April 14, 1951; *New York Times*, April 19, 1951; *Philadelphia Inquirer*, April 14, 1951; *Philadelphia Inquirer*, April 19, 1951; *Philadelphia Evening Bulletin*, April 14, 1951; *Philadelphia Tribune*, April 17, 1951; *Philadelphia Afro American*, April 21, 1951; *New York Post*, April 15, 1951; *Sunday Compass*, April 15, 1951; *Pittsburgh Courier*, April 21, 1951; all located in RPA Box 36 Folder 20; Josephine Baker to RPA, RPA Box 36 Folder 20; *Pittsburgh Courier*, April 7, 1951, RPA Box 36 Folder 20. Baker and the FBI, see Dudziak, *Cold War Civil Rights,* 68.

15. *Trentonian*, April 23, 1951; *Trentonian*, April 20, 1951; *Trenton Evening Times*, April 20, 1951; *Trenton Evening Times*, April 26, 1951; *New York Post*, April 26, 1951; all located in RPA Box 36 Folder 21.

16. *Philadelphia Afro American*, May 5, 1951; RPA Box 36 Folder 19; *Trentonian*, May 2, 1951,

RPA Box 36 Folder 20; *Trentonian*, May 3, 1951, RPA Box 36 Folder 20; *Trenton Evening Times*, May 1, 1951, RPA Box 36 Folder 20; *Pittsburgh Courier*, May 5, 1951, RPA Box 36 Folder 20; Pittsburgh Courier, May 19, 1951, RPA Box 36 Folder 19; *Philadelphia Inquirer*, May 5, 1951, RPA Box 36 Folder 20; *Daily Compass*, May 6, 1951, RPA Box 36 Folder 20; *New York Post*, RPA Box 36 Folder 19.

17. *Trenton Sunday Times-Advertiser*, May 6, 1951, RPA Box 36 Folder 18; *Trentonian*, May 17, 1951, RPA Box 36 Folder 19; *Trentonian*, May 10, RPA Box 36 Folder 19; *Trenton Evening Times*, May 17, 18, 1951, RPA Box 36 Folder 19; *Pittsburgh Courier*, May 12, 1951, RPA Box 36 Folder 19; *Philadelphia Tribune*, May 19, 1951, RPA Box 36 Folder 19; *Philadelphia Inquirer*, May 22, 1951, RPA Box 36 Folder 19.

18. *Philadelphia Inquirer*, May 24, 26, 1951; *Trenton Evening Times*, May 25, 1951; *Pittsburgh Courier*, May 26, 1951; *Trentonian*, May 25, 30, 1951; *New York Post*, May 27, 1951, *Daily Compass*, May 27, 1951; all located in RPA Box 36 Folder 19. *Trentonian*, June 1, 1951, New York Post, June 1, 1951; *Pittsburgh Courier*, June 2, 1951; *Trenton Evening Times*, June 1, 1951; all located in RPA Box 36 Folder 19.

19. RPA to Marshall, June 6, 1951, RPA Box 36 Folder 25.

20. *Nation*, 173 (September 1, 1951), 52; Walter White's editorial, NT (ca. June 1951); in RPA Box 36 Folder 21. *Philadelphia Tribune*, June 16, 1951; *Trenton Evening Times*, June 15, 1951; RPA Box 36 Folder 21. *Newark Evening News*, June 15, 1951; *New Jersey CIO News* ca. (June 1951), RPA Box 36 Folder 21; *The Crisis*, 58 (June/July 1951), 372–73; *Charleston Daily Mail* June 16, 1951; *Pittsburgh Courier*, July 7, 1951; in RPA Box 36 Folder 21.

21. Theodore Spaulding to RPA, June 13, 1951, RPA Box 36 Folder 21; Francis E. Rivers to RPA, June 21, 1951, RPA Box 36 Folder 21; Moore to RPA, June 28, 1951, RPA Box 36, Folder 21; Francis S. Katzenbach III to RPA, July 12, 1951, RPA Box 36 Folder 21; RPA to Moore, June 27, 1951, RPA Box 36 Folder 21; Moore to RPA, June 28, 1951, RPA Box 36 Folder 21; J. Mercer Burrell to RPA, July 5, 1951, RPA Box 36 Folder 21.

22. RPA to Marshall, June 21, 1951, RPA Box 36 Folder 21.

23. RPA to Marshall, June 21, 1951; RPA Box 36 Folder 21; RPA to Moore, June 27, 1951, RPA Box 36 Folder 21; Katzenbach to RPA, July 12, 1951, RPA Box 36 Folder 21; Burrell to RPA, July 5, 1951, Box 36 Folder 25.

24. "Six Minus Four: Trenton's Way Out" *The Nation* 173 (September 1951), 53; RPA to Moore, July 23, 1951, RPA Box 36 Folder 21; RPA to Marshall, July 23, 1951, RPA Box 36 Folder 21; Henry Lee Moon to J. Mercer Burrell, July 31, 1951, RPA Box 36 Folder 25; *The Nation*, 173 (September 22, 1951), 248; *New Republic*, 47 (October 22, 1951), 14, *New Republic*, 47 (November 11, 1951), 2–3; Marshall to RPA, October 23, 1951, RPA Box 36 Folder 25.

25. RPA to Louis Levinthall, July 29, 1949; RPA Box 17 Folder 10; RPA to William L. Dawson, January 3, 1939, RPA Box 10 Folder 8; Alexander to Dawson, January 13, 1948, RPA Box 17 Folder 6; Alexander to Earl Chudoff, January 13, 1949, RPA Box 17 Folder 6; RPA to Marshall Shepard, January 13, 1949, RPA Box 17 Folder 6; RPA to Channing Tobias, January 10, 1949, RPA Box 10 Folder 8.

26. *Philadelphia Inquirer*, January 23, 1949, RPA Box 17 Folder 8; RPA to James A. Finnegan, January 17, 1949, RPA Box 17 Folder 6; *Philadelphia Afro American*, January 15, 1949, *Philadelphia Tribune*, January 18, 1949; *Philadelphia Evening Bulletin*, January 27, 1949, all located in RPA Box 17 Folder 11.

27. *Philadelphia Inquirer*, July 20, 1949, RPA Box 17 Folder 6; RPA to Carl Murphy;

August 9, 1949, RPA Box 17 Folder 10..RPA to E. Washington Rhodes, August 9, 1949; RPA to Mary McLeod Bethune, August 9, 1949; RPA to Channing Tobias, August 10, 1949; all in RPA Box 17 Folder 10; *Philadelphia Tribune*, August 9, 1949.

28. RPA to Walter Annenberg, August 1, 1949, RPA Box 17 Folder 10; *Philadelphia Tribune*, July 12, 1949.

29. RPA to Marshall Shepard, September 26, 1949, RPA Box 10 Folder 10.

30. RPA to Annenberg, August 26, 1949, RPA to Isaac D. Levy, RPA Box 17 Folder 9; RPA to David Niles, September 2, 1949, RPA Box 17 Folder 9; Anderson, *Eyes off the Prize*, 155.

31. Neil A. Lewis notes that in order to avoid the Congress and Senate federal judge confirmation vote a president can issue a recess appointment. Hastie, Thurgood Marshall, and A. Leon Higginbotham Jr. were all presidential recess appointments. *New York Times*, December 28, 2000, A 18. This tactic enabled Truman to avoid opposition from Dixiecrats who opposed black judges.

32. Ware, *Grace Under Pressure*, 225; *Philadelphia Tribune*, October 18, 1949, RPA Box 17 Folder 9; *Pittsburgh Courier*, October 22, 1949, RPA Box 17 Folder 9; *Philadelphia Afro American*, October 27, 1949, RPA Box 17 Folder 9; Goldman, *Picking Federal Judges*, 98–101.

33. Krenn, *Black Diplomacy*, 17–20, 47–50.

34. RPA to Myers, October 28, 1949, RPA Box 17 Folder 9. William H. Gray Jr. to Myers, October 28, 1949; Gray to Truman, October 28, 1949; RPA Box 17 Folder 9. *Philadelphia Tribune*, October 29, 1949; *Daily News*, St. Thomas, U.S. Virgin Islands, January 3, 1950; RPA Box 17 Folder 14.

35. Dudziak, *Cold War Civil Rights*, 61.

36. Roy Garvin to RPA, November 2, 1949, RPA Box 17 Folder 9; RPA to William L. Dawson, November 1, 1949, RPA Box 17 Folder 9.

37. Alexander, "Report on the Negro Soldier" (October 1950), 9–12, RPA Box 79 Folder 26; *Pittsburgh Courier*, October 28, 1950, RPA Box 17 Folder 14.

38. Earl Chudoff to William Boyle, November 15, 1950, RPA Box 17 Folder 14. Chudoff to Dawson, December 6, 1950; Chudoff to Boyle, December 6, 1950; Chudoff to Truman, December 11, 1950; all located in RPA Box 10 Folder 11.

39. Chudoff to Truman, January 17, 1951; William Boyle Jr. to Chudoff, January 22, 1951; Boyle to Frank Meyers, January 23, 1951; James A. Finnegan to RPA, February 1, 1951; all located in RPA Box 10 Folder 7. *Pittsburgh Courier*, January 27, 1951, RPA Box 10 Folder 18. *Philadelphia Afro American*, February 10, 1951, RPA Box 10 Folder 18.

40. Chudoff to RPA, April 4, 1951, RPA Box 10 Folder 7; Chudoff to William Boyle, April 4, 1951, RPA Box 10 Folder 18; Boyle to Chudoff, April 9, 1951, RPA Box 10 Folder 17; *Pittsburgh Courier*, April 4, 1951, RPA Box 10 Folder 19.

41. RPA to Christine Ray Davis, April 17, 1951, RPA Box 10 Folder 7; Committee of Negro Leaders, see Krenn, *Black Diplomacy*, 56–65.

42. Curtis C. Carson to RPA, September 15, 1949, RPA Box 8 Folder 41; Richardson Dillworth to Arthur Jones, September 16, 1949, RPA Box 10 Folder 10; Dillworth to Reverend D. Ward Nichols, September 29, 1949, RPA Box 10 Folder 10; Joseph S. Clark Jr. to Nichols, September 30, 1949, RPA Box 10 Folder 10; Jones to Boyle, September 15, 1949, RPA Box 17 Folder 10; Jones to David A. Lawrence, September 14, 1949, RPA 17 Folder 10.

43. RPA to James Finnegan, October 13, 1949; RPA to Richardson Dillworth, October 13, 1949; RPA to Joseph S. Clark Jr., October 13, 1949; Dillworth to RPA, October 14, 1949;

Finnegan to Dilworth, October 14, 1949; all in RPA Box 10 Folder 10; *Philadelphia Inquirer*, October 26, 1949, RPA Box 17 Folder 9.

44. *Philadelphia Tribune*, October 1949, RPA Box 17 Folder 9; *Pittsburgh Courier*, October 30, 1949, RPA 17 Folder 9; RPA to Hastie, October 24, 1949, RPA Box 17 Folder 12; RPA to Myers, October 25, 1949, RPA Box 17 Folder 12; RPA to Roy Garvin, RPA Box 17 Folder 9; *Philadelphia Inquirer*, October 26, 1949, RPA Box 17 Folder 9. Williams, *American Revolutionary*, 161–66.

45. McKenna, "Negro Vote in Philadelphia Elections," 74–75.

46. *Pittsburgh Courier*, May 19, 1951, RPA Box 36 Folder 20; *Pittsburgh Courier*, May 26, 1951, RPA Box 36 Folder 20; *Pittsburgh Courier*, June 2, 1951, RPA Box 36 Folder 20; *Philadelphia Evening Bulletin*, May 29, 1951, RPA Box 30 Folder 51; *Philadelphia Tribune*, June 2, 1951, RPA Box 36 Folder 20; Adams et al., *Philadelphia*, 126.

47. RPA to J. Austin Norris, July 26, 1951, RPA Box 17 Folder 17. *Philadelphia Inquirer*, July 26, 1951; RPA to Marshal Shepherd, July 30, 1951; RPA Box 17 Folder 17. RPA to Pettigrew, July 27, 1951, Box 17 Folder 17. RPA to Earl Chudoff, October 4, 1951, RPA Box 17 Folder 17. RPA to Finnegan, October 11, 1951, RPA Box 17 Folder 17.

48. *Philadelphia Tribune*, October 10, 1951; *Philadelphia Tribune*, ca. 1951; RPA Box 109 Folder 1. E. Luther Cunningham to Democrats, November 1951, RPA Box 17 Folder 14.

49. *Philadelphia Evening Bulletin*, November 7, 1951, RPA Box 17 Folder 16; R. R. Wright Jr. to RPA, November 16, 1951, RPA Box 10 Folder 13; Dorothy Height to RPA, November 25, 1951, RPA Box 10 Folder 16; *Philadelphia Daily News*, November 26, 1951, RPA Box 10 Folder 25; *New York Amsterdam News*, November 24, 1951, RPA Box 17 Folder 16; *Atlanta Daily World*, December 1, 1951, RPA Box 17 Folder 16; Walter H. Annenberg to RPA, November 25, 1951, RPA Box 10 Folder 16; Sadie T. M. Alexander to Eustace Gay, December 3, 1951, RPA Box 10 Folder 7; RPA to John Saunders, December 8, 1951, RPA Box 10 Folder 20; Ekstrom, "Electoral Politics of Reform and Machine," 90–98.

Chapter Five

1. Raymond Pace Alexander quoted in Early, *This Is Where I Came In*, 102.
2. Klarman, "How Brown Changed Race Relations," 89.
3. Ibid., 83.
4. Countryman, *Up South*, 101–12.
5. Ibid., 120–79; Willis, *Cecil's City*.
6. *Philadelphia Tribune*, October 1, 1957.
7. *Philadelphia Tribune*, September 14, 1957.
8. Ibid., 1.
9. Hirsch, "Massive Resistance in the Urban North"; Sugrue, "Crabgrass-Roots Politics."
10. No Name, October 8, 1957, Girard College Hate Letters Box A, Richardson Dilworth City Archives.
11. *Philadelphia Tribune*, September 28, 1957.
12. Kenneth E. Carpenter, "Stephen Girard: Myths and Realties," paper presented at the Haitian Studies Association Conference, in possession of the author. An urban legend surrounds the relationship between Stephen Girard and Haitian leader Toussaint Louverture. The myth goes as follows. Louverture purchased "25,000–30,000 rifles" and thirty million

dollars' worth of arms from Girard to invade Africa. Napoleon's brother LeKlerk had invited Louverture to France; he was captured by the French, where he had died in prison. Louveture's money remained in the National Bank of Philadelphia. In 1877, Thomas Prosper Gragnon-LaCoste, a French scholar, published the book *Toussaint Louverture, general, en cheef del'armee de Saint-Dominque surnomme le Premier des Noris.* Carpenter contends that Gragnon-LaCoste used the rumor to get control of Louverture's will and to obtain money from the French government. Joel A. Rogers, a black historian and author of *100 Amazing Facts about the Negro,* cited Gragnon-Lacoste's work and mentions Girard and Louverture's relationship. The only document is a letter between Girard and Louverture that has Girard informing Louverture that some of his ships were coming to Haiti. There is no evidence of any financial dealings between the men (14–20; 30–35). Girard's will quoted in Alexander's "Statement of Raymond Pace Alexander: Sponsor of resolution #433 RE: Girard College" in Raymond Pace Alexander's Papers, Box 32 Folder 46.

13. *Philadelphia Tribune,* May 19, 1953; RPA to Robert Stern, June 10, 1953, RPA Box 35 Folder 21; RPA to Registrar, July 3, 1953, RPA Box 35 Folder 22.

14. *Philadelphia Inquirer,* July 25, 1953.

15. Gillen, May 11, 1957, RPA Papers Box 32 Folder 24; Milo A. Manly to RPA, July 31, 1953, RPA Box Folder; RPA to George Schermer, September 25, 1953, Box 33 Folder 2; RPA to Melville Ferguson, August 6, 1953, RPA Papers Box 34 Folder 5.

16. *Philadelphia Inquirer,* July 12, 1953; George J. Amonitti to RPA, May 12, 1954, RPA Papers Box 33 Folder 22; Bright to RPA, January 4, 1954, RPA Papers, Box 33, Folder 31.

17. RPA to Robert Poindexter, January 13, 1954; RPA to no name, March 31, 1954, RPA Box 33 Folder 1; "Excerpt From Minutes: Board of Directors of City Trusts," March 19, 1954, RPA Papers, Box 33 Folder 23; RPA to Floyd Logan, April 9, 1954, RPA Papers Box 33 Folder 22.

18. RPA to Lawrence Smith, September 29, 1955, RPA Papers, Box 33 Folder 28; RPA to Marshall Shepard, December 7, 1956, RPA Papers, Box 34 Folder 21; RPA to Maurice B. Fagan, n.d. circa 1956, RPA Papers, Box 34 Folder 21.

19. *Philadelphia Evening Bulletin,* April 30, 1957; Dent to RPA, April 30, 1957, RPA Papers, Box 35 Folder 4; *Saturday Evening Post,* June 22, 1957; King to RPA, June 3, 1957, RPA Papers, Box 35 Folder 4; *Tallahassee Democrat,* May 13, 1957, in RPA Papers, Box 35 Folder 1.

20. Walter Sienkiewicz to Richardson Dillworth, May 3, 1957; Disgusted Democrat to Dillworth, September 12, 1957; Was a Friend, September 12, 1957; all in Dillworth Papers City Archives Box A 499.

21. Bewildered White Democrat to RPA, May 8, 1957, RPA Papers Box 35 Folder 4; No Name to RPA, n.d., RPA Papers, Box 35 Folder 5; White Girl to RPA, August 2, 1957, RPA Papers, Box 35 Folder 5.

22. Countryman, *Up South,* 83.

23. Saunders, *100 Years After Emancipation,* 117–18.

24. *Philadelphia Tribune,* January 7, 1958; *Philadelphia Tribune,* March 1, 1958.

25. *Philadelphia Tribune,* January 18, 1958.

26. Ibid., May 24, 1958.

27. Countryman, *Up South,* 86.

28. *Philadelphia Tribune,* November 8, 1958.

29. *Philadelphia Tribune,* December 2, 1958; *Philadelphia Inquirer,* November 26, 1958.

30. Joseph Varbalow to George Leader, December 11, 1958; James J. Regan Jr. to RPA, February 12, 1959, both in RPA Box 86 Folder 43.

31. Saunders, *100 Years After Emancipation*, 128–32; *Philadelphia Tribune*, January 6, 1958,

32. "The Noose Is Crime" series, *Philadelphia Tribune*, December 18, 22, 25, 1956; *Philadelphia Tribune*, April 30, 1957; *Philadelphia Tribune*, May 7, 1958.

33. "The Spiritual Rehabilitation Program," RPA Box 98 Folder 28, 39, 40. *Philadelphia Afro American*, February 7, 1959; *Philadelphia Afro American*, February 7, 1959; *Sunday Evening Bulletin*, January 13, 1959; *Atlanta Daily World*, February 4, 1959; *Pittsburgh Courier*, February 7, 1959; *Dallas Morning News*, January 14, 1959; *Florida Times Union*, (Jacksonville, FL), January 14, 1959; all in RPA Box 2 Folder 3.

34. RPA, "Are We Too Soft on Criminals," RPA Box 98 Folder 15.

35. E. Washington Rhodes to RPA, February 3, 1960, RPA Box 12 Folder 16; RPA to Rhodes, March 9, 1959, RPA Box 12 Folder 16; SRP Executive Committee Report, 1960, Box 75 Folder 26, 21; RPA to Carl Murphy, March 2, 1960, RPA Box 12 Folder 26.

36. RPA, Address Before the National Bar Association, Box 98 Folder 12; George K. Henshaw to RPA, July 22, 1959, RPA Box 98 Folder 12.

37. Alexander, "Commencement Address at William Penn H.S." (June 1958), RPA Box 98 Folder 11.

38. Hershberg et al., "Tale of Three Cities," 477–78; Alexander, "The Future of Philadelphia," RPA Box 99 Folder 63.

39. Marshall to RPA, August 16, 1960, RPA Box 12 Folder 26; RPA to Marshall, September 26, 1960, RPA Box 12 Folder 26; King Jr. to RPA, November 10, 1960, RPA Box 12 Folder 26. Carson, *In Struggle*; Chafe, *Civilities and Civil Rights*.

40. *Ebony* 21 (January 1963), 228; Green, *Selling the Race*, 141; *Philadelphia Tribune*, January 1, 1963.

41. Countryman, *Up South*, 126–29.

42. *Philadelphia Tribune*, January 12, 1963.

43. *Philadelphia Tribune*, January 19, 1963; *Philadelphia Tribune*, January 22, 1963; *Philadelphia Tribune*, January 26, 1963; *Philadelphia Tribune*, February 16, 1963; *Philadelphia Evening Bulletin*, January 24, 1965.

44. Lermack, "Politics of Negro Pressure Group Organization," 147; Willis, *Cecil's City*, 119–31.

45. *Philadelphia Tribune*, January 4, 1964.

46. In 1964, the Brooklyn chapter of Congress for Racial Equality (CORE) organized a "stall-in" during the opening day of the 1964 World's Fair, which was being held in Queens, New York. According to Brian Purnell, motorists planned to "run out of gas and block traffic on major roadways" to Queens. The protest did not prevent the World's Fair from opening, but the publicity alerted the nation to the civil rights issues in New York City. CORE used civil disobedience and protest politics to expose institutional racism in New York City. Brian Purnell, "Drive Awhile for Freedom: Brooklyn CORE's 1964 Stall-In and Public Discourses on Protest Violence," in Theoharis and Woodard, *Groundwork*, 45–77.

47. "Anger and Guilt," *Newsweek*, May 1964, 46; *Time*, May 1, 1964; RPA to the Editor of *New York Times*, June 1, 1964; all located in RPA Box 98 Folder 52.

48. King to RPA, May 21, 1964; Sidney R. Redmond to RPA, June 22, 1964; Charles A. Hall to RPA, June 25, 1964; all located in RPA Box 13 Folder 25.

49. RPA to King, July 20, 1964, RPA Box 13 Folder 25.
50. King to RPA, July 30, 1964, RPA Box 13 Folder 25.
51. "The Talk Is Race" *Time*, 84 (August 1964), 24–25; "Black Rage in New Jersey," *Time*, 84 (August 1964), 19; "They Got Too Mad," *Time* 84 (August 1964), 17; *Philadelphia Tribune*, September 2, 1964; *Philadelphia Inquirer*, July 16, 1964.
52. *Philadelphia Evening Bulletin*, July 22, 1964; Esther Eyer to RPA, July 22, 1964; Lois Stalvey to RPA, July 25, 1964; Charles R. Weiner to RPA, July 27, 1964; Julian Goldberg to RPA, July 28, 1964; all located in RPA Box 13 Folder 26.
53. Countryman, *Up South,* 154–74; *Philadelphia Inquirer*, August 30, 1964; RPA to Maurice Litman, September 15, 1964, RPA Box 98 Folder 53.
54. RPA to Maurice Litman, September 15, 1964, RPA, "We Salute Them Proudly," Box 98 Folder 55; "The Goddam Boss," *Time* 84, September 11, 1964, 24.
55. *Philadelphia Inquirer*, September 2, 1964.

Chapter Six

1. Early, *This Is Where I Came In*, 129.
2. Alexander, "Five Civil Rights Groups."
3. Wilkins, *Standing Fast*, 314–15.
4. Julian Bond, "The Politics of Civil Rights History," in Robinson and Sullivan, *New Directions in Civil Rights Studies*, 9.
5. Brown, *Fighting for US*; Ogbar, *Black Power*; Joseph, *Waiting 'Til The Midnight Hour*; Jeffries, *Black Power in the Belly of the Beast*; Tyson, *Radio Free Dixie*; Countryman, *Up South*.
6. Judson L. Jeffries, "An Unexamined Chapter of Black Panther History," in Jeffries, *Black Power in the Belly of the Beast*, 185.
7. Wilkins, *Standing Fast*, 318.
8. Edward P. Morgan, "Media Culture and the Public Memory of the Black Panther Party," in Lazerow and Williams, *In Search of the Black Panther Party*, 328.
9. Joseph, *Waiting 'Til the Midnight Hour*, 147; Harley, "Chronicle of a Death Foretold."
10. Feldstein, "'I Don't Trust You Anymore,'" 1367.
11. D'Emilio, *Lost Prophet*, 433.
12. Alexander, "We Still Have a Dream" (December 1966), 15–16.
13. Ibid., 18–20.
14. *Philadelphia Inquirer*, February 19, 1968; *Philadelphia Evening* Bulletin, February 19, 1968; *Atlanta Journal and Constitution*, March 4, 1968.
15. *Philadelphia Inquirer*, February 19, 1968.
16. Alexander, "The Negro Lawyer and His Responsibility in the Urban Crisis," RPA Box 99 Folder 38; Alexander, December 31, 1968, RPA Box 99 Folder 38.
17. Ibid., 8.
18. Ibid., 5.
19. RPA to Timothy Jenkins, November 21, 1968, RPA Box 87 Folder 20.
20. Ogbar, *Black Power*, 142–43.
21. Robert L. Carter to RPA, February 11, 1969. Attached to this letter is the NCBL's "Declaration of Concern and Commitment," RPA Box 87 Folder 20.

22. RPA to Robert L. Carter, March 6, 1969, RPA Box 14 Folder 19.

23. *Report of the National Advisory Commission on Civil Disorders* (1968).

24. Wilkins, *Standing Fast*, 335.

25. Alexander, "The Future of Philadelphia," RPA Box 99, Folder 63, 10.

26. Ibid., 12.

27. Jennifer H. Lansbury, "Alice Coachman: Quiet Champion of the 1940s," in Wiggins, *Out of the Shadows*, 147–62. Coachman won the gold medal in the high jump during the 1948 Olympics.

28. Mark Dyreson, "Jesse Owens: Leading Man in Modern American Tales of Racial Progress and Limits," in Wiggins, *Out of Shadows*, 118.

29. Zirin, *Welcome to the Terrordome*, 128.

30. *Philadelphia Inquirer*, September 13, 1972.

31. Ibid.

32. Sugrue, "Affirmative Action from Below," 169–71.

33. *Philadelphia Inquirer*, November 20, 1972; Sugrue, "Affirmative Action form Below," 171; Deslippe, "Do Whites have Rights?"

34. Davis, *Brutal Need*, 1.

35. Alexander, "The American Negro's New World and New Purpose." 1, 8–9, RPA Box 98 Folder 64.

36. Ibid., 10–12.

37. Gaines, *American Africans in Ghana*, 117.

38. Alexander, "The American Negro's New World and Purpose," RPA Box 98 Folder 64, 14–16.

39. Lyndon B. Johnson, "To Fulfill These Rights," quoted in Katznelson, *When Affirmative Action Was White*, 176.

40. Ibid., 179; Steinberg, *Turning Back*, 120.

41. Alexander, "In Our Other America," 4–5, RPA Box 98 Folder 66.

42. Conley, *Being Black Living in the Red*; Shapiro, *Hidden Cost of Being African American*.

43. Lemann, *Big Test*, 163.

44. Ibid., 113–19; RPA, "In Our Other America," Box 98 Folder 66.

45. Alexander, Address, Annual Conference of the National Legal Aid and Defender Association, October 4, 1966, 7, RPA Box 77 Folder 29.

46. Ibid., 9.

47. Ibid., 10.

48. Ibid., 12.

49. Dickerson, *Militant Mediator*, 270.

50. To RPA, July 23, 1965, RPA Box 68 Folder 15.

51. Alexander, RPA Box 99 Folder 4.

52. Ibid., 34.

53. Ibid., 34–35.

54. Alexander, "Civil Rights, The Negro Protest and the War on Poverty: Efforts to Cure America's Social Ills," *New York State Bar Journal* 41 (February 1969), 90–100, RPA Box 99 Folder 46.

55. RPA to Edward Brooke, January 20, 1969; RPA to Ralph Bunche, February 3, 1969; RPA to Andrew F. Brimmer, February 3, 1969; all in RPA Box 14 Folder 19.

56. Edward P. Morgan, "Media Culture and the Public Memory of the Black Panther Party," in Lazerow and Williams, *In Search of the Black Panther Party*, 327.

57. *Philadelphia Evening Bulletin*, January 24, 1965.

58. Claude Lewis, "Our City's New Negro Leaders Draw Their Power From the People," *Philadelphia Evening Bulletin*, October 22, 1967.

59. RPA to Morley Cassidy, February 1, 1965, RPA, Letter to the *Philadelphia Bulletin*, Box 98 Folder 62; RPA to Cassidy, February 2, 1965, RPA Box 98 Folder 62; Alexander to Editor of the *Bulletin*, ca. October 1967.

60. Janken, *Rayford W. Logan*, 233.

61. Robert J. Levine to RPA, March 18, 1970, RPA Box 99 Folder 59; RPA to Levine, April 8, 1970, RPA Box 99 Folder 59; Alexander, "Blacks and the Law," *Verdict: The Philadelphia Trial Lawyers Association* 6 (September 1970), 3. *Negro History Bulletin* 34 (May 1971), 109–14; *New York State Bar Journal* 43 (January 1971); *Pennsylvania Bar Association Quarterly* 61 (October 1971).

62. Alexander, "Blacks and the Law," *Verdict* (1971), 5.

63. Ibid., 4–5.

64. Higginbotham, "To the Scale and Standing of Men," 380; *Commonwealth of Pennsylvania et al. v. Local Union No. 542;* International Union of Operating Engineers et al.

65. Constance Baker Motley to Derrick Bell, October 30, 1974, RPA Box 16 Folder 8; Baker Motley to Helen Edmonds, November 1, 1974, RPA Box 16 Folder 8; RPA to Baker Motley, November 22, 1974, RPA Box 16 Folder 11; *Philadelphia Inquirer*, November 26, 1974; *Congressional Record* 20 (November 26, 1974), 374–84.

66. *Philadelphia Tribune*, November 26, 1974; *Philadelphia Tribune*, November 30, 1974; *Philadelphia Evening Bulletin*, November 25, 1974; *Philadelphia Inquirer*, November 25, 1974.

67. King, *Where Do We Go From Here*, 162.

68. "Death of Raymond Pace Alexander" 20 *Congressional Record* 37484 (December 26, 1974), 1897–98.

69. Gaines, *American Africans in Ghana*.

Conclusion

1. Alexander, NAACP Testimonial Dinner (1971), RPA Box 100 Folder 71.

2. Hall, "Long Civil Rights Movement."

3. Delaney, *Condition, Elevation, Emigration, and Destiny*, Preface.

4. Gaines, *Uplifting the Race*, ix-xxi; Higginbotham, *Righteous Discontent*.

5. Hacker, *Two Nations*, 102.

6. Jackson, *From Civil Rights to Human Rights*, 251.

7. Countryman, *Up South*, 330.

8. Austin, *Getting in Wrong*, 9, 42.

BIBLIOGRAPHY

Manuscript Collections

Raymond Pace Alexander and Sadie Tanner Mossell Alexander Papers, University of
  Pennsylvania Archives
Floyd L. Logan Papers, Temple University Urban Archives
The Philadelphia Branch of the NAACP Papers, Manuscript Division, Library of Congress,
  Washington D.C.
The City Archives of Philadelphia

Newspapers and Magazines

Crisis
National Bar Journal
New York Post
New York Times
Opportunity
Philadelphia Afro American
Philadelphia Independent
Philadelphia Inquirer
Philadelphia Tribune
Pittsburgh Courier
The Nation
New Republic
Trentonian
Time
Trenton Evening Times

Dissertations

Bates, Beth Thompkins. "The Unfinished Task of Emancipation: Protest Politics Comes of Age in Chicago, 1925–1943." Ph.D. diss., Columbia University, 1997.

Biondi, Martha. "The Struggle for Black Equality in New York, 1945–1955." Ph.D. diss., Columbia University, 1997.

Hale, William, H. "The Career Development of the Negro Lawyer in Chicago." Ph.D. diss., University of Chicago, 1949.

Haley, Charles T. "To Do Good and Do Well: Middle Class Blacks and the Depression in Philadelphia 1929–1941." Ph.D. diss., State University of New York Binghamton, 1980.

Hardy, Charles III. "Race and Opportunity: Black Philadelphia During the Era of the Great Migration, 1916–1930." Ph.D. diss., Temple University, 1989.

Hardin, Clara A. "The Negroes of Philadelphia: The Cultural Adjustment of a Minority Group." Ph.D. diss., Bryn Mawr, 1945.

Hatfield, Eugene. "The Impact of the New Deal on Black Politics in Pennsylvania, 1928–1936." Ph.D. diss., University of North Carolina, 1979.

Miller, James E. "The Negro in Pennsylvania Politics: With Special Emphasis on the Years Between 1927 and 1940." Ph.D. diss., University of Pennsylvania, 1945.

Nelson, Viscount H., Jr., "Race and Class Consciousness of Philadelphia Negroes With Special Emphasis on the Years Between 1927 and 1940." Ph.D. diss., University of Pennsylvania, 1969.

Porter, Aaron C. "The Career of a Professional Institution: Study of Norris, Schmidt, Green, Harris, Higginbotham, and Associates." Ph.D. diss., University of Pennsylvania, 1993.

White, Vibert. "Developing a School of Civil Rights Lawyers: From the New Deal to the New Frontier." Ph.D. diss., Ohio State University, 1988.

Published Sources

Adams, Carolyn, et al., eds. *Philadelphia: Neighborhoods, Division, and Conflict in a Post-Industrial City.* Philadelphia: Temple University Press, 1991.

Anderson, Carol. *Eyes Off of the Prize: The United Nations and the African American Struggle for Human Rights, 1944–1955.* Cambridge: Cambridge University Press, 2003.

Auerbach, Jerold S. *Unequal Justice: Lawyers and Social Change in Modern America.* New York: Oxford University Press, 1976.

Austin, Algernon, *Getting in Wrong: How Black Public Intellectuals Are Failing Black America.* New York: iUniverse, Inc, 2006.

Banks, William M. *Black Intellectuals: Race and Responsibility in American Life.* New York: Norton, 1996.

Bartlett, Paul M. *The Good Black: A True Story of Race in America.* New York: Dutton, 1999.

Bates, Beth Thompkins, *Pullman Porters and the Rise of Protest Politics in Black America, 1925–1945.* Chapel Hill: University of North Carolina Press, 2001.

Bauerlein, Mark, *Negrophobia: A Race Riot in Atlanta, 1906.* San Francisco: Encounter, 2001.

Bauman, John. *Public Housing, Race and Renewal: Urban Planning in Philadelphia 1920–1970.* Philadelphia: Temple University Press, 1974.

Bell, Derrick. *Faces at the Bottom of the Well: The Permanence of Racism.* New York: Basic Books, 1992.

Berman, William C. *The Politics of Civil Rights in the Truman Administration*. Columbus: Ohio State University Press, 1970.

Biondi, Martha. *To Stand and Fight: The Struggle for Civil Rights In Postwar New York City*. Cambridge: Harvard University Press, 2003.

Blakely, Robert J. *Earl B. Dickerson: A Voice for Freedom and Equality*. Chicago: University of Illinois Press, 2006.

Boyle, Kevin. *Arc of Justice: A Saga of Race, Civil Rights, and Murder in the Jazz Age*. New York: Henry Holt, 2004.

Branch, Taylor. *At Canaan's Edge: America in the King Years, 1965–1968*. New York: Simon and Schuster, 2006.

Brandt, Nat. *Harlem at War: The Black Experience in WWII*. Syracuse: Syracuse University Press, 1996.

Brisbane, Robert H. *The Black Vanguard: Origins of the Negro Social Revolution 1900–1960*. Valley Forge, Penn.: Judson Press, 1970.

Brown, Scot. *Fighting for US: Maulana Karenga, The US Organization and Black Cultural Nationalism*. New York: New York University Pres, 2003.

Brundage, W. Fitzhugh. *Lynching in the New South: Georgia and Virginia, 1880–1930*. Urbana: University of Illinois Press, 1993.

Capeci, Dominic, Jr. *The Harlem Riot of 1943*. Philadelphia: Temple University Press, 1997.

———. *The Lynching of Cleo Wright*. Lexington: University Press of Kentucky, 1999.

Carson, Clayborne. *In Struggle: SNCC and the Black Awakening of the 1960s*. Cambridge: Harvard University Press, 1981.

Carter, Dan T. *Scottsboro: A Tragedy of the American South*. Baton Rouge: Louisiana State University Press, 1969.

Chafe, William H. *Civilities and Civil Rights: Greensboro, North Carolina and the Black Struggle for Equality*. New York: Oxford University Press, 1980.

Cohen, William. *At Freedom's Edge: Black Mobility and the Southern White Quest for Racial Control, 1861–1951*. Baton Rouge: Louisiana State University Press, 1991.

Collier-Thomas, Bettye, and V. P. Franklin. *A Chronology of The Civil Rights Era in the U.S. and in Philadelphia*. Philadelphia: Packard Press, 1994.

———. *Sisters in the Struggle: African American Women in the Civil Rights–Black Power Movement*. New York: New York University Press, 2001.

Conley, Dalton. *Being Black, Living in the Red: Race, Wealth, and Social Policy*. Berkeley: University of California Press, 1999.

Cooper, George. *Poison Widow: A True Story of Witchcraft, Arsenic and Murder*. New York: St. Martin's Press, 1999.

Countryman, Matthew. *Up South: Civil Rights and Black Power in Philadelphia*. Philadelphia: University of Pennsylvania Press, 2007.

Cruse, Harold. *The Crisis of the Negro Intellectual: Historical Analysis of the Failure of Black Leadership*. New York: Quill, 1967.

Davis, Martha. *Brutal Need: Lawyers and the Welfare Rights Movement, 1960–1973*. New Haven: Yale University Press, 1993.

Delaney, Martin R. *The Condition, Elevation, Emigration, and Destiny of the Colored People of the United States*. Baltimore: Black Classic Press, 1993.

D'Emilio, John. *Lost Prophet: The Life and Times of Bayard Rustin*. New York: Free Press, 2003.

Dickerson, Dennis. *Militant Mediator: Whitney M. Young, Jr.* Lexington: University of Kentucky Press, 1998.

Dittmer, John. *Local People: The Struggle for Civil Rights in Mississippi.* Chicago: University of Illinois Press, 1995.

Douglas, Davison M. *Jim Crow Moves North: The Battle Over Northern School Segregation, 1865–1954.* Cambridge: Cambridge University Press, 2005.

Drake, St. Clair, and Horace R. Cayton. *Black Metropolis: A Study of Negro Life in a Northern City.* New York: Harcourt Brace, 1945.

DuBois, W. E. B. *The Philadelphia Negro: A Social Study.* Philadelphia: University of Pennsylvania, 1899.

Dudziak, Mary L. *Cold War and Civil Rights: Race and the Image of American Democracy.* Princeton: Princeton University Press, 2000.

Dyson, Michael Eric. *I May Not Get There with You: The True Martin Luther King Jr.* New York: Free Press, 2000.

Early, Gerald. *This Is Where I Came In: Black America in the 1960s.* Lincoln: University of Nebraska Press, 2003.

Ekstrom, Charles A. "The Electoral Politics of Reform and Machine: The Political Behavior of Philadelphia's Black Wards, 1943–1969." In Miriam Ershkowitz and Joseph Zikmund II, eds., *Black Politics in Philadelphia.* New York: Basic Books, 1973.

Ellsworth, Scott. *Death in a Promised Land: The Tulsa Race Riot of 1921.* Baton Rouge: Louisiana State University Press, 1982.

Ershkowitz, Miriam, and Joseph Zikmund II, eds. *Black Politics in Philadelphia.* New York: Basic Books, 1965.

Fairclough, Adam. *Race and Democracy: The Civil Rights Struggle in Louisiana, 1915–1972.* Athens: University of Georgia Press, 2001.

Finkleman, Paul, ed. *The Era of Integration and Civil Rights, 1930–1990.* New York: Garland, 1992.

———, ed. *African Americans and the Legal Profession in Historical Perspective.* New York: Garland, 1992.

Fox, Stephen R. *The Guardian of Boston: William Monroe Trotter.* New York: Atheneum, 1970.

Franklin, V. P. *The Education of Black Philadelphia: The Social and Educational History of a Minority Community.* Philadelphia: University of Pennsylvania Press, 1979.

———. "The Philadelphia Race Riot of 1918." In Kenneth Kusmer, ed., *The Great Migration and After 1917–1930. Volume 2.* New York: Articles-Garlan, 1991.

Gaines, Kevin. *American Africans in Ghana: Black Expatriates and the Civil Rights Era.* Chapel Hill: University of North Carolina Press, 2006.

———. "The Historiography of the Struggle for Black Equality Since 1945." In Jean-Christophe Agnew and Roy Rosenzweig, eds., *A Companion to Post-1945 America.* New York: Wiley-Blackwell, 2003.

———. *Uplifting the Race: Black Leadership, Politics, and Culture in the Twentieth Century.* Chapel Hill: University of North Carolina Press, 1996.

Garrow, David. *Bearing the Cross: Martin Luther King Jr. and the Southern Christian Leadership Conference.* New York: Vintage Books, 1988.

Gatewood, Willard B. *Aristocrats of Color: The Black Elite 1880–1920.* Bloomington: Indiana University Press, 1990.

Goggin, Jacqueline. *Carter G. Woodson: A Life in Black History.* Baton Rouge: Louisiana State University Press, 1993.

Goings, Kenneth W. *"The NAACP Comes of Age": The Defeat of Judge John J. Parker.*
Bloomington: Indiana University Press, 1990.

———, and Raymond A. Mohl. *The New African American Urban History.* New York: Sage, 1996.

Goldman, Sheldon. *Picking Federal Judges: Lower Court Selection From Roosevelt Through Reagan.*
New Haven: Yale University Press, 2000.

Graham, Lawrence Otis. *Our Kind of People: Inside America's Black Upper Class.* New York:
Harper Collins, 1999.

———. *The Senator and the Socialite: The True Story of America's First Black Dynasty.* New York:
Harper Perennial, 2006.

Green, Adam, *Selling the Race: Culture, Community, and Black Chicago, 1940–1955.* Chicago:
University of Chicago Press, 2007.

Greenberg, Cheryl Lynn. *Or Does It Explode: Black Harlem in the Great Depression.* New York:
Oxford University Press, 1991.

Gregg, Robert. *Sparks from the Anvil of Oppression: Philadelphia's African Methodists and
Southern Migrants, 1890–1940.* Philadelphia: Temple University Press, 1993.

Hacker, Andrew. *Two Nations: Black and White, Separate, Hostile, Unequal.* New York: Dutton,
1995.

Hahn, Steven. *A Nation Under Our Feet: Black Political Struggles in the Rural South From Slavery
to the Great Migration.* Cambridge: Harvard University Press, 2003.

Hamby, Alonzo L. *Liberalism and Its Challengers from F.D.R. to Bush.* New York: Oxford
University Press, 1992.

Hamilton, Charles V. *The Political Biography of an American Dilemma: Adam Clayton Powell Jr.*
New York: Collier Books, 1991.

Harley, Sharon. "Chronicle of a Death Foretold: Gloria Richardson, the Cambridge Movement,
and the Radical Black Activist Tradition." In Bettye Collier-Thomas and V. P. Franklin,
Sisters in the Struggle: African American Women in the Civil Rights-Black Power Movement.
New York: New York University Press, 2001.

Harris, Paul. *Black Rage Confronts the Law.* New York: New York University Press, 1997.

Haynes, Robert V. *A Night of Violence: The Houston Riot of 1917.* Baton Rouge: Louisiana State
University Press, 1976.

Hershberg, Theodore, et al. "A Tale of Three Cities: Blacks, Immigrants, and Opportunity in
Philadelphia, 1850–1880, 1930, 1970." In Theodore Hershberg, ed., *Philadelphia: Work, Space,
and Family and Group Experience in the Nineteenth Century.* New York: Oxford University
Press, 1981.

Higginbotham, A. Leon, Jr. *In the Matter of Color: Race and the American Legal Process.* New
York: Oxford University Press, 1978.

———. *Shades of Freedom: Racial Politics of Presumptions of the American Legal Process.* New
York: Oxford University Press, 1996.

Higginbotham, Evelyn Brooks. *Righteous Discontent: The Women's Movement in the Black Baptist
Church 1880–1920.* Cambridge: Harvard University Press, 1993.

Hine, Darlene Clark. "Black Lawyers and the Twentieth-Century Struggle for Constitutional
Change." In John Hope Franklin and Genna Rae McNeil, eds. *African Americans and the
Living Constitution.* Washington, D.C.: Smithsonian Institution Press, 1995.

Hirsch, Arnold. *The Making of the Second Ghetto: Race and Housing in Chicago, 1940–1960.*
Cambridge: Cambridge University Press, 1983.

Horne, Gerald. *Communist Front? The Civil Rights Congress.* London: Associated University Press, 1988.

Jackson, Kenneth T. *The Ku Klux Klan in the City, 1915–1930.* New York: Oxford University Press, 1967.

Jackson, Thomas F. *From Civil Rights to Human Rights: Martin Luther King Jr. and the Struggle for Economic Justice.* Philadelphia: University of Pennsylvania Press, 2007.

James, Winston. *Holding Aloft the Banner of Ethiopia: Caribbean Radicalism in Early Twentieth-Century America.* New York: Verso, 1998.

Janken, Robert. *Rayford W. Logan and the Dilemma of the African American Intellectual.* Amherst: University of Massachusetts Press, 1993.

Johnson, Charles S. *The Negro College Graduate.* New York: Negro Universities Press, 1928.

Joseph, Peniel E. *Waiting 'Til the Midnight Hour: A Narrative History of Black Power In America.* New York: Henry Holt, 2006.

Jeffries, Judson, ed. *Black Power in the Belly of the Beast.* Chicago: University of Illinois Press, 2006.

Katznelson, Ira. *When Affirmative Action Was White: An Untold History of Racial Inequality in Twentieth-Century America.* New York: Norton, 2005.

Kellogg, Charles Flint. *NAACP: A History of the National Association for the Advancement of Colored People: Volume I, 1909–1920.* Baltimore: Johns Hopkins Press, 1967.

Kilson, Martin. "Political Change in the Negro Ghetto 1900–1940s." In Nathan Huggins, Martin Kilson, and Daniel M. Fox, eds., *Key Issues in the Afro American Experience.* New York: Harcourt Brace Jovanich, 1971.

King, Martin Luther, Jr. *Where Do We Go From Here: Chaos or Community?* New York: Harper and Row, 1967.

Kirby, John B. *Black Americans in the Roosevelt Era: Liberalism and Race.* Knoxville: University of Tennessee Press, 1980.

Kluger, Richard. *Simple Justice: The History of Brown v. Board of Education and Black America's Struggle for Equality.* New York: Knopf, 1976.

Kornweibel, Theodore, Jr. *Seeing Red: Federal Campaigns Against Black Militancy, 1919–1925.* Bloomington: Indiana University Press, 1998.

Korstad, Robert. *Civil Rights Unionism: Tobacco Workers and the Struggle for Democracy in the Mid-Twentieth Century South.* Chapel Hill: University of North Carolina Press, 2003.

Krenn, Michael L. *Black Diplomacy: African Americans and the State Department, 1945–1969.* New York: M. E. Sharpe, 1999.

Kusmer, Kenneth. "African Americans in the City Since World War II." In Kenneth Goings and Raymond Mohl, eds. *The New African American Urban History.* New York: Sage Publication, 1996.

———. "The Black Urban Experience in American History." In Darlene Clark Hine, ed. *The State of Afro-American History: Past, Present, and Future.* Baton Rouge: Louisiana State University Press, 1986.

———. *A Ghetto Takes Shape: Black Cleveland, 1870–1930.* Urbana: University of Illinois Press, 1976.

Labaree, David F. *The Making of an American High School: The Credentials Market and the Central High School of Philadelphia, 1838–1939.* New Haven: Yale University Press, 1988.

Lane, Roger. *Roots of Violence in Black Philadelphia, 1860–1900.* Cambridge: Harvard University Press, 1986.

———. *William Dorsey's Philadelphia and Ours: On the Past, Future of the Black City in America.* New York: Oxford University Press, 1991.

Lazerow, Jama, and Yuhuru Williams, ed. *In Search of the Black Panther Party: New Perspectives on a Revolutionary Movement.* Durham: Duke University Press, 2006.

Lemann, Nicholas. *The Big Test: The Secret History of American Meritocracy.* New York: Farrar, Straus, and Giroux, 1999.

Leonard, Walter, J. *Black Lawyers: Training and Results, Then and Now.* Boston: Senna Shih, 1977.

Lermack, Paul. "The Politics of Negro Pressure Group Organization: Cecil B. Moore and the Philadelphia Branch of the NAACP." In Miriam Ershkowitz and Joseph Zikmund II, eds., *Black Politics in Philadelphia.* New York: Basic Books, 1973.

Lewis, David Levering. *W. E. B. DuBois: A Reader.* New York: Henry Holt, 1995.

———. *When Harlem Was in Vogue.* New York: 1979.

Lewis, Earl. *In Their Own Interests: Race, Class, and Power in Twentieth-Century Norfolk, Virginia.* Berkeley: University of California Press, 1991.

Litwack, Leon. *Trouble in Mind: Black Southerners in the Age of Jim Crow.* New York: Knopf, 1998.

Locke, Alain, ed. *The New Negro: Voices of the Harlem Renaissance.* New York: Albert and Charles Boni, 1925.

Loewen, James W. *Sundown Towns: A Hidden Dimension of American Racism.* New York: New Press, 2005.

Logan, Rayford W. *The Betrayal of the Negro: From Rutherford B. Hayes to Woodrow Wilson.* New York: Da Capo Press, 1997.

Massey, Douglass S., and Nancy Denton. *American Apartheid: Segregation and the Making of the Underclass.* Cambridge: Harvard University Press, 1993.

McKenna, William J. "The Negro Vote in Philadelphia Elections." In Miriam Ershkowitz and Joseph Zikumd II, *Black Politics in Philadelphia.* New York: Basic Books, 1973.

McNeil, Genna Rae. *Groundwork: Charles Hamilton Houston and the Struggle for Civil Rights.* Philadelphia: University of Pennsylvania, 1983.

Meier, August. *Negro Thought in America, 1880–1915.* Ann Arbor: University of Michigan Press, 1963.

Meier, August, and Elliot Rudwick. "Attorneys Black and White: A Case Study of Race Relations Within the NAACP." In Meier and Rudwick, *Along the Color Line: Explorations in the Black Experience.* Urbana: University of Illinois Press, 1976.

———. *CORE: A Study in the Civil Rights Movement, 1942–1968.* Chicago: University of Illinois Press, 1973.

———. "The Origins of Nonviolent Direct Action in Afro-American Protest: A Note on Historical Discontinuities." In Meier and Rudwick, *Along the Color Line*, 312–13.

Mohraz, Judy. *The Separate Problem: Case Studies of Black Education in the North, 1900–1930.* London: Greenport, 1979.

Moreno, Paul J. *From Direct Action to Affirmative Action: Fair Employment Law and Policy in America, 1933–1972.* Baton Rouge: Louisiana State University Press, 1997.

Morris, Aldon. *The Origins of the Civil Rights Movement: Black Communities Organizing for Change*. New York: Macmillan, 1984.

Motley, Constance Baker. *Equal Justice Under Law: An Autobiography by Constance Baker Motley*. New York: Farrar, Straus and Giroux, 1998.

Murray, Pauli, ed. *State's Laws on Race and Color*. Athens: University of Georgia Press, 1997.

Nelson, H. Viscount. *Black Leadership's Response to the Great Depression in Philadelphia*. Lewiston, N.Y.: Mellon, 2006.

Nicolaides, Becky M. *My Blue Heaven: Life and Politics in the Working-Class Suburbs of Los Angeles, 1920–1965*. Chicago: University of Chicago Press, 2002.

O'Brien, Gail Williams. *The Color of the Law: Race, Violence, and Justice in the Post-World War II South*. Chapel: University of North Carolina Press, 1999.

Ogbar, Jeffrey, O. G. *Black Power: Radical Politics and African American Identity*. Baltimore: Johns Hopkins University Press, 2004.

Osofsky, Gilbert. *Harlem: The Making of a Ghetto, 1890–1930*. New York: Harper and Row, 1966.

Painter, Nell Irvin. *Exodusters: Black Migration to Kansas After Reconstruction*. New York: Knopf, 1976.

Payne, Charles. *I've Got the Light of Freedom: The Organizing Tradition and the Mississippi Freedom Struggle*. Berkeley: University of California, 1995.

Perlmann, Joel. Ethnic *Differences: Schooling and Social Structure Among the Irish, Italians, Jews and Blacks in an American City, 1880–1935*. Cambridge: Cambridge University Press, 1988.

Pfeffer, Paula *A. Philip Randolph: A Pioneer of the Civil Rights Movement*. Baton Rouge: Louisiana State University Press, 1990.

Pierce, Richard B. *Polite Protest: The Political Economy of Race in Indianapolis, 1920–1970*. Bloomington: Indiana University Press, 2005.

Plummer, Brenda Gayle. *Rising Wind: Black Americans and U.S. Foreign Affairs, 1935–1960*. Chapel Hill: University of North Carolina Press, 1996.

Rabinowitz, Howard N. *Race Relations in the Urban South 1865–1890*. Urbana: University of Illinois Press, 1980.

Ralph, James Jr. *Northern Protest: Martin Luther King, Jr., Chicago, and the Civil Rights Movement*. Cambridge: Harvard University Press, 1993.

Ransby, Barbara. *Ella Baker and the Black Freedom Movement: A Radical Democratic Vision*. Chapel Hill: University of North Carolina Press, 2003.

Reed, Christopher R. *The Chicago NAACP and the Rise of Black Professional Leadership, 1910–1966*. Bloomington: Indiana University Press, 1997.

Robinson, Armstead, and Patricia Sullivan, eds. *New Directions in Civil Rights*. Charlottesville: University Press of Virginia, 1991.

Rudwick, Elliott M. *Race Riot in East St. Louis, July 2, 1917*. Carbondale: Southern Illinois University Press, 1963.

Saunders, John A. *100 Years After Emancipation: History of the Philadelphia Negro, 1787–1963*. Philadelphia: *Philadelphia Tribune*, 1964.

Schneider, Mark R. *Boston Confronts Jim Crow, 1890–1920*. Boston: Northeastern University Press, 1997.

———. *We Return Fighting: The Civil Rights Movement in the Jazz Age*. Boston: Northeastern University Press, 2002.

Segal, Geraldine R. *Blacks in the Law: Philadelphia and the Nation.* Philadelphia: University of Pennsylvania Press, 1983.

Self, Robert. *American Babylon: Race and the Struggle for Post War Oakland.* Princeton: Princeton University Press, 2003.

Shapiro, Thomas. *The Hidden Cost of Being African American: How Wealth Perpetuates Inequality.* New York: Oxford University Press, 2004.

Singh, Nikhil Pal. *"Black Is A Country": Race and the Unfinished Struggle for Democracy.* Cambridge: Harvard University Press, 2004.

Sitkoff, Harvard. *A New Deal for Blacks: The Emergence of Civil Rights as a National Issue: The Depression Decade.* New York: Oxford University Press, 1978.

Smith, J. Clay, Jr. *Emancipation: The Making of the Black Lawyer, 1844–1944.* Philadelphia: University of Pennsylvania Press, 1993.

———. *Rebels in Law.* Ann Arbor: University of Michigan Press, 1998.

Sollors, Werner, Caldwell Titcomb, and Thomas A. Underwood, eds. *Blacks at Harvard: A Documentary History of African-American Experience at Harvard and Radcliff.* New York: New York University Press, 1993.

Spear, Allan H. *Black Chicago: The Making of a Negro Ghetto, 1890–1920.* Chicago: University of Chicago Press, 1967.

Steinberg, Steven. *Turning Back: The Retreat from Racial Justice in American Thought and Policy.* Boston: Beacon Press, 1995.

Stephenson, Gilbert Thomas. *Race and Distinction in American Law.* New York: D. Appleton, 1910.

Styles, Fitzugh Lee. *Negroes and the Law in the Race's Battle for Liberty, Equality and Justice Under the Constitution of the United States.* Boston: Christopher Publishing House, 1937.

Sugrue, Thomas. *The Origins of the Urban Crisis: Race and Inequality in Post War Detroit.* Princeton: University of Princeton Press, 1996.

———. *Sweet Land of Liberty: The Forgotten Struggle for Civil Rights in the North.* New York: Random House, 2008.

Taylor, Henry Louis Jr., and Song-Ho Ha. "A Unity of Opposites: The Black College Educated Elite, Black Workers, and the Community Development Process." In Henry Louis Taylor Jr. and Walter Hill, eds., *Historical Roots of the Urban Crisis.* New York: Routledge, 2000.

Taylor, Henry Louis, and Walter Hill, eds. *Historical Roots of the Urban Crisis.* New York: Routledge, 2000.

Theoharis, Jeanne, and Komozi Woodward, eds., *Freedom North: Black Freedom Struggles Outside the South, 1940–1980.* New York: New York University Press, 2003.

———. *Groundwork: Local Black Freedom in America.* New York: New York University Press, 2005.

Thomas, Richard W. *Life for Us Is What We Make It: Building Black Community in Detroit, 1915–1945.* Bloomington: Indiana University Press, 1992.

Tompkins, Beth Bates. *Pullman Porters and the Rise of Protest Politics in Black America, 1925–1945.* Chapel Hill: University of North Carolina Press, 2001.

Trotter, Joe Jr. "African Americans in the City: The Industrial Period, 1900–1950." In Kenneth Goings and Raymond Mohls, eds., *The New African American Urban History.* New York: Sage Publications, 1996.

———. *Black Milwaukee: The Making of an Industrial Proletariat, 1915–1945.* Urbana: University of Illinois Press, 1985.

Tuck, Stephen G. N. *Beyond Atlanta: The Struggle for Racial Equality in Georgia, 1940–1980.* Athens: University of Georgia Press, 2001.

Tushnet, Mark V. *The NAACP's Legal Strategy Against Segregated Education, 1925–1950.* Chapel Hill: University of North Carolina Press, 1987.

Tuttle, William Jr. *Race Riot: Chicago and Red Summer of 1919.* New York: Atheneum, 1970.

Tyson, Timothy. *Radio Free Dixie: Robert F. Williams and the Roots of Black Power.* Chapel Hill: University of North Carolina Press, 1999.

Upton, James N. *Urban Riots in the 20th Century: A Social History.* Bristol, Ind.: Wyndham Hall Press, 1989.

Van De Burg, William L. *New Day in Babylon: The Black Power Movement and American Culture, 1965–1975.* Chicago: University of Chicago Press, 1992.

Von Eschen, Penny M. *Race Against Empire: Black Americans and Anti-colonialism, 1937–1957.* Ithaca: Cornell University Press, 1997.

Ware, Gilbert. *From the Black Bar: Voices for Equal Justice.* New York: G. P. Putnam's Sons, 1976.

———. *William Hastie: Grace Under Pressure.* New York: Oxford University Press, 1984.

Washington, Linn. *Black Judges on Justice: Perspectives from the Bench.* New York: New Press, 1994.

Weems, Robert E. Jr. *Desegregating the Dollar: African American Consumerism in the Twentieth Century.* New York: Oxford University Press, 1998.

Wiese, Andrew. *Places of Their Own: African American Suburbanization in the Twentieth Century.* Chicago: University of Chicago Press, 2004.

Weisenfeld, Judith. *African American Women and Christian Activism: New York's Black YWCA, 1905–1945.* Cambridge: Harvard University Press, 1997.

Weiss, Nancy J. *Farewell to the Party of Lincoln: Black Politics in the Age of FDR.* Princeton: Princeton University Press, 1983.

Wiggins, David K., ed. *Out of the Shadows: A Biographical History of African American Athletes.* Fayetteville: University of Arkansas Press, 2006.

Winch, Julie. *Philadelphia's Black Elite: Activism, Accommodation, and the Struggle for Autonomy, 1787–1848.* Philadelphia: Temple University Press, 1988.

Wilkins, Roy, with Tom Matthews. *Standing Fast: The Autobiography of Roy Wilkins.* New York: Viking Press, 1982,

Williams, Juan. *Thurgood Marshall: American Revolutionary.* New York: Times Books, 1998.

Williamson, Joel. *The Crucible of Race: Black White Relations in the American South Since Emancipation.* New York: Oxford University Press, 1984.

Willis, Arthur C. *Cecil's City: A History of Blacks in Philadelphia, 1639–1979.* New York: Carton Press, 1990.

Woodson, Carter G. *The Negro Professional Man and the Community with Special Emphasis on the Physician and the Lawyer.* New York: Negro Universities Press, 1928.

Woodward, C. Vann. *Origins of the New South, 1877–1913.* Baton Rouge: Louisiana State University Press, 1971.

———. *The Strange Career of Jim Crow.* New York: Oxford University Press, 1966.

Wright, Bruce. *Black Robes White Justice: Why Our Legal System Doesn't Work for Blacks.* New York: Carol Publishing Group, 1987.

Zirin, Dave. *Welcome to the Terrordome: The Pain, Politics, and Promise of Sports.* Chicago: Haymarket Books, 2007.

Articles

Alexander, Raymond Pace. "Blacks and the Law," *Verdict* 6 (September 1970), 1.

———. "Comments From Bench, Bar and Press on Our First Issue of Journal." *National Bar Journal* (October 1941): 162–73.

———. "The Five Civil Rights Groups Should Combine Forces Now." *Negro Digest* 14 (June 1965): 4.

———. "The Negro Lawyer." *Opportunity* 20 (September 1931): 268–71.

———. "The Thomas Mattox Extradition Case." *National Bar Journal* 2 (June 1944): 1–16.

———. "Voices from Harvard's Own Negroes." *Opportunity* 1 (March 1923).

Banner-Haley, Charles Pete. "*The Philadelphia Tribune* and the Persistence of Black Republicanism during the Great Depression." *Pennsylvania History* 65 (Spring 1998): 190–202.

Clark-Hine, Darlene. "Black Professionals and Race Consciousness: Origins of the Civil Rights Movement, 1895–1950." *Journal of American History* 89 (March 2003).

Dale, Elizabeth. "Social Equality Does Not Exist Among Themselves, nor Among Us": Baylies vs. Curry and Civil Rights in Chicago, 1888." *American Historical Review* 102 (April 1997): 311–40.

Deslippe, Dennis A. "Do Whites Have Rights? White Detroit Policeman and 'Reverse Discrimination' Protests in the 1970s." *Journal of American History* 91 (December 2004): 932–60.

Eagles, Charles. "Toward New Histories of the Civil Rights Era." *Journal of Southern History* 46 (November 2000): 815–48.

Fainstein, Norman, and Susan Nesbit. "Did the Black Ghetto Have a Golden Age?: Class Structure and Class Segregation in New York City, 1949–1979." *Journal of Urban History* 23 (November 1996): 3–29.

Feldstein, Ruth. "'I Don't Trust You Anymore': Nina Simone, Culture, and Black Activism In the 1960s." *Journal of American History* 91 (March 2005).

Fleming, G. James. "A Philadelphia Lawyer." *Crisis* 46 (November 1939): 329–31, 347.

Gaines, Kevin. "Rethinking Race and Class in African-American Struggles for Equality, 1885–1914." *American Historical Review* 102 (April 1997): 377–88.

Hall, Jacquelyn. "The Long Civil Rights Movement and the Political Uses of the Past." *Journal of American History* 91 (March 2005): 1233–63.

Hastie, William H. "Toward an Equalitarian Legal Order: 1930–1970." *Annals of the American Academy of Political and Social Science* 407 (May 1973): 18–32.

Higginbotham, A. Leon Jr. "To the Scale and Standing of Men." *Journal of Negro History* 60 (July 1965): 340–80.

Hine, Darlene Clark. "Black Professionals and Race Consciousness: Origins of the Civil Rights Movement, 1890–1950." *Journal of American History* 89 (March 2003): 1279–80.

Hirsch, Arnold. "Massive Resistance in the Urban North: Trumbull Park, Chicago, 1953–1966." *Journal of American History* 82 (September 1995): 522–50.

Johnson, James Weldon, and Herbert J. Seligmann. "Legal Aspects of the Negro Problem."
    Annals of the American Academy of Political and Social Science 80 (November 1928): 90–97.
Jones-Ross, Felecia G. "Mobilizing the Masses: *The Cleveland Call and Post* and the Scottsboro
    Incident." *Journal of Negro History* 84 (Winter 1999): 48–61.
Kaplan, Benjamin. "The Legal Front: Some Highlights of the Past Year." *Crisis* 47 (July 1940):
    206–8.
Katz, Michael, et al. "The New African American Inequality." *Journal of American History* 92
    (June 2005): 75–108.
Klarman, Michael J. "How Brown Changed Race Relations: The Backlash Thesis." *Journal of
    American History* 81 (June 1994).
Leonard, Walter J. "The Development of the Black Bar." *Annals of the American Academy of
    Political and Social Science"* 407 (May 1973): 134–43.
Liacourus, Peter J. "Report on Pennsylvania Bar Admission Procedures." *Temple Law Quarterly*
    44 (Winter 1971): 143–258.
Mack, Kenneth. "Law and Mass Politics in the Making of the Civil Rights Lawyer, 1931–1941."
    Journal of American History 93 (June 2006).
———. "Rethinking Civil Rights Lawyering and Politics in the Era Before Brown." *Yale Law
    Journal* 115 (2005).
Marshall, Thurgood. "Equal Justice Under the Law." *Crisis* 46 (July 1939): 199–201.
McGee, Henry W. "Black Lawyers and the Struggle for Racial Justice in the American Social
    Order." *Buffalo Law Review* 20 (Winter 1971): 423–34.
McBride, David. "Mid-Atlantic State Courts and the Struggle With the 'Separate But Equal'
    Doctrine: 1880–1939." *Rutgers Law Journal* 17 (Spring 1986): 569–89.
Mollison, Irvin C. "Negro Lawyers in Mississippi." *Journal of Negro History* 15 (January 1930):
    283–95.
Nelson, Viscount H. Jr. "The Philadelphia NAACP: Race Versus Class Consciousness During
    the Thirties." *Journal of Black Studies* 5 (March 1975): 255–75.
Odum, Howard. "Negro Children in the Public Schools of Philadelphia." *Annals of the
    American Academy of Political and Social Sciences* 49 (September 1913): 189–99.
Sitkoff, Harvard. "Racial Militancy and Interracial Violence in the Second World War." *Journal
    of American History* 58 (December 1971): 661–81.
Smith, J. Clay Jr. "The Black Bar Association and Civil Rights." *Creighton Law Review* 15
    (Spring 1981): 651–79.
Sugrue, Thomas. "Affirmative Action from Below: Civil Rights, the Building Trades, and the
    Politics of Racial Equality in the Urban North, 1945–1969." *Journal of American History* 91
    (June 2004): 145–73.
———. "Crabgrass-Roots Politics, Race, Rights, and Reaction Against Liberalism in the Urban
    North, 1940–1964." *Journal of Urban History* 82 (September 1995); 551–78.
Wolcott, Victoria W. "Recreation and Race in the Postwar City: Buffalo's 1956 Crystal Beach
    Riot." *Journal of American History* 93 (June 2006): 63–90.
Work, Monroe. "The Negro in Business and the Professions." *Annals of the American Academy of
    Political and Social Science* 80 (November 1928): 138–45.

INDEX

Abbott, Robert S., 40, 65
Abolishment of Peonage Committee, 77
Abraham, Henry J., 14
Acheson, Dean, 115
Adams, Carolyn, 118
affirmative action, 20, 169, 172, 173, 185
African American attorneys, 191–92; African
    Americans and, 23, 25, 70–71; and civil
    rights, 91; and the Pennsylvania Bar
    Exam, 20; in the south, 71
African Americans: affirmative action
    and, 169, 172; education and, 7, 12;
    Great Depression and, 40, 62; Great
    Migration and, 61–62; at Harvard, 18–
    19; Jews and, 16–17; New Deal and, 90;
    politics and, 38, 53, 54, 62, 66; poverty,
    crime, and, 141–42; presidential election
    (1948) and, 63–64; segregation and, 46;
    social and political progress and, 160;
    unemployment and, 145; urban renewal
    and, 147; white violence and, 13, 40–41,
    76, 77, 93; World War I and, 12, 13, 17,
    61–62; World War II and, 62–63, 74–75,
    80, 90
Alexander, Ellen, 3
Alexander, Hillard, Jr., 6
Alexander, Hillard Boone, 3, 4–5, 6, 7
Alexander, Irene, 6
Alexander, James, 3
Alexander, Raymond Pace: academic honor

societies and, 14–15; affirmative action
    and, 169, 173, 185; African American
    crime and, 142–43; African American
    studies and, 9–10, 26, 164, 181, 190;
    on African Americans and black
    attorneys, 70–71; American diplomacy
    and, 112–16, 176–78; and the Arsenic
    Widow Case, 72; ASNLH and, 163,
    183–84; on attorneys and civil rights,
    165; Berwyn Desegregation Case and,
    46–54; birth of, 3; on Black attorneys,
    36–37; Black Power movement and,
    160, 162, 163–64, 167, 168–69, 175, 181–82,
    186, 192; Black separatism and, 182; on
    Black soldiers in Europe, 113–14; Brown
    Case and, 41–45, 191; Carter and, 167;
    Carter G. Woodson Award and, 163;
    Chew Case and, 24; childhood of,
    6–9; church and, 7, 9, 11; CIO and,
    70; City-Wide Colored Citizens
    Committee and, 69; civil rights cases
    and, 72, 74; civil rights movement
    tactics and, 156, 158, 159, 166, 167, 170,
    180, 189, 193; civil rights protests and,
    145–46, 148, 149–50, 153–54; Cold War
    and, 95, 96, 106–7, 120; Communist
    Party and, 39; Community Legal
    Services and, 127–28; crime, poverty
    and, 170, 172–75, 192; crimes by youth
    and, 141; death of, 184–85; early career

of, 21; education of, 7–8, 10, 11–13, 14,
15, 16, 17, 20; exposure to white elite
of, 8–9; FBI and, 94, 95; Fellowship
Commission and, 96; foreign policy
and, 117; Girard College Desegregation
Case and, 125–26, 128, 130–34, 135–36;
on Harvard, 16; hate mail to, 80, 83,
131–32, 133; Henry Case and, 23–24;
ILD and, 39, 43, 54, 97; John Mercer
Langston Law Club and, 29; judgeship
of, 127, 140; judgeships sought by, 61, 63,
64, 65–66, 76, 108, 109–11, 137, 138–40;
King and, 151, 152–53; law practice of,
34–36; LDEF and 98, 99; Lewis and,
10–11, 15; and litigation and civil rights,
17–18, 27, 28, 39, 55–56, 57; on lynching,
40, 41; Madison Square Garden Case
and, 17–18; Malcolm X and, 170–71;
marriage of, 25; Mattox Case and, 76–
80; military service and, 14; Mississippi
Freedom Summer and, 151–52; on
Moore, 148, 179; NAACP and, 29–30,
32–34, 40, 46, 48–50, 78, 79, 80, 96, 97,
98–99, 104, 106; *National Bar Journal*
and, 72–73; NBA and, 29, 36–40, 69–71,
72–73, 91–92, 165; NCBL and, 167; New
Negro movement and, 10, 19, 26, 27, 28,
29, 56, 148, 161, 163, 167, 181–82, 189, 190,
192; Nile Club and, 19–20; NNC and,
95; NOI and, 170–71; Olympics (1972)
and, 168; personal injury suits and, 23;
Philadelphia race riot and, 155–56; on
police brutality, 40–41, 42; political
protest and, 51–52; politics and, 38, 61,
64–66, 67–69, 89–90, 91, 108–9, 110,
114, 116–19, 120, 136–37; Popular Front
and, 94, 97; on poverty, 170; Rounds
Case and, 30–34, 191; Scottsboro Case
and, 39; socialism and, 165, 186, 192;
Spiritual Rehabilitation Program and,
127–28; Sykes Case and, 82–89; Thomas
Case and, 22–23; Trenton Six Case
and, 96, 97–101, 191; unemployment
and, 144–45; United States Supreme
Court and, 87, 134; Woodson and, 9,

11; World War I and, 12; World War II
and, 74–75
Articles: "Blacks and the Law," 182–83;
"The Five Civil Rights Groups
Should Combine Forces Now," 159;
"New Deal Has Given Lip Service to
Negro Aspirations," 90; "Voices from
Harvard's Own Negroes," 18–19
Speeches: "The Future of the American
Negro," 11–12; "In Our Other America,"
173; "Let My People Live," 73–74;
"The Negro Lawyer: His Duty in a
Rapidly Changing, Social, Economic
and Political World," 37–38; "The New
Negro Fights for Justice," 27; "On to
College," 26; "What about National
Preparedness for the Negro," 74
Alexander, Sadie Tanner Mossell, 126, 180,
192; CCR and, 63, 90; CORR and,
51; education of, 17, 25; Fellowship
Commission and, 96; law practice of,
35–36; marriage of, 25; and politics, 108,
120; racial discrimination against, 12,
55–56
Alexander, Samuel, 3, 4, 6
Alexander, Schollie, 6
Alexander, Virginia (sister), 6
Alexander, Virginia Pace (mother), 3–4, 5, 6
Alpha Kappa Alpha, 190
Alpha Phi Alpha, 26, 190
American Bar Association, 72
American Bar Association Journal, 73
American Civil Liberties Union (ACLU),
49, 78, 80, 106, 107
American Federation of Labor (AFL), 70
American Negro Labor Conference, 201n49
Amonitti, George J., 132
Amsterdam News, 119
Anders, Jean, 57
Anderson, Carol, 110–11
Anderson, Marion, 72
Annenberg, Walter, 109, 110
"Appeal to the Common Sense of Colored
Citizens, An," 90
Armstrong, Louis, 128

Arsenic Widow Case, 72

Association for the Study of African
    American Life and History (ASALH),
    181, 183–84

Association for the Study of Negro Life and
    History (ASNLH), 9, 10

Association of Black Sociologists, 166

Atlanta Constitution, 163–64

Attucks, Crispus, 12

Austin, Algernon, 193

Bagnall, Robert, 30, 47

Baker, Joe, 119

Baker, Josephine, 102

Baldi, Frank, 76

Baldwin, James: *Go Tell It on the Mountain*,
    150; *Blues for Mr. Charlie*, 150–51

Ball, John C., 79

Baltimore Afro-American, 40, 88

Barristers Club, 119

Belafonte, Harry, 146

Bell, Derrick, 166, 184

Bell, John C., 87

Belton, Catherine, 56

Beresin, Jack, 8

Berwyn Desegregation Case, 46–54

Beta Gamma Sigma, 14

Bethune, Mary McLoud, 62, 109, 115

Black Cabinet, 62

Black Panthers, 161, 162

Black Power movement, 160–61, 163–64, 167,
    175, 181, 182, 192

Black Studies, 164

Blanc, Victor A., 129–30

Bliven, Bruce, 107

Bok, Curtis, 67

Bond, Julian, 160

Boston, African Americans in, 15

Boston Guardian, 15

Bowser, Charles, 180

Boyle, William, 113, 114, 115

Bradford, Odessa, 154

Brandeis, Louis, 139

Bright, John, 132

Brimmer, Andrew F., 178

Brock, Essie, 47

Brodsky, Joseph, 38

Brooke, Edward W., 178

Brotherhood of Sleeping Car Porters, 159

Brown, Francis Schuck, 82, 86

Brown, William E. "Willie." *See* Willie
    Brown Case

Brown V. Board of Education, 125

Bruce, Roscoe Conkling, Jr., 18

Brumbaugh, Martin G., 7

Brundage, Fitzhugh, 77

Bryan, Helen, 51, 56, 57

Bulger, Robert, 134

Bulletin Forum, The, 143

Bunche, Ralph, 51, 94, 114, 115, 176, 178

Burbank, B., 16

Burrell, J. Mercer, 98–99, 105–6

Burroughs, Nannie H., 65

Burton, Nathan, 77

Butterfield, Roger, 71

Butts, R. C., 74

Cahn, Edgar, *The War on Poverty: A Civilian
    Perspective*, 170

Cahn, Jean, *The War on Poverty: A Civilian
    Perspective*, 170

Cambridge Non-Violent Action Committee,
    162

Capeci, Dominic, 80

Carlos, John, 168

Carmichael, Stokely, 159, 160–62, 175

Carrier, R. E., 88

Carroll, Vincent A., 82, 83, 84, 85, 86, 87

Carson, Curtis C., 116

Carson, Saul, 49

Carter, Elmer, 72

Carter, Robert, 166–67

Carver, George Washington, 72

Cayton, Horace R., 74

Central High School (Philadelphia), 8

Central High School (Little Rock), 128

Cheatham, Harry, 53

Cheney, Pauline, 48

Chew, William, 24

Chicago Defender, 40

Chudoff, Earl, 114, 115, 117, 118, 129, 136, 137

Churchill, Winston, "From Stettin in the Baltic to Trieste in the Adriatic," 93

Citizens Committee Against Juvenile Delinquency and Its Causes (CCAD), 138

Citizens Republican Club, 65

City-Wide Colored Citizens Committee, 78

Civil Rights Act (1964), 152, 153, 160

Civil Rights Congress (CRC), 94, 120; and the Trenton Six Case, 96, 97, 98, 99–100, 104–5, 106

civil rights movement, 160; Cold War and, 94–95, 115–16, 120; Jews and, 16–17; litigation and, 190–91; media and, 160, 176, 179; tactics of, 127; white backlash and, 129

Clark, Granville, 118

Clark, Joseph S., 116, 117, 118, 119, 136, 137

Clay, Fair, 78

Cleveland, Mark, 76

Coachman, Alice, 168

Cobb, O. B., 47, 49, 50

Cold War, and civil rights, 94–95, 115–16, 120

Coleman, William, 95, 183

Collett, Wayne, 168

Colored American Citizens Organization, 65

Commmission on Human Relations (CHR), 126

"Committee of One Hundred," 4

Committee on Civil Rights (CCR), *To Secure These Rights*, 63–64, 90–91

Committee on Race Relations (CORR), 47–48, 51, 56

Committee to Support the Southern Freedom Struggle, 146

Communist Party, 39, 43, 44, 49, 93, 94, 95, 98, 99, 120, 201n49

Community Action Programs (CAP), 178

Community Legal Services (CLS), 127–28

Congress of Industrial Organizations, 70

Congress of Racial Equality (CORE), 159, 211n46

Connor, Eugene "Bull," 161

Cooke, Jay, 65, 66

Cooper, Ralph, 98, 99, 100, 101, 102, 103, 104, 106

Corlo, George, 100

Corlo, Mario, 101

Cornell, Wilbur, 75, 77

Cornell Law Journal, "Blacks and the Law," 182–83

Corwin, Edward S., 99

Cosmopolitan Club, 16

Countryman, Matthew, 95, 96, 147, 148, 160, 192

Crisis, The, 13, 18; "The Philadelphia Lawyer," 72; "Segregation," 51

Crosby, Primus, 47

Cunningham, Luther, 136, 142

Daily Compass, The, 97

Darrow, Clarence, 39

Dash, Samuel, 148

Davis, Ben, Jr., 94

Davis, Christine Ray, 115

Davis, Lania, 52

Davis, Mamie, 56

Davis, Martha, 170

Dawson, William, 91, 108, 110, 113, 115

Day, Edmund E., 16

Delaney, Michael, 189–90

Delate, Andrew F., 100

Delta Sigma Theta, 190

Democratic Party: African Americans and, 54, 62, 64; convention (1964), 160

Denby, Herbert, 33

Dent, A. W., 134

Dewey, Thomas, 109

Dickens, Helen O., 103

Dickerson, Earl, 98

Dickerson, G. Edward, 64, 70

Diemond, John A., 132

Dilworth, Richardson, 116, 117, 118, 119, 134–35, 136

Dixiecrat Party, 63, 64

"Don't Buy Where You Can't Work" campaign, 39, 62, 127

Double V Campaign, 63, 74, 80

Drake, St. Clair, 74

Drayden, Gladys, 57
Dreiser, Theodore, 38
DuBois, Shirley Graham, 186
DuBois, W. E. B., 19; Alexander and,
    114–15; Brown Case and, 44; civil rights
    strategy of, 28; foreign policy and,
    62, 113; Great Depression and, 62; on
    Philadelphia, 5, 6; politics and, 109;
    "Segregation," 51; white attorneys and,
    25; World War I and, 13–14
Duch, Andrew, 101
Dudley, Edward, 96, 112, 116
Dudziak, Mary, 94, 102, 113
Dunbar Law Club, 16
Dye, Wilbur, 76
Dyreson, Mark, 168

Earle, George, 53, 54, 68, 158; Alexander and,
    69, 109; Equal Rights Bill (1935), 55
East St. Louis riot, 13
Ebony, 146
Educational Equality League (EEL), 49, 52
Eisenhart, Roy, 103
Eisner, Herman, 33
Eliot, Charles, 18
Ellis, Francis, 65
English, Collis, 98, 99, 100, 101, 102, 103, 104,
    106
English, George, 102–3
English, Rube, 103
Erkstom, Charles A., 119
Eyre, Ester, 154

Fagan, Maurice, 133
Fair Employment Practices Act, 95
Fair Employment Practices Commissions,
    63, 91
Farmer, James, 159
Faubus, Oral, 128
Fauset, Arthur H., 68, 89
Felder, Ivan, 132
Feldstein, Ruth, 162
Fenerty, Clare G., 76, 78, 79
Ferguson, Melville, 132
Ferguson, William C., 22

Finnegan, Alex A., 108
Finnegan, James, 114, 116, 117, 119
Fleck, John J., 131
Forrest, McKinley, 98, 99, 100, 101, 103, 104
Foster, Marcus, 155
Fox, Edward, 64
Frankfurter, Felix, 73, 75, 183
Freedom Schools, 190

Gaffney, Joseph P., 134
Gaines, Kevin, 94, 171, 190–91
Garvey, Marcus, 19, 20, 25, 163
Garvin, Roy, 113
Gay, Eustace, 15, 54, 119
Gay, Walter A., 108, 109
Gillen, John, 131
Girard, Stephen, 130, 209n12
Girard College Desegregation Case, 96,
    125–26, 128, 130–34, 135–36, 158
Goggin, Jacqueline, 10, 19–20
Goldwater, Barry, 128, 152, 153, 154
Goodwin, Richard, "The Negro Family: The
    Case for National Action," 172
Gordon, James, 31, 32
Gordon, R. Howard, 78
Gragnon-LaCoste, Thomas Prosper, 210n12
Graham, David, 103
Grape-Vine (Central State College), 170
Gray, William H., Jr., 148
Great Depression, 40, 62, 189
Great Migration, 61–62
Green, Adam, 146
Green, Edward T., 24–25
Green, Norman J., 46
Green, William, Jr., 136, 137, 140
Greene, Harry, 117
Gregg, Robert, 3
Groce, Earl, 25

Ha, Song-Ho, 14
Hacker, Andrew, 191
Haggerty, Eugene, 136–37
Hall, Charles A., 151–52
Hall, Jacqueline Dowd, 62
Hall, Robert, 79

Hamilton, Charles, 91
Hardin, Clara, 69
Hare, Daniel, 57
Haring, J. Howard, 103
Harlem Liberator, 51
Harlem Renaissance, 164
Harr, Luther, 67
Harriman, Averill, 178
Harrington, Michael, *The Other America: Poverty in the United States*, 170
Harrison, Earl, 109
Harvard University, 18–19, 20
Hastie, William, 119; ambassadorship of, 91; education of, 10; judgeship of, 110, 111; "Negro Discrimination and the Need for Federal Action," 77; Popular Front and, 94
Hause, J. Frank E., 47
Hays, Arthur Garfield, 99, 100, 107
Henderson, Purvis, 103
Henry, Edward, 65, 66–67, 137
Henry, Mrs. W. R., 23–24
Henson, Matthew, 12
Hershberg, Theodore, 145
Heubner, D., 14
Higginbotham, A. Leon, 184
Higginbotham, Evelyn Brooks, 191
Hine, Darlene Clark, 29
Hines, W. W., 48
Hirsch, Arnold, 129
Holderman, Carl, 105
Hoover, J. Edgar, 19
Hoover Dam Project, 40
Horn, J. V., 55–56
Horn and Hardart (restaurant), 55–56, 57
Horne, Gerald, 94, 98
Horner, William, 97, 102
Houston, Charles Hamilton, 51, 165; Alexander and, 16, 56; education of, 10, 16; ILD and, 45; Mattox Case and, 78; Nile Club and, 19; Phi Beta Kappa and, 14; Popular Front and, 94
Houston, William L., 65
Howard, Perry, 28, 65
Hubbard, Maceo, 35, 109

Huff, William Henry, 77
Hunton, Alphaeus, 186

International Labor Defense (ILD): Alexander and, 54; Berwyn Case and, 49, 51, 52; Brown Case and, 44; NAACP and, 43, 44–45; NBA and, 39–40; Trenton Six Case and, 97
Iowa Colored Bar Association, 29
Irelan, Tillie, 85
Irvin, James H., 65

Jackson, Thomas, 192
James, Arthur, 78
Janken, Kenneth, 15, 182
Jeffries, Judson, 160
Jenkins, Timothy L., 166
Jim Crow, 4, 37, 49, 52, 92, 126, 170, 172
John Mercer Langston Law Club, 29, 65, 111, 119
Johnson, Arthur, 81
Johnson, Charles S., 12
Johnson, James Weldon, 76
Johnson, Lyndon B., 159, 178; affirmative action and, 169, 173; Civil Rights Act (1964) and, 152, 153; election (1964) and, 154; King and, 176; "To Fulfill These Rights," 172; War on Poverty and, 160
Johnson, W. A., 77
Johnson, W. L., 49, 50, 52
Joint Committee to Secure a Fair Trial for the Trenton Six, 98
Jones, Arthur, 116
Jones, Ruth, 56
Joseph, Peniel, 162
Journal of Negro History, 184
juvenile delinquency, 140–41

Kasper, John, 129
Katzenback, Frank, III, 99, 100, 105
Katznelson, Ira, 62
Keller, William, 78, 79
Kelley, James C. (Jaycee), 81–82, 84–85, 87
Kelly, John, Sr., 136
Kelly, John B., 30, 67

Kelly, John J., 105
Kelsy, P., 14
Kerner Report, 167
King, Martin Luther, Jr., 156; Alexander
    and, 146, 151, 152–53; assassination of,
    164; Black Power and, 162; *Chaos or
    Community: Where Do We Go From
    Here*, 186; Civil Rights movement and,
    159; Democratic Convention (1964)
    and, 160; Girard Desegregation Case
    and, 134; March Against Fear, 161;
    media and, 161; poverty, race and, 192;
    Vietnam War and, 176
Klarman, Michael, 126
Klein, Charles, 128
Kornweibel, Theodore, 19
Krenn, Michael L., 112, 113
Ku Klux Klan, 49, 171
Kulp, D., 82

Landon, Alf, 66
Lane, Roger, 3, 4, 6
Lawrence, Joseph, 52
Leader, George, 127, 137, 138, 139–40
League of Struggle for Negro Rights
    (LSNR), 49, 51, 201n49
Lee, Blanche, 41
Lee, Tommie, 168
LeKlerk, Charles, 210n12
Lemarck, Paul, 149
Levine, Robert, 182
Levinson, Abraham, 85
Levinthall, Louis E., 108, 140
Lewis, Claude, 179–80, 185
Lewis, John, 153, 159, 162
Lewis, William H., 9, 10–11, 15
Lipschutz, Ephraim, 82, 86
Lipscomb, Alice, 180
Litman, Maurice, 155
Locke, Alain, 51
Logan, Floyd, 49, 52, 133
Logan, Rayford, 15, 73, 79, 112, 182
Lord, John W., Jr., 82
Louis, Joe, 168
Louise Thomas Case, 22–23

Louverture, Toussaint, 209n12
Lowell, Abbot Lawrence, 18
Lutz, Dorothy, 41, 42
lynching, 13, 40–41, 77, 78, 79, 80, 93

M Street High School (Washington, D.C.),
    10
Mack, Kenneth, 28, 39, 94
MacKenzie, John, 98, 101, 103, 104
Maddox, Lester, 175
Madison Square Garden Case, 17–18
Magloire, Paul Eugene, 115
Mahoney, George, 175
Main Line Daily Times, 47
Malcolm X, 170–71
Manly, Milon A., 131
Manning, Peyton "Scrappy," 100
Marbles v. Creecy, 80
March Against Fear, 161–62
Marshall, George, 173
Marshall, Thurgood, 13, 117, 119, 165;
    Alexander and, 65; civil rights
    protests and, 145–46; Girard College
    Desegregation Case and, 131; Mattox
    Case and, 78; "Negro Discrimination
    and the Need for Federal Action," 77;
    Trenton Six Case and, 104, 106, 107
Martin, Alexander, 66, 67
Martin, Edward, 79, 87–88
Martin, Freeman L., 72, 73
Martin, Isadore M., 30, 31, 32–33, 50, 54
Mattox, Emmy, 75
Mattox, Gussie, 75
Mattox, Lester, 76
Mattox, Thomas. *See* Thomas Mattox Case
Maxey, George W., 44, 73
Mayfield, Julian, 186
McDevitt, Harry S., 44
McDevitt, Henry, 86
McGill, Ralph, 163–64
McKenna, William J., 117
McKissick, Floyd, 166
McLendon, James D., 18
McNeil, Genna Rae, 16, 19
Meier, August, 26, 46

Methodist Ministers Conference, 65

Metropolitan Opera House, 8

Millen, Herbert, 13, 66, 108; Berwyn
    Desegregation Case and, 52, 53; Brown
    Case and, 43; ILD and, 44

Millen Judicial Party, 66

Miller, Henry, 100

Miller, James, 67

Millison, Irvin C., 91, 96

Minnick, Thomas J., Jr., 22

Mississippi Freedom Democratic Party, 160

Mississippi Freedom Summer, 151

Montgomery Bus Boycott, 121, 145, 164

Moon, Henry Lee, 107

Moore, Acel, 184

Moore, Cecil B.: Alexander and, 153, 154,
    192; background of, 146–47; civil rights
    protests and, 127, 128, 142, 148–49, 154,
    158, 178–79; politics and, 138; race riot
    (1964) and, 128, 155, 156

Moore, Clifford R., 98–99, 105, 106, 107

Moore, E. W., 9

Moore, Lewis Tanner, 35

Morgan, Edward P., 161

Mossell, Nathan, 67, 131

Mossell, Sadie Turner. See Alexander, Sadie
    Turner Mossell

Motley, Constance Baker, 184

Mound City Bar Association, 29

Moynihan, Daniel Patrick, "The Negro
    Family: The Case for National Action,"
    172

Murer, John H., 77, 78, 79

Murphy, Carl, 40, 109

Murray, Pauli, 40, 109

Myers, Francis, 117; Alexander and, 109, 111,
    112, 114, 116; Hastie and, 110, 111

Nabrit, James A., 178

Nation, The, 104, 107

Nation of Islam (NOI), 170–71

National Association for the Advancement
    of Colored People (NAACP):
    Alexander and, 29–30, 32–34, 36, 40,
    48–50, 78, 79, 80, 96, 97, 98–99, 104,
106; Berwyn Desegregation Case
    and, 46, 48–50; black attorneys and,
    29–30, 40; Brown Case and, 34; civil
    rights litigation and, 190; civil rights
    movement and, 159; civil rights protests
    and, 145; Cold War and, 120; criminal
    cases and, 42–43; extradition cases
    and, 76–77; Girard Case and, 133; ILD
    and, 43, 44–45; Legal Defense and
    Educational Fund (LDEF), 98, 99,
    106; Mattox Case and, 76–77, 78, 79,
    80; NBA and, 40; Pennsylvania Equal
    Rights Law (1935) and, 55; Rounds
    Case and, 30, 32–34; Trenton Six Case
    and, 96, 97, 99–100, 104, 105–6

National Bar Association (NBA): Alexander
    and, 66, 69–71, 164, 165, 190; CIO
    and, 70; founding of, 29; ILD and, 39;
    Mattox Case and, 78; NAACP and, 40

National Bar Journal, 69, 72–73, 79

National Conference of Black Political
    Scientists, 166

National Council of Black Lawyers
    (NCBL), 166

National Institute of Administration of
    Saigon, 176

National Lawyers Guild (NLG), 77, 80, 94

National Negro Bar Association (NNBA),
    28

National Negro Business League (NNBL),
    28

National Negro Congress (NNC), 94, 95

National Urban League (NUL), 159, 176

Negro Digest, "The Five Civil Rights Groups
    Should Combine Forces Now," 159

Nelson, H. Viscount, 42–43

New Deal, 62, 90

New Jersey CIO News, 105

New Negro movement, 13, 180–81; African
    American history and, 19, 163;
    Alexander and, 190; attorneys and, 20,
    27–28; Black Power movement and,
    160, 161; civil rights movement and, 189,
    192; principles of, 26; Woodson and, 10

New Orleans Times Picayune, 134

New Republic, 107
New York Herald Tribune, 101
New York Law Journal, 166
New York Post, 101
New York State Equal Rights Law, 18
New York Times, 101, 151, 161
Newark Evening News, 105
Newsweek, 150, 161
Newton, Huey, 162
Nile Club, 19–20, 26
Niles, David, 110, 111
Nix, Robert C., Jr., 185
Nix, Robert C., Sr.: Alexander and, 185;
    Brown Case and, 42, 44, 55; leadership
    and, 185; Moore and, 148; politics and,
    120, 136, 137–38; race riot (1964) and, 128,
    155; World War II and, 74
Nixon, Richard, 169, 178
Norris, J. Austin: Alexander and, 185;
    leadership and, 179; Moore and, 148;
    politics and, 108, 120, 136

Odum, Howard W., 7
Office of Economic Opportunity (OEO),
    178
Office of Federal Contract Compliance of
    the Department of Labor, 169
Ogbar, Jeffery, 166
Olympics (1968), 168
Olympics (1972), 168
Omega Psi Phi Fraternity Incorporated, 190
Opportunity, 18; "The Negro Lawyer," 38
Owens, Jesse, 166

Pace, Alice, 6
Pace, Georgia Chandler, 6, 7
Pace, Jenne, 3
Pace, John Schollie, 3, 6, 7
Pace, Thomas, 3
Pace, Virginia. *See* Alexander, Virginia Pace
Parker, Heloise T., 81
Parker, John, 52
Parks, Rosa, 191
Patterson, William L., 39, 45, 94, 98, 120
Pearson, Drew, 156–57

Pellettieri, George, 99, 100, 102, 105, 106
Pennsylvania Bar Exam, 20
Pennsylvania Equal Rights Law (1887), 25
Pennsylvania Equal Rights Law (1935), 28,
    54–57
Peppers, Alice, 73
Perry, Michael, 134
Pettygrew, J. Thompson, 118
Phi Beta Kappa, 14
Philadelphia: affirmative action and, 169;
    African Americans in, 3, 4–5, 6; Board
    of Directors of City Trusts, 128, 130, 133;
    city politics of, 64; police brutality in,
    26, 31, 34, 40, 42, 43, 119, 145, 154, 155, 181;
    politics and race in, 4–5; race relations
    in, 4, 5–6, 21, 26, 126–27, 129–30; race
    riots in, 13, 128, 154–56, 181, 192; school
    segregation in, 45–46; transit strike
    in, 63
Philadelphia Afro American: "Give
    Others a Chance," 114–15; Spiritual
    Rehabilitation Program and, 143;
    Trenton Six Case and, 101, 102
Philadelphia Bulletin: Girard College
    Desegregation Case and, 125; Sykes
    Case and, 81
Philadelphia Committee for Defense of
    Political Prisoners (PCDPP), 49
Philadelphia Council for Community
    Advancement (PCCA), 147, 148
Philadelphia Courier, 24
Philadelphia Evening Bulletin: Alexander
    and, 143, 153, 185; black leadership and,
    179–80; Girard College Desegregation
    Case and, 132, 134; Trenton Six Case
    and, 101
Philadelphia Independent, 54, 148
Philadelphia Inquirer, 109, 117; Alexander and,
    72, 108, 138, 163, 169, 185; Girard College
    Desegregation Case and, 132; Mattox
    Case and, 79; Olympics (1972) and,
    168; on race relations, 153, 156–57; race
    riot (1964) and, 155; Sykes Case and, 81,
    83–84, 85, 86, 88; Trenton Six Case and,
    100, 101

Philadelphia Plan, 169

Philadelphia Rapid Transit Corporation
(PRTC), 23, 24

Philadelphia Record, 53–54

Philadelphia Tribune: on African Americans
and crime, 141–42; Alexander and, 15,
64, 66, 67, 68, 117, 136, 137, 138, 146, 185;
on appointment of federal judges,
109; Berwyn Case and, 46, 50, 52,
53, 54; Brown Case and, 44; Chew
Case and, 24; on the city council
race (1951), 118, 119; on crime, 65;
on desegregation of Central High
(Little Rock), 128; "The Future of the
American Negro," 11; Girard Case
and, 128–29, 131; Green Case and, 24;
on the Hastie appointment, 111; on
housing conditions, 147; on Moore,
149; NBA and, 70; on the Pennsylvania
Equal Rights Law (1935), 55; on racial
violence, 129, 130; Robinson and, 150;
Rounds Case and, 31; on segregation,
21; Sykes Case and, 83, 84, 86, 87, 88;
Thomas Case and, 22–23; Trenton Six
Case and, 100, 104

Pinchot, Gifford, 52

Pittsburgh Courier: Alexander and, 79, 114; on
city council race (1951), 118; Double V
Campaign and, 63, 80; on Ethiopia, 114;
on the Foreign Service, 112, 115; on the
Hastie appointment, 111, 117; Mattox
Case and, 79; Thomas Case and, 22;
Trenton Six Case and, 100, 102, 103

Poitier, Sidney, 146

police brutality, 41, 91, 97, 101, 162. *See also*
Philadelphia: police brutality in

Popper, Martin, 73

Popular Front, 94, 95, 96, 127

Pound, Dean Roscoe, 20, 39

Powell, Adam Clayton, Jr., 147, 156–57, 162

Princeton Committee for the Defense of the
Trenton Six, 99, 104, 107

Progressive Party, 63

Purnell, Brian, 211n46

race riots, 62, 193; in northern cities, 153, 156,
160, 192; poverty and, 145; whites and,
13, 63, 129–30. *See also* Philadelphia:
race riots in

Rainey, Joseph, 74, 95, 127, 136

Randolph, A. Philip: Black Power and, 162;
civil rights movement and, 159; Cold
War and, 115; Committee to Support
the Southern Freedom Struggle and,
146; election (1964) and, 153; Fair
Employment Practices Commissions
and, 63; poverty, civil rights and, 62;
white attorneys and, 25

Rankin, Frances, 57

Ransom, Leon, 79

Ray, James Earl, 164

Reagan, Ronald, 163

Redmond, Sidney, 151, 152

Regan, James J., 139

Republican Party, African Americans and,
38, 53, 64–65, 66

Reynolds, Hobson, 54–55, 67, 69

Rhodes, E. Washington, 50; on African
Americans and crime, 141–42;
Alexander and, 114; Girard Case and,
131; Moore and, 148; politics and, 64, 68

Rice, John K., 118

Richardson, Gloria, 162

Ricks, Willie, 162

Rivers, Frances E., 90, 105

Rizzo, Frank, 185

Robeson, Paul, 109, 113

Robinson, Jackie, 150

Rogers, Joel A., 79, 210n12

Roosevelt, Eleanor, 146

Roosevelt, Franklin Delano, 19, 54, 62, 63, 75

Roosevelt, Theodore, 10, 174

Rounds, Walter Lee. *See* Walter Rounds
Case

Rudwick, Elliot, 46

Rustin, Bayard, 162, 163, 186

Salus, Samuel, 55

Sampson, Faith, 171

Sanders, Jack, 138
Saturday Evening Post, 134
Saunders, John, 137, 139, 185
Saxe, Michael, 82
Schermer, George, 131
Schmidt, Harvey, 114, 120, 137
Schnader, William, 47, 48, 49, 52, 53, 54
Schroeder, Irene, 85
Scott, Amos, 181
Scott, John R. K., 21
Seaboard White Citizens Council, 129
Seale, Bobby, 162
Segal, Bernard G., 183
Segal, Geraldine, 20
Seligmann, Herbert J., 43, 76
Shelby, Earl, 125
Shepherd, Marshall, 110, 118, 133, 136, 138
Shields, Charles, 56
Sickel, Carlton, 175
Sienkiewicz, Walter V., 135
Simone, Nina, "Mississippi Goddamn," 162
Singh, Nikhil, 62
Sitkoff, Harvard, 62
Smalley, Judge, 101, 102, 103
Smith, J. Clay, 28
Smith, L. C., 77
Smith, Lawrence, 133
Smith, Robert, 56
Smith, Zelmon, 77
Society of Friends (Quakers), 47
Southern Christian Leadership Conference (SCLC), 152, 153, 159
Spaulding, Theodore, 95, 105, 114, 137
Spingam, Arthur, 33, 43
Spiritual Rehabilitation Program (SRP), 127–28
Stalvey, Lois Mark, 154
Starkosh, Charles, 24–25
Steinberg, Stephen, 172
Stern, Howard, 86
Stern, Robert, 131
Stoddard, Margaret McPherson, 30–31
Stouffer's Restaurant, 56
Stradford, C. Francis, 37, 70, 71

Student Army Training Corps (SATC), 14
Student Non-Violent Coordinating Committee (SNCC), 159, 175–76, 190
Styles, Fitzhugh Lee, *Negroes and the Law*, 71
Sugrue, Thomas, 129, 169
Sullivan, J. Minor, 100, 101, 102
Sullivan, Leon, 7, 121, 127
Sykes, Corrine. *See* Sykes Case
Sykes, Florence, 85
Sykes Case, 81–89

Tallahassee Democrat, 134
Talmadge, Eugene, 77
Tanner, Henry O., 35
Tate, James, 128, 155
Taylor, Henry Louis, Jr., 14
Temple, Priscilla, 47
Temple Law Journal, 79
Thomas, Louise. *See* Louise Thomas Case
Thomas Mattox Case, 75–80
Thompson, Robert Ellis, 11
Thorpe, James, 98, 99, 100, 101
Thurmond, Strom, 64
Till, Emmett, 150
Time: on black attorneys, 71; on the civil rights movement, 161; on Moore, 179; on race riots, 153, 156
Tobias, Channing, 63, 90, 108, 109
Toure, Kwame. *See* Carmichael, Stokely
Tracey, James W., Jr., 88
Trenton Evening Times, 102, 103, 105
Trenton Six Case, 96, 97–107, 191
Trenton Times, 97–98
Trentonian, The, 100, 102, 103
Trotter, William Monroe, 15
Truman, Harry S.: African American appointments and, 108, 110, 111, 112; civil rights and, 63, 90–91, 95–96; Cold War and, 93, 95–96
Tyson, Timothy, 160

Ulio, J. A., 74
United States Information Agency (USIA), 113

United States Supreme Court, 87, 125, 134
Universal Negro Improvement Association
    (UNIA), 19

Vandevere, W. T., 47–48
Vann, Robert, 54
Varbalow, Joseph, 139
Vare, Bill, 64
Vietnam War, 162–63, 175–76
Volpe, Mario, 100, 101, 102
Voting Rights Act, 160

Wagner, Robert, 153
Walden, Austin Thomas, 71
Wallace, Henry, 63, 109, 111
Wallace, Mike, *The Hate that Hate Produced*,
    171
Walter Rounds Case, 30–34, 191
War on Poverty, 160, 162, 170, 178
Ware, Gilbert, 20
Washington, Booker T., 15, 28, 173
Watson, James, 51, 68
Weise, Andrew, 46
Wetzel, Mr., 48
Wheller, John R. C., 14
White, Walter: Berwyn Case and, 46, 48, 54;
    black attorneys and, 40; Brown Case
    and, 42, 44; ILD and, 39–40, 43, 44–45;
    Mattox Case and, 79; Rounds Case
    and, 30, 31, 32–34; Trenton Six Case
    and, 104–5, 106
white backlash, 63, 64, 126, 129, 186
White Crusaders, 55
Wilkins, Roy: Berwyn Case and, 47, 48,
    49, 50, 52; Black Power and, 161, 162,
    167; Brown Case and, 43; civil rights
    movement and, 159, 186; civil rights
    protests and, 145; election (1964) and,
    153; Mattox Case and, 78
Williams, James O., 179
Williams, John Francis, 24, 35
Williams, Josephine, 24
Willie Brown Case, 39, 41–45, 191
Williston, Samuel, 20
Willkie, Wendell, 89, 90

Wilson, Horace, 98, 100, 103, 104
Wilson, Woodrow, 139
Wodlinger, Freeda, 81
Wodlinger, Harry M., 80–81
Woodson, Carter G., 23; Alexander and,
    9–10, 19, 163, 190; on black attorneys,
    36; Garvey and, 20
Woodson, George, 29
World War I, 12, 13–14, 17, 61–62
World War II, 62–63, 74–75, 80, 90
World's Fair (1964), 211n46
Wright, Cleo, 80
Wright, R. R., Jr., 119, 180
Wright, Richard, 162

Yale Law Journal, 79
Yeargan, Max, 51
Young, Whitney, 159, 176, 186

CPSIA information can be obtained at www.ICGtesting.com
Printed in the USA
LVOW06s0535130116

470404LV00001B/51/P